PENNSYLVANIA SPORTS TRIVIA

PENNSYLVANIA SPORTS TRIVIA

Marky Billson
and
J. Alexander Poulton

OVER TIME BOOKS

The Publisher: OverTime Books is an imprint of Éditions de la Montagne Verte

Library and Archives Canada Cataloguing in Publication

Billson, Marky, 1971–
     Pennsylvania sports trivia / Marky Billson, J. Alexander Poulton.

ISBN 978-1-897277-64-5

     1. Sports—Pennsylvania—Miscellanea. I. Poulton, J. Alexander (Jay Alexander), 1977– II. Title.

GV584.P4B56 2011   796.09748   C2010-907909-4

Project Director: J. Alexander Poulton
Project Editor: Nicholle Carrière
Cover Images: baseball glove, © Bobbiholmes / Dreamstime.com; football, © Toddtaulman / Dreamstime.com; track sprinter, © Jupiterimages; boxing gloves, © Zedcor Wholly Owned; golfer, © iStockphoto.com / Sergey Kashkin; basketball hoop, © 2011 Thinkstock; cyclist, © Václav Volráb / Dreamstime.com; Heinz Field, © 2011 Sean Pavone / Dreamstime.com; Citizens Bank Park, © 2011 Ffooter / Dreamstime.com; all other photos, © Photos.com.

We acknowledge the financial support of the Government of Canada through the Canada Book Fund (CBF) for our publishing activities.

Government of Québec—Tax Credit for book publishing—Adminstered by SODEC

 Canadian Heritage   Patrimoine canadien   **SODEC** Québec

PC: 1

Contents

Dedication

To my mother, Dr. Vida Joyce Hull. She never understood my fascination with sports, but I can never repay her for moving to Pennsylvania in my youth.

—Marky Billson

Acknowledgments

Thanks go to Terry Shields, my former editor at the *Pittsburgh Post-Gazette*, who patiently allowed me to develop as a writer, and Don Clegg, another former editor of mine at the *Wheeling Intelligencer*, who taught me a sense of style.

Additional thanks go to OverTime Books for giving me the opportunity to write this book together with J. Alexander Poulton.

Finally, thanks to Mike Mastovich at the *Johnstown Tribune-Democrat*, who provided information to me on Point Stadium for this book.

—Marky Billson

Introduction

A common question posed by American sports fans is: "What is the best sports town in the country?"

The problem with this question is that it is subjective. Fans will always say, rightly or wrongly, that their metropolis is the best and will use whatever criteria they can to support their claim.

So let's try this question on for size: "What's the best sports *state* in the country?"

Oh, that's easy. It's Pennsylvania. No question about it.

Cynics will claim that the second question is just as subjective as the first, but this author begs to differ.

This is a state that doesn't name just streets and arenas after athletes, but entire towns (for example, Jim Thorpe, Pennsylvania).

This is a state where, in the 1980s, Harrisburg's WHTM-TV, located among the many farms of central Pennsylvania, placed sports news ahead of the weather forecast on their newscasts, an extreme rarity among local news programs.

"Should I plant my crops tomorrow? My livelihood depends on it, but first I *gotta* know how the Hershey Bears did!"

When WHTM did air the weather during this period of time, Saturday forecasts included a segment known as the "Steelers Forecast," which told the people of Harrisburg what the weather would be like...in Pittsburgh.

Pennsylvania...

- Can claim to be the birthplace of not only pro football, but also Arena Football and college basketball

- Is the home of not only the first Major League Baseball World Series, but also the Little League and Pony League World Series

- Not only produces Kentucky Derby winners (Smarty Jones), but at least one Kentucky Derby winner was named after a Pennsylvania city (1939 winner Johnstown, to say nothing of Apollo, Baden-Baden or Proud Clarion)

- Has produced the same number of university teams that have gone to the Rose Bowl as...California

- Has more licensed deer hunters than any other state in the country

- Is where Sylvester Stallone set *Rocky*, Susan Dowd set *Slap Shot*, Dorothy Kingsley set *Angels in the Outfield* and someone who wanted to share Julius Erving with all of Pennsylvania set *The Fish That Saved Pittsburgh*

- Gave us the first play-by-play sportscast, the first sports arena with a retractable roof and the first concrete-and-steel sports stadium

- Has produced more Major League Baseball players than any other state except California—and that's only because California has three times the population

- Is a state whose high school football all-star game, "The Big 33," has produced at least one player in every Super Bowl that has ever been played

- Has produced not only the National Football League franchise with the most Super Bowl victories (Pittsburgh Steelers), but the franchise with the most USFL Championship Game appearances (Philadelphia Stars) as well

- Is where Immaculata University established women's basketball, and the Pittsburgh Crawfords and Homestead Grays established the Negro Baseball Leagues

- Is the state whose teams not only introduced double-knit baseball uniforms, but also numbers on football jerseys

- Gave us "Gettysburg Eddie" (Eddie Plank), "The Reading Rifle" (Carl Furillo) and "The Pittsburgh Kid" (Billy Conn or Paul Spadafora, take your choice)

- Is a state where all of the existing major professional sports franchises have won world championships, as did the two existing relocated franchises while they were in Pennsylvania

- Is where not only have both of the BCS colleges (Pitt, Penn State) won national football championships, but the lone FCS university with a full allotment of football scholarships (Villanova) has won one as well

- Is where Mario Lemieux became the only player in the history of the National Hockey League to score five goals five different ways in a game; where Wilt Chamberlain became the only player in the history of the NBA to score 100 points in a game; and where Lou Gehrig, Chuck Klein and Pat Seery tied an MLB record by hitting four home runs in a game.

Certainly no other state ties as much of its culture to sports, has a population that's as interested in sports or is as knowledgeable about sports as Pennsylvania.

Care to debate?

First, how many states have a Major League Baseball franchise, a National Football League franchise, a National Basketball Association franchise and a National Hockey League franchise playing within their confines?

I'll save you the trouble. The answer is 13. In addition to Pennsylvania, there are Arizona (provided the Phoenix Coyotes don't leave), California, Colorado, Florida, Georgia, Illinois, Massachusetts, Michigan, Minnesota, New York, Ohio and Texas. And though it's not a state but a district (whatever that means), we'll include the District of Columbia as well. Perhaps the Washington Redskins no longer play within the confines of the district, but it seems a bit petty to exclude them.

So 13 states and a district make the first cut. Now, how many of those states also have a NASCAR track?

Goodbye Colorado, Massachusetts, Minnesota, Ohio and the District of Columbia. Landover, Maryland, may be part of the Beltway area, but Richmond isn't.

Of the remaining nine states, how many have hosted one of the three major American events on the Pro Golfers Association Tour? Goodbye Arizona.

How many have both a major thoroughbred and a harness horse racing track? Georgia and Texas are out.

How many have a Major League Soccer franchise? Bye, bye, Florida, Illinois and Michigan.

Has California ever hosted the NCAA lacrosse championships? No?

Has a New York university ever played for an NCAA field hockey title?

And then there was one.

True, a Californian or New Yorker could ask, "How many Olympic Games have there been in Pennsylvania?" but the Olympics are more of an international competition rather than an American one. And though we may begrudgingly have to give surfing to California, everyone this side of Brian Wilson and Greg Brady is asking, "So what?"

The Quaker State, meanwhile, will even this up with bowling superiority. Maybe other states have bowling alleys, but the natives don't demand that presidential candidates roll a few frames on campaign stops the way they do in Pennsylvania.

Furthermore, California cannot compete with the tradition and legacy of sports that Pennsylvania has. The Bay Area may have the Golden State Warriors and the Oakland Athletics, but they had to take them, directly or indirectly, from Philadelphia. And, hey, there wouldn't be a Willie Stargell Field or Avenue in Oakland if it wasn't for his exploits in Pittsburgh.

It's time for the writer to share a bit of personal background to relate the cultural experience of sports in Pennsylvania. I was born into a family of intellectuals, an only child who was separated from his father by divorce, but only after his travels took me to Rhode Island and Germany. Afterward, my family relocated for educational and professional reasons to North and South Carolina, Florida, Tennessee, the DC suburbs and four different parts of Pennsylvania.

Nowhere else did I find the passion, the interest or the ability to strike up a conversation in public by asking if the home team could win than when our travels took us to Pittsburgh, Shippensburg, Huntingdon and the Main Line suburbs to live. My mother had no interest in sports; her passions were art, science fiction and animals. I had no siblings or father to play catch or shoot hoops with. So why did I become such a passionate sports fan that I would embark on a career as a sportswriter?

Because in Pennsylvania, if a young boy wants to get along with his male counterparts, he simply has to be able to talk sports.

Sure, there were sports fans in the other places I lived; Columbia, South Carolina, for example, is a great sports town. The rivalry between the University of North Carolina and North Carolina State travels along the same white-collar/blue-collar social lines that the famed New York Yankees–Brooklyn Dodgers rivalry once did in New York. But nowhere else did the boys in school want to debate the merits of the Pirates vs. the Phillies like they did in Shippensburg, where the subject seemed to be a daily, and venomous, argument that rivaled any romantic story that Roger Kahn or Larry King told about what the Yankees, Dodgers and Giants meant to New York City in the 1950s.

But it's easy to argue and cheer for your team when they're battling for pennants every year, as the New York baseball teams of that era always were. We were *true* fans, disputing the merits of the fifth- and sixth-place teams in the six-team National League East Division. New York in the 1950s can have Yogi Berra vs. Roy Campanella. *We* had Johnny Ray vs. Juan Samuel!

And besides, didn't Yogi's son Dale wind up playing for the Pirates? Didn't Campy go to Simon Gratz High?

But growing up in Pennsylvania hardly meant the major sports teams were always coming up short. Upon moving to Pittsburgh in 1979, I was greeted with the Pirates and Steelers winning world championships. Then, after moving to Huntingdon, the Phillies, Eagles, Flyers and Sixers all played for world championships the next season.

For 12 seasons, from 1970 to 1981, either the Pirates or the Phillies went to the baseball playoffs for the National League East 11 times. And if that wasn't enough, in 1982, the University of Pittsburgh Panthers began the college football season ranked number one, only to see the Penn State Nittany Lions finish as the national champions.

Winning obviously breeds interest, but the romanticism of sports in Pennsylvania stays with you for life.

Let Willie Mays play stickball with the kids. Let everyone a half-century ago in Baltimore feel like they were neighbors to a Colt. Me? One week in Pittsburgh, I picked up *Sports Illustrated* in the Linden Elementary school library and saw Stargell on the cover, named "Sportsman of the Year" with Terry Bradshaw—the same Willie Stargell that lived at the bottom of the hill and only a few blocks away from Linden on Conover Road. The next week, it was L.C. Greenwood on the cover of *SI*, shown leading the Steelers to the Super Bowl— the same L.C. Greenwood who lived one street over from Linden on Dallas Avenue. My state wasn't just the center of the sports world then, but my *neighborhood* was, and perhaps like no other place before or since.

Of course, not everyone in Pennsylvania came into life's awareness in Pittsburgh's Point Breeze neighborhood during 1979 or 1980. And my friends in other Keystone State locales all seemed to be as rabid a fan as I was.

Where did their interest come from?

Perhaps it came down from previous generations, when great-grandparents came out of a mine or mill to play baseball or football on a town team during the weekend. This source of entertainment for the entire community was not only eagerly anticipated for days before the event, but also provided a sense of identity to all those who participated or watched.

But those days are long gone, and Pennsylvania is in a transition from a blue-collar to a white-collar workforce. Yet the interest in sports remains.

Perhaps it's because, as future generations make their living more with their minds and less with the sweat of their brows, a different appeal is discovered. Sports provide an intellectual escape, one filled with strategy, statistics and history.

Pennsylvania is a very diverse state, offering the full slate of American culture like no other state can. Consider that there are no more rustic or conservative people than the Amish, and no trendier people than those living in Pittsburgh's Shadyside neighborhood. The height of ritziness can be found in the aforementioned Point Breeze neighborhood in Pittsburgh, whereas the height of urban blight can be found in Philadelphia's Point Breeze neighborhood.

Pennsylvania is as complex as the computer lab at Carnegie-Mellon University and as simple as a farm in Saxon. It's Poison and Cinderella rocking their way up the charts in the late '80s, while Will Smith rapped his way up. It's where broadcasting was born and the Declaration of Independence was signed. It's where electricity was discovered and the polio vaccine was invented. It's a bellwether state in a presidential election, yet by the time the primaries roll around, the parties have already decided who they'll run in November.

But the one thing that links all these differences together in Pennsylvania, in a way that music or theater or politics never could, is sports.

And even my mother, who knew nothing of sports or of life in Pittsburgh, told me prior to our move to the soon-to-be christened "City of Champions" for her fellowship at Pitt, "You better get ready, Marky. They care about their football teams out there." If a non-fan from Ohio knows of the state's reputation, the rest of the population can hardly refute it.

This book is the story, the history and a compendium of unique facts about sports in Pennsylvania. Perhaps from them, we can see some of the future of sports in Pennsylvania, which, quite objectively, is the best sports state in the country.

–*Marky Billson*

Chapter One

The Three States of Pennsylvania: Eastern, Central and Western

Pittsburgh vs. Philly

"Pennsylvania is Philadelphia on one end, Pittsburgh on another and Alabama in the middle."

When James Carville gave the above description of the Keystone State, he presumably wasn't referencing Alabama with the sort of romanticism Lynyrd Skynyrd did. But just as Tennessee often refers to its totality as having "three grand divisions," Pennsylvania can say the same—eastern, central and western.

To be fair, northern Pennsylvania cities such as Scranton and Erie probably have more in common culturally with a place like Harrisburg than any other part of the state, so perhaps it's wise to refer to the "grand divisions" of Pennsylvania as southeastern, central and southwestern. Yet the latter term is rarely used in Pittsburgh, and when a Pittsburgher says "western Pennsylvania," he or she is usually referring to the greater Pittsburgh vicinity and not Erie or Du Bois.

Pittsburgh and Philadelphia are different, much like Los Angeles and San Francisco, Baton Rouge and New Orleans, or Memphis and Nashville are. Yet they also have their similarities. Maybe in Pittsburgh the sandwiches come with coleslaw and

French fries, while in Philly, cheesesteaks are all the rage. But the bottom line is that both cities' distinct cuisines, for better or worse, are sandwiches, and sandwiches that outsiders probably have to learn to love, at that. Similarly, both cities are known throughout America as great sports towns. But which one is better? And where does central Pennsylvania fit in?

Traditionally, in Pennsylvania, the old adage goes that fans east of Harrisburg root for Philadelphia teams, and those west of the capital root for Pittsburgh. This is not an absolute rule, as the Pitt Panthers have had a radio affiliate in Philadelphia, the Pirates have had radio affiliates in Carlisle and Harrisburg, and in 2010, the Steelers had them in locations such as Chambersburg, Scranton, Gettysburg and Williamsport. The Phillies historically have had radio affiliates as far west as State College, as well.

On television, since the Eagles and Steelers are in different conferences, they rarely have scheduling conflicts in the center of the state. The Baltimore Ravens usually get precedence in south-central Pennsylvania when they play at the same time as the Steelers on television stations, though during the final few seasons that the Colts were in Baltimore, this did not happen because of kickoff times (the Colts kicked off an hour after the rest of the NFL when playing at home because of Maryland blue laws) and the fact the Steelers were championship caliber while the Colts were just plain lousy at the time.

Root Sports allows sports fans throughout the state to see live Pirates and Penguins games, save for the Philadelphia metro region. Similarly, CSN Philly is carried in the eastern part of the state into State College, though Flyers games are blacked out in rural central Pennsylvania areas like Huntingdon to avoid conflict with the Penguins.

Still, it is not uncommon for a central Pennsylvanian to adopt, say, the Phillies as his favorite baseball team and the Steelers as his favorite football squad. Yet it is safe to say that these actions would be considered blasphemous in either Pittsburgh or Philly.

Philadelphia will boast that they have professional basketball (76ers) and Pittsburgh does not. Pittsburgh will counter that they have major college football (Pitt Panthers) and Philadelphia does not, which may seem like a slap to Temple and the Army–Navy game, but is technically correct since these two entities are not part of the BCS.

Philadelphia has thoroughbred racing (Penn National and Philadelphia Park), just as Erie does (Presque Isle), while Pittsburgh has harness racing (The Meadows).

Field hockey has always been more prevalent in central and eastern Pennsylvania, though in 2009, 20 high schools in the Western Pennsylvania Interscholastic Athletic League (WPIAL) participated in the sport. But with Pittsburgh's three rivers, rowing has taken off in that area, with the Three Rivers Rowing Association winning "Club of the Year" honors from USRowing in 2002 and 2010.

The central part of the state lives up to the "red state" reputation that James Carville tagged it with, but has the sports that capture the nation's eye. Long Pond has a NASCAR track that hosts two Nextel Championship Races a year, and Penn State, located in State College, is traditionally a major college football power. The Little League Baseball World Series is held annually in Williamsport.

If Philadelphia and Pittsburgh fans are extremely cynical, central Pennsylvania sports fans are exceedingly optimistic; witness the phrase "If God isn't a Penn State fan, why is the sky blue and white?" The fact that the University of North Carolina's colors are also blue and white is irrelevant.

All this is well and good, but there comes a time when every central Pennsylvania sports fan has to take sides—does he or she root for the Pirates or the Phillies? The Steelers or the

Eagles? The Penguins or the Flyers? And, to a lesser extent, for Pitt or Villanova come college basketball season? A fan's choice of which Pennsylvania city to align him- or herself with may reveal more of that fan's character than anything else.

Critical Fans

Both Pittsburgh and Philadelphia sports fans can be, and usually are, critical. Steelers fans were known to boo Terry Bradshaw; Phillies fans did the same to Mike Schmidt.

Philadelphia sports fans have a reputation for being more violent. A search on YouTube will provide clips of Philadelphia fans overturning parked cars after the Phillies won the 2008 World Series. In the years that followed, Citizens Bank Park saw one fan get tasered when he ran out onto the field, and another was arrested when he gagged himself and vomited on an 11-year-old girl after her father asked him to temper his profanity.

Veterans Stadium was so violent for Eagles games that a makeshift court and jail was set up for unruly fans during its final seasons. Eagles followers once broke the leg of famed Washington Redskins fan Zema "Chief Zee" Williams during a 1983 game, and, prior to holding the office, even Pennsylvania governor Ed Rendell was said to take part in throwing snowballs at opponents on the field.

Perhaps the most notable incident occurred in 1968, when fans at Franklin Field, disappointed by the Eagles' abysmal 2–11 record, booed and threw snowballs at Frank Olivo, who was dressed as Santa Claus during a halftime show.

There have, however, been two violent incidents of note in Pittsburgh during celebrations. In 1991, a fan accidentally fell to his death as a mob greeted the Pittsburgh Penguins at the Greater Pittsburgh International Airport upon returning home from winning the Stanley Cup. Another fan perished at the hands of a hit-and-run driver following the Steelers' 36–33 playoff victory at Heinz Field against Cleveland in 2003.

And while Philadelphia fans at The Vet cheered as Dallas Cowboys receiver Michael Irvin lay motionless with the neck injury that ended his career in 1999, there were incidents in which Steelers fans at Three Rivers cheered when their own players were injured—most recently, quarterback Bubby Brister in 1991.

Philadelphia fans, however, may be more forgiving than Pittsburgh fans. For instance, Mitch "Wild Thing" Williams will forever be known to Phillies fans as the pitcher who gave up Joe Carter's World Series–ending home run in 1993. In the days that followed, he received death threats and his home was pelted with eggs. Later that offseason, he was traded to Houston. But upon his return to Philadelphia in 1994, Williams was given a standing ovation. He later became a local sportscaster, even hosting his own talk show during the 2008 World Series.

Compare this to Stan Belinda, who is best known in Pittsburgh for giving up Francisco Cabrera's game-winning pinch-hit with two out in the bottom of the ninth inning in the seventh game of the 1992 National League Championship Series to give Atlanta the pennant, 3–2. The following year, the *Pittsburgh Post-Gazette* published a letter from a fan demanding that Belinda, an Alexandria native who grew up rooting for the Bucs, apologize for losing the game. The request was so outlandish that, during a game broadcast, Braves announcer Pete Van Wieren even questioned the *Post-Gazette*'s editorial decision to publish such a letter.

The Rumor Mill

Further ugliness is found in the endless supply of unsubstantiated rumors surrounding many of Pittsburgh's sports heroes. The star at Pitt slumps in his final season, so he must have a drug problem. A retired Steelers great injures himself at home, so he must have been beat up by the mob. A former Pirates pitcher's skills disappear, so he must have caught his wife in bed with a tcammate. Personal rumors regarding Steelers quarterback Kordell Stewart were so prevalent that he went from being the most marketed player in the NFL in 1997 to a vilified figure in 1998, and he finally felt compelled to address the gossip in *ESPN Magazine* in 2001.

While Pittsburgh may not have a monopoly on unsubstantiated rumors surrounding its sports heroes, it certainly seems to have many.

Media Darlings

In 1980, NFL Films called the Steelers fan base "the loudest, most loyal in the league." And it's true that the Steelers have sold out every home game since 1972, save for a single game featuring replacement players at Three Rivers Stadium during an NFL players' strike in 1987.

But what goes in Philadelphia might not fly in Pittsburgh.

Case in point: in 2004, the Philadelphia Eagles were playing in their third straight NFC championship game. They'd lost the previous two against the St. Louis Rams and Tampa Bay Buccaneers. Yet on WIP, one of the country's first all-sports radio stations, legendary Eagles play-by-play broadcaster Merrill Reese gave commentaries and updates surrounding the Eagles. He spoke of how the 2003 Eagles had "captured a place in our hearts." Granted, Reese is a play-by-play broadcaster, not a journalist. Still, outside a game broadcast, the comment seemed a bit sappy.

Pittsburgh sports talk radio is a bit different. While, historically, Steelers broadcaster Myron Cope led cheers with his invention, "The Terrible Towel," even he was known to be critical—witness his 1991 Christmas carol, "'Twas a Season the Steelers Should Have Spent in Prison," sung on WTAE-TV after a year in which the Steelers missed the playoffs. The Steelers' record that season was not 2–14, but rather 7–9, and they only missed the playoffs by one game. In many markets, Cope's song would be cause for dismissal, but in Pittsburgh, it only made him more popular.

More recently, Mark Madden has been a sports-talk leader in Pittsburgh, helping create a boom in popularity for the Penguins, but hardly without controversy. A former bad-guy professional wrestler, Madden took that persona to the airwaves and has used it to forge a long career, often harshly criticizing beloved local sports figures in the process.

The point is, it would be hard to imagine a commentator talking about how the Steelers had won a place in their fans' hearts after two straight conference championship losses during the week of an appearance in the third. No, it's more likely that Pittsburgh fans and media would wait until the Super Bowl was in the bag before anyone claimed that the Steelers had won a place in their hearts.

Similar, Yet Oh, So Different

The perception is that Pittsburgh teams have been more successful than Philadelphia ones. Philadelphia has, as of 2010, won 16 major sports championships (including the NBA championship, the Super Bowl and the Stanley Cup), while Pittsburgh has won 14, largely because Philadelphia has more teams than Pittsburgh.

From the Pittsburgh standpoint, this analogy does not take into account the nine national championships the Pitt football team has won, Negro League titles won by the Crawfords or the Grays, or even something like western Pennsylvania's dominance in winning the Pennsylvania Cup, which is given to the high school hockey state champions every year. This statistic also registers the Philadelphia Warriors' 1947 NBA title but doesn't count the championship won by the ABA Pittsburgh Pipers in 1967–68.

From a Philadelphia standpoint, this analogy fails to recognize championships won by, say, the United States Football League Stars in 1984, Villanova's miracle 1985 NCAA men's basketball tournament championship or titles won by minor professional sports teams such as the Major Indoor Lacrosse League Wings or the Arena Football League's Soul.

And it poses the question, does an NFL championship won in 1948 by the Eagles hold the same weight as a Super Bowl won by the Steelers in 2008? If not, then certainly the Pirates' 1909 World Series championship would not have the same weight as the Phillies' 2008 crown. But if that's the case, then should the Athletics' five world championships, won between 1910 and 1930, be counted at all?

Philly Flops

At the beginning of the 21st century, it often seemed as though Pittsburgh sports teams had all the luck in Pennsylvania. The Steelers won their sixth Super Bowl in 2008 and have the most Super Bowl wins in NFL history, but the Eagles haven't won any. The Flyers may have won the Stanley Cup in 1974 and 1975, but the Penguins have won it three times since then, in 1991, 1992 and 2008.

True, following the 2010 season, the Pittsburgh Pirates had not had a winning season since 1992, the longest such losing streak in major professional sports history. But until the Phillies won the 2008 World Series, Philadelphia had gone

25 years without a major sports championship. And historically, the Bucs' streak is not as lengthy as what the Phillies endured from 1918 to 1948, when the Phils posted a losing record in 30 of 31 seasons, save for a 78–76 mark in 1932. And the Phillies wouldn't have even posted a winning record that year except that the New York Giants gave up six unearned runs in a season-ending 6–3 Philadelphia victory that was called off early because of darkness!

Perhaps it goes hand in hand with the critical nature of their fan base, but Philadelphia does have the reputation for being a haven for losing sports franchises. For instance:

- The Phillies were the first major league team to lose 10,000 games in their history; they also own the longest losing streak in modern baseball history (23 games in 1961) and the greatest pennant collapse in history (the 1964 Phillies had a 6.5 game lead with 12 games left in the season, only to lose 10 straight while St. Louis won eight in a row to take the pennant).

- In 1973, the 76ers finished 9–73, the worst record in modern NBA history; as of 2010, they had not won the NBA championship in 27 years.

- As of 2011, the Eagles had never won a Super Bowl and did not have a winning record from 1967 to 1977.

- The A's, easily the premier franchise in the American League after the 1931 season, with the most pennants and world championships, quickly saw the New York Yankees pass them by; they eventually left town in 1954, a shadow of their former selves, after 23 straight pennant-less seasons.

- The Flyers, as of 2011, have won no Stanley Cup championships for 36 years.

- The Temple football team, a long-time loser, was kicked out of the Big East Conference in 2004 for being uncompetitive.

Losing Is the Pitts

Pittsburgh has had their droughts as well. In addition to the Pirates' streak of consecutive losing seasons at the beginning of the 21st century, they went 32 years, from 1928 to 1959, without winning the pennant.

Prior to Chuck Noll becoming their head coach in 1969, the Steelers were regarded as the biggest losers in the NFL. From their inception in 1933 until 1971, they'd never won a division title (which meant playing for a championship in the pre–Super Bowl era of the NFL) and really only sniffed one twice, in 1947 and 1963. The Steelers were so bad that it took the franchise 10 seasons to even score 28 points in a game— a 35–7 victory against Detroit on November 8, 1942.

Finally, before Mario Lemieux rescued them, the Penguins were an afterthought, struggling to play in front of half-capacity crowds at the Pittsburgh Civic Arena. They failed to post a winning record until their eighth season, 1974–75, only to blow a 3–0 lead to the New York Islanders in a best-of-seven playoff series and then declare bankruptcy. From 1983 through 1988, the Penguins failed to make the playoffs despite playing in an era where the top four finishers in their six-team division qualified—and they had Lemieux for four of those seasons!

Evening the Score

Ultimately, as of 2010, the Pirates have won the World Series five times and the Phillies twice, and the Penguins have won the Stanley Cup three times and the Flyers twice. Most importantly, the Steelers have the most Super Bowl victories, and the Eagles have the least.

Perhaps that's why Philadelphia sports fans would be more apt to, according to Merrill Reese, take an Eagles team that couldn't win the Super Bowl but came close to their hearts, yet, theoretically at least, Pittsburgh fans would demand more than just a Final Four appearance from the Steelers before recognizing that team as being truly special.

Or how about this—in 1979, Pittsburgh began referring to themselves as "The City of Champions" after the Pirates won the World Series and the Steelers won the Super Bowl. Philadelphia then took the nickname the next year, as all four of Philadelphia's pro sports franchises played for a world championship—yet only the Phillies actually won a world championship.

However, there are many similarities between Pittsburgh and Philadelphia. They both have reputations for being blue-collar towns, yet their manufacturing industries have been in decline for some time now, and both cities have so many prestigious universities and white-collar interests that one wonders when conventional wisdom will allow the two cities to escape the tag. Both have an impressive array of discoveries, inventions and firsts to their historical credit, a diverse blend of ethnicities and religions among their populations, and sports fans who are known to put pro football first and have a hard edge to their support.

Then there are the things between Philly and Pittsburgh that are similar, yet different. Pittsburghers identify a group with "yinz." Philadelphians say "youse." Pittsburgh is Bob Prince's loud sports coat; Philadelphia is Howard Eskin's furs. Pittsburgh is Carnegie-Mellon; Philadelphia is the University of Pennsylvania. Pittsburgh is Myron Cope; Philadelphia is Dave Zinkoff. Pittsburgh is Stan and Guy on *Sportsbeat*; Philadelphia is Don Henderson on WCAU.

In Philadelphia, every historic home seems to claim that George Washington slept there. In Pittsburgh, George Washington discovered, then surveyed the area for the British! In Pittsburgh, Point Breeze is the ritziest neighborhood in the city; in Philadelphia, Point Breeze is perhaps the toughest slum.

Philadelphia is David Brenner for Schmidt's; Pittsburgh is Frank Nicotero for Iron City. We'd give that one to Philadelphia, except that Iron City is still made in western Pennsylvania, while Schmidt's seems to be living out its final days as a brand— it's now brewed in Woodridge, Illinois.

In Philadelphia, when Phillies manager Danny Ozark let the greatest home-run hitter in franchise history, Mike Schmidt, lead off in nine games during the 1978 pennant race and National League Championship Series, the press said he was dumb, and he was fired the following season after winning three straight division championships. In Pittsburgh, when Pirates manager Jim Leyland let the greatest home-run hitter in baseball history, Barry Bonds, lead off for four straight seasons at the start of his career, the press called him a genius. The Bucs finished second in the division in three of those years, and then the media continued to heap praise on Leyland when he finally moved Bonds into a batting-order position where he could drive in runs, thus resulting in three straight Pirates division titles from 1990 to 1992.

Philadelphia sports fans are more apt to embrace basketball. Forget the Sixers or the Big Five—just consider how much attention Kobe Bryant received when he was playing at Lower Merion High. This was a player who was able to not only enter the NBA draft and forgo college, but also take Brandy Norwood to the prom!

Pittsburgh embraces hockey. The city has a professional legacy that dates back more than 100 years, but more recently, the sport has enjoyed a huge wave of popularity that can be traced to the arrival of Mario Lemieux playing for the Penguins in 1984.

At the time of Lemieux's arrival, there were less than a dozen indoor hockey rinks in western Pennsylvania, including locations beyond Pittsburgh, where aspiring hockey players could skate. Some, such as the rink at Monroeville Mall, were even being closed. However, in 2010, the Pennsylvania Interscholastic Hockey League listed 26 ice rinks in western Pennsylvania that host games. Western Pennsylvania has become fertile ground for producing hockey players, and the players from the area who learned to skate during Mario Lemieux's playing career, which lasted off and on from 1984 to 2005, are often referred to as "Lemieux babies."

Furthermore, in 2009–10, the Penguins had the highest local television ratings of any American NHL franchise and sold out every home game at the Mellon Arena. With Sidney Crosby and Evgeni Malkin poised to lead Pittsburgh on the ice into the second decade of the 21st century, the Penguins have become the team of choice for many young Pittsburghers.

In Conclusion

All this is fine, well and good, but which one, Philadelphia or Pittsburgh, is the *better* sports city?

That's like asking who's prettier, Christina Aguilera or Kelly Monaco? It's a subjective argument, and likely the side taken depends on where one lives or which team one roots for.

Chapter Two

Pro Football

Wednesday Night Football

Just before dusk on September 28, 1892, in Mansfield, the Wyoming Seminary football team took to the home field of Mansfield State Normal School to play in the first nighttime football game in history.

Smythe Park, the home stadium of Mansfield Normal, wasn't equipped with a lighting system, so one had to be installed in order for the players and the spectators to be able to see the action. Grounds crews put in a series of poles along both sidelines and in the end zones, hoping it would be enough to fight back the fading light. As the two teams took to the field, it appeared that the lighting would work, but as the game progressed and darkness fell all around, it turned out to be completely inadequate.

The quarterbacks could just see a few yards in front of them, and fans had difficulty making out plays on opposite ends of the field. Things were made even worse after several players slammed directly into some of the light poles, making the field even darker. After only 20 minutes and 10 plays, both teams agreed to end the game at halftime. Neither side had scored a single point.

Although the game was a complete bust, it began a tradition of night football that has lasted to this day. In celebration of that historic game, a yearly re-enactment of the original game is played between Wyoming Seminary and Mansfield State Normal School during the fall festival known as "Fabulous 1890s Weekend." On September 28, 1992, *Monday Night Football* celebrated "100 years of night football" with a game between the Los Angeles Raiders and the Kansas City Chiefs.

The Birthplace of Pro Football

While the first recorded college football game took place in New Jersey in 1869, the first instance of professional football occurred in Pittsburgh in 1892. One must understand that in the late 19th century, the idea of professional athletics was not universally accepted by the public. Purists believed sports should be a strictly amateur affair and that money would only corrupt the competition.

But those thoughts were changing. Professional baseball had existed since 1869, and football teams, called "athletic associations," were sprouting up throughout the country and would often pay their players "double expenses," though a player could accept such a payout and still be considered an amateur.

William "Pudge" Heffelfinger, a three-time All-American guard at Yale, was generally regarded as the best lineman in football at the time. After playing for the Elis, he suited up for the Chicago Athletic Association for the general double expenses rule.

Back in Pittsburgh, the Allegheny Athletic Association (AAA) and the Pittsburgh Athletic Club (PAC) had a fierce rivalry, and when the PAC used Penn State's captain for an October game against the AAA, the Alleghenies cried foul and demanded a rematch. The PAC agreed and decided that this time, they'd go after Heffelfinger to play for their team, and pay him $250 to boot. However, the negotiations were covered in the *Pittsburgh Press*. To counter the PAC offer, the AAA promised Heffelfinger double what the PAC would pay him, and Pudge agreed.

So, on November 12, 1892, Heffelfinger shocked the PAC when he showed up in an AAA uniform, then scored the game's only touchdown after he forced a fumble, giving the AAA a 4–0 victory.

After that, paying football players was no longer taboo, and pro football was born.

The Bicycle Club Football Championships

If you think modern-day football with its devastating hits and hulking athletes is a sport of brutality, it doesn't compare to the no-holds-barred violence that occurred in the early days of the sport. One of the best examples of these blood-filled rivalries occurred between two of Philadelphia's bicycle clubs.

Cycling is not something that one automatically associates with football, but in the late 19th century, cycling was extremely popular as a sport as well as a leisure activity. This popularity gave rise to clubs, which sprang up across the city and the country. Cycling competitions between rival clubs were intense affairs, and one of the fiercest rivalries in Philadelphia was between the Century Wheelmen and the Park Avenue Wheelmen. When weather did not permit cycling, the organizations often branched out to other forms of athletic expression, including football.

As the air began to chill in the autumn of 1892, the Century Wheelmen were forced to put away their bicycles, but the desire for athletic competition led them to organize a football team. After some practice and a few lessons on the rules of the sport, they played their first game against the Athletic Association of Camden and lost 22–6. The loss, however, did not dampen their egos, and the next day, the Wheelmen posted a notice in the *Philadelphia Record* aimed directly at their bitter rivals that read, "The Century Wheelmen think they can do the Park Avenue football team to the tune of 100 to 0." Three weeks later, the teams met at the Phillies' Ball Park, which ironically was equipped with a bicycle track that may have led to its later name, the Baker Bowl.

The spectators who turned up to watch a football game saw something that more closely resembled a prizefight. From the first kickoff to the last play of the game, players punched, kicked, scratched and delivered devastating body checks that left several men unconscious on the field. Three players even had to be revived with buckets of cold water. With the teams evenly matched and equally beaten, bruised and broken, the game ended in a scoreless tie, far from the "100 to 0" score that the Wheelmen had promised. The next day, the *Philadelphia Record* ran a headline over an article about the game that read, "No One Killed, Several Wounded. Good Blood Spilled and Bad Blood Made."

The teams met again in the autumn of the following year, and more blood was shed on the gridiron. Despite their violence and unorganized nature, matches such as these were being played across the country, establishing the game of football in the American sports landscape and laying the foundations of its rabid fan base in Pennsylvania.

The Philadelphia Pros

From its inception, football was a game played primarily by amateurs from local sporting clubs like the Century Wheelmen. More prizefight than football, early games often lacked the refinement and regulation that would bring in regular fans. But by 1900, many of those amateur clubs began to pay their better players, leading to the rise of professional teams. Philadelphia was a hub for amateur football teams, but it wasn't until 1901, with the establishment of the Philadelphia Football Club, that the city got its first taste of pro football. Often referred to in the press as the Philadelphia Stars, All-Stars, Quakers or Phillies, the city's team was most commonly known as the Philadelphia Pros.

Composed mainly of former University of Pennsylvania players, the Pros began their inaugural season with a game against the Conshohocken Tigers and promptly disposed of the challengers with a 6–0 shutout. The Pros went on to play teams such as the Orange, the N.J. Athletic Club and the Homestead Library and Athletic Club from western Pennsylvania, who were their toughest opponents that season.

Homestead defeated the Pros in the championship game, both teams having finished the season with an identical number of wins and losses. But the Homestead squad was too solid on their defense for the Pros to get more than a few yards per down. The great rivalry between the cities of Pittsburgh and Philadelphia might have started in those very games. However, the Pros' outstanding season and drive for the championship had pushed the idea of professional football into the minds of the Philly faithful and paved the way for future pro clubs to develop and thrive.

The Forgotten Frankford Yellow Jackets

In May 1899, in the parlor of the Suburban Club in the Philadelphia neighborhood of Frankford, members organized themselves into the Frankford Athletic Association, thus bringing football to the small town. They began by organizing matches against other club and college teams. The association played under the name Yellow Jackets and had success in the following years but disbanded some time before 1912. Players moved on to steady careers and families because football was not the lucrative undertaking that it is today. However, a core group of players persisted and started a new team called the Loyola Athletic Club, which, later, in honor of their old team, renamed themselves the Frankford Athletic Club and played football under the name Yellow Jackets.

By the early 1920s, the Yellow Jackets were one of the premiere teams in the region. Competition with other city clubs was fierce, but every year, the Yellow Jackets managed to put together a winning team. The club's good fortune continued in 1922, when the Philadelphia city champions, the Union City Quakers, were disbanded, and the Yellow Jackets absorbed some of the Quakers' star players.

The club remained independent but played several well-documented games against teams from the fledgling National Football League. With financial backing to support the league, the NFL attracted some of the best players from across the country and could put together high-quality teams. However, in exhibition games against the Frankford Yellow Jackets, NFL teams had a losing record of 2–6–1. The Yellow Jackets were so good that they joined the NFL at the league's request in 1924.

In their first official game as a member of the NFL, the Jackets defeated the Rochester Jeffersons, 21–0. Under the coaching of Punk Berryman, a former All-American player with Penn State, the team finished their inaugural season with the third best record in the league, just behind the Cleveland Bulldogs and the Chicago Bears.

The following season, the Jackets finished with a decent record but again missed the top spot, though the club did have a hand in deciding the 1925 NFL championship. Nearing the end of the 1925 season, the NFL-leading Pottsville Maroons played a game outside the league against the Notre Dame

All-Stars in Philadelphia. The Yellow Jackets caused a stir when they complained to the league that the Maroons had infringed on their territorial rights in the city. This was a violation of the NFL rules, and the league was forced to suspend the Maroons with several games left in the season, thereby allowing the Chicago Cardinals to take the 1925 title.

The Yellow Jackets would get their moment to shine in the 1926 season, finishing in first place with a record of 14–1–2, thus giving them the championship. The Yellow Jackets were the first Pennsylvania team to win the NFL crown. The next few years in the league were not so kind to the club as the Yellow Jackets suffered a string of losing seasons. The team's dismal record, combined with the Great Depression, made it hard for them to stay in business. The club struggled through the 1929 and 1930 seasons, but before the start of the next season, a fire severely damaged Frankford Stadium, sounding the death knell for the franchise. With negative revenues at the gates, the team folded at the end of the 1931 season. Philadelphia, however, remained a viable market, and two years after the Yellow Jackets' demise, the Philadelphia Eagles were born.

The Philadelphia Eagles and the NRA

The Philadelphia Eagles joined the NFL in 1933 as a replacement team in the city for the defunct Frankford Yellow Jackets. The city—and the country—still had not pulled out of the Depression, but the recovery process through President Roosevelt's New Deal put the country on the path toward recovery.

The New Deal was a series of economic programs that were instated during Roosevelt's first term as president and focused on what has become known as the three Rs: relief, recovery and reform. One of the lead government bodies in charge of turning the country around was the National Recovery Administration, or the NRA (*not* affiliated with the National Rifle Association). The NRA pushed through a series of measures to help boost consumer purchasing power and increase employment. To get their message out to the American public, they launched the Blue Eagle campaign. Businesses that subscribed to the government's recovery programs were permitted to display a poster with the NRA Blue Eagle along with the announcement, "We Do Our Part." The poster could be seen in every city across the country, including Philadelphia, with the Blue Eagle's outspread wings and talons grasping a wheel (symbolizing industry) in one foot and lightning bolts (symbolizing power) in the other. The Blue Eagle was the creation of Hugh Johnson, head of the NRA, who famously said of the symbol, "When every American housewife understands that the Blue Eagle on everything that she permits into her home is a symbol of its restoration to security, may God have mercy on the man or group of men who attempt to trifle with this bird."

It was from this symbol and the power it stood for that the new owners of the Philadelphia NFL franchise drew inspiration, naming their new team the Eagles and emblazoning blue wings on the players' uniforms.

The Steagles

When World War II erupted on September 1, 1939, the United States decided to remain out of what it considered to be a European problem. However, when the Japanese attacked Pearl Harbor on December 7, 1941, the country was thrust into the war, and young American men enlisted to fight, including many professional athletes. The NFL lost 600 players, and many clubs considered folding or suspending operations until the end of the conflict. However, following a statement by President Roosevelt that the country needed sports entertainment to maintain the people's morale, teams found ways to continue.

The Pittsburgh Steelers and the Philadelphia Eagles had a problem, though. Neither club had enough players to put on the gridiron. The Steelers, in fact, were left with just six players, and the Eagles had 16. It was just prior to the start of the 1943 season that Steelers owner Art Rooney Sr. came up with the idea of merging his club with the state-rival Philadelphia Eagles. At first, Eagles owner Lex Thompson was not happy with the idea because he could run his team with the 16 players he still had under contract, even if this number was not optimal. But after some time to consider the difficulty of operating a club with the bare minimum of players, Thompson agreed to the merger. Three home games would be played at Shibe Park in Philadelphia and two at Forbes Field in Pittsburgh. The team would officially be known as the Eagles (sans location designation), though the press and history has given them the moniker "Steagles." The team colors were Philly's green and white instead of Pittsburgh's black and gold.

But when it came time to decide who would run the team on the field, both coaches wanted to install their system of play. Neither Eagles coach Alfred "Greasy" Neale nor Steelers coach Walt Kiesling would hand power over to the other, and the two men simply hated one another. This division between the coaches plagued the team for the entire season, and with disharmony on the sidelines, the team suffered on the scoreboard. Adding to the chaos was the strange requirement that players on both teams hold full-time jobs on top of their commitment to pro football. All the players worked on wartime defense projects, and one of the Pittsburgh players, Ted Doyle, worked on the Manhattan Project, the U.S.'s secret effort to build the first atomic bomb. With all these distractions, the Steagles (only in Philadelphia did the media insist on calling them the Eagles) had set themselves up for a disastrous season, but the players managed to come together, and the team finished with a 5–4–1 record.

The following season, the NFL was back on solid ground because the army had declared that men over 26 would no longer be drafted into service. But now, with a surplus of players and teams returning to the league, the NFL had 11 teams—one more than the pre-war norm—and had to reduce the number to 10. Still without an operational number of players, the Steelers merged yet again, this time with the Chicago Cardinals for the 1944 season, creating a team that was known as Card-Pitt.

Card-Pitt

With both teams facing depleted rosters, the Chicago Cardinals and the Pittsburgh Steelers were forced to merge for the start of the 1944 season. The Steelers had just come out of a semisuccessful merger with the Philadelphia Eagles in the 1943 season but didn't want to return for another season as the Steagles because of friction among personnel and the intense regional rivalries between the clubs.

Finding another team to merge with proved difficult. At the annual NFL meetings before the start of the season, the Steelers' most logical choice for a merger was either Cleveland or the Brooklyn Tigers because of their geographical proximity. Steelers owner Art Rooney Sr. pushed aside both options in favor of joining with the Chicago Cardinals, who were winless in 1943. Although the team would be placed in a tough division with the Green Bay Packers and the Chicago Bears, Rooney felt there was nowhere to go but up with a team that had such poor results the previous season. With a fresh influx of players and ideas, the Card-Pitt alliance began the season with the hope of stringing together a number of wins. But things did not exactly turn out that way.

Ironically, Card-Pitt's first challenge was against the Philadelphia Eagles in an exhibition game. The Eagles taught Card-Pitt a lesson in offensive football, scoring three touchdowns in the first quarter on their way to a 22–0 victory. Despite the humiliating defeat, the team reined in their defense for their next game but still lost to the Washington Redskins, 3–0. For the start of the regular season, Card-Pitt played the Cleveland Rams before a crowd of 21,000 spectators at Forbes Field in Pittsburgh, but all the fans left the field unhappy, as Card-Pitt ended up losing the game 28–23. The rest of the season was downhill from that point. Two days before the team's second game, their starting quarterback was drafted into the army, and the replacement was a 155-pound rookie from St. Francis, John McCarthy. The team finished the 10-game season without a single triumph. For the start of the 1945 NFL season, the teams mercifully went their separate ways, and Pittsburgh once again had a Steelers team to call its own.

Chuck Bednarik

One word comes to mind when Chuck Bednarik is mentioned, tough. He often referred to himself as "Mr. Philadelphia" after playing for Bethlehem's Liberty High School, then for the University of Pennsylvania and his entire 14-year professional career with the Eagles. Bednarik started at both center and linebacker throughout his career, the last player to do so on a full-time basis. His crushing tackle on Frank Gifford in 1960 kept Gifford out of football for 18 months and was so brutal that onlookers initially were concerned that Gifford had died.

The biggest tackle Bednarik made that season, however, was in the NFL championship game at Franklin Field, when he tackled Green Bay's Jim Taylor at the Eagles' eight-yard line on the final play of the game, thus preserving Philadelphia's 17–13 victory. As of 2011, it is still the last NFL championship the Eagles have won.

Bednarik also was an All-Pro eight times, was twice All-American at Penn, won the Maxwell Award as a Philadelphia Quaker in 1947 and was named the NFL's greatest center of all time in 1969. Prior to playing pro football, he flew 30 missions in World War II as a B-24 waist gunner with the Army Air Corps, winning the Air Medal.

The Mean Joe Greene Commercial

In "Mean Joe" Greene's day, the Steelers defensive tackle was known as one of the most dominant defensive players in the history of the NFL and was the cornerstone of Pittsburgh's legendary "Steel Curtain" that terrified offenses across the league through the 1970s. He brought such energy and fierceness to each game that he earned a reputation on the field as someone not to mess with. This reputation as a surly, fierce, mean player is what the Coca-Cola Company used to their advantage in creating one of the most memorable commercials in television history.

First aired on September 1, 1979, the commercial shows a beaten and battered Greene walking to the dressing room after a game. A little boy, played by nine-year-old Tommy Okon, approaches Greene, offers him encouragement and gives him his Coke. Mean Joe guzzles the entire bottle, then smiles and gives the kid his jersey, saying those famous words: "Hey, kid, catch." Greene later recalled, "It's very hard to gulp down an entire bottle of Coca-Cola and then speak clearly. The first three takes we did, when I finished the bottle, I looked at the kid and said, 'Hey, kid...*Urrrp!*' It wasn't intentional. I just couldn't say the line without burping."

The ad became so successful that it was later adapted to other countries. In Argentina, soccer legend Diego Maradona played the role of Greene; in Brazil, the ad featured soccer star Zico; and in Italy, it was soccer star Dino Zoff. The commercial has been parodied, written about and copied hundreds of times since it originally aired and even was remade for Super Bowl XLIII, when the Pittsburgh Steelers met the Arizona Cardinals, with Steeler Troy Polamalu playing the role of Greene.

The Birth of Arena Football

A more streamlined version of regular football, arena football was first played in Pittsburgh in 1987. On June 19, 1987, the Pittsburgh Gladiators defeated the Washington Commandoes, 48–46, at the Civic Arena in front of 12,117 fans—the first game in Arena Football League (AFL) history.

Arena football was the brainchild of Jim Foster, who envisioned a game played on a 50-yard field in a hockey arena with eight men per side. Punting would be outlawed, all of the players except quarterbacks, kickers and a defensive specialist (usually a defensive back) would have to play both ways, and balls that went wide of the goalposts, be they kicks or passes, would bounce off netting strung up to the side of the posts and be considered live balls.

Other rules included goalposts that were 15 feet high and twice as narrow as their NFL counterparts, kickoffs from the goal line, three-yard penalties for minor infractions and earning an extra point on a conversion or field goal if a drop-kick was attempted. In 1987, all four teams in the AFL were originally owned by the league, and each team was given a $50,000 per year salary cap for the entire 15-player roster.

But this did not mean that teams were filled with local beer-league talent. The Gladiators' quarterback, Mike Hohensee, was an All-American at Minnesota. Linebacker Craig Walls and lineman Earnest Adams had played for the United States Football League's Pittsburgh Maulers, and wide receiver Greg Best previously played for the Steelers, setting a since-broken franchise record for the longest fumble recovery for a touchdown when he raced 90 yards with the ball in a 1983 victory against the Cleveland Browns.

The first game was not only sold to three-quarter capacity at the Igloo, but was also nationally televised in primetime on ESPN, roughly six weeks before the network would air their first NFL game, with Lee Corso giving color commentary.

Back in Pittsburgh, future Penguins play-by-play announcer Paul Steigerwald and longtime college football commentator Beano Cook called the action on KQV-AM, while famed Meadows track announcer Roger Huston manned the public-address microphone.

On the first play from scrimmage, Russell Hairston, a former defensive back for the Kentucky Wildcats, caught a 45-yard touchdown pass from Hohensee, setting the tone for the AFL's high-scoring, pass-happy feel, not to mention Hairston's own MVP season.

Other highlights included Walls' brother Kendall suiting up against him (both had played at Peabody High School in Pittsburgh) for the Commandoes, future Arizona Wildcats head football coach Mike Stoops as Pittsburgh's possession receiver (met with cries of "Stooooooooooops" whenever he caught a pass), the unusual stance of center Scott Dmitrenko, who cocked one arm at a 23-degree angle prior to snapping the ball, and future Atlanta Falcons defensive coordinator Joe Haering, a native of the Pittsburgh neighborhood of Morningside, as the Gladiators' head coach. Bob Harrison, who later became a Steelers assistant, was Washington's coach, thus becoming the first black head pro football coach since 1922.

The Gladiators won their first four games, then suffered their first loss to the Denver Dynamite, 32–31, under the open roof of the Pittsburgh Civic Arena in front of 14,644 fans. This is still the only outdoor arena football game in history.

Pittsburgh also led the Arena Football League in attendance in 1987, averaging 12,856 fans to earn the right to host the first-ever Arena Bowl. It was a rematch of Pittsburgh and Denver, and again Hairston caught a long touchdown pass in the first quarter. But the score was called back because of a penalty, setting the tone for the day. The Gladiators did not score for three quarters and lost, 45–16.

The Gladiators played for four years in Pittsburgh before moving to Tampa, where they became the Tampa Bay Storm and are still in operation today.

Semipro Football

Think of semipro football, and perhaps an image of the movie *The Longest Yard* sprouts up. Other ideas might be of a romantic, long-ago notion of a team like the Bloomfield Rams in Pittsburgh, where a player like Johnny Unitas could get $6 a game playing on a dusty field to keep his career alive before being signed by the Baltimore Colts, or the old Hope-Harvey team of the early 1930s that evolved into the Pittsburgh Steelers franchise.

But semipro football still lives on. The players play for no money, just the hope of recognition and the love of the game after their high school, college and sometimes even professional careers are over.

Two of the more successful semipro franchises in America are the Central Penn Piranha and the Pittsburgh Colts.

The Piranha, formed in 1995, have never lost more than two games in a season, which always lasts a minimum of 13 games and a maximum of 19. They have won two national championships, 10 league titles and finished undefeated four times. They are generally accepted as the best semipro football organization of the first decade of the 21st century behind such players as Dan McMunn, believed to be the all-time career sack leader in minor league football with 150, and linebacker Melik Brown, who signed with the Arena Football League's Philadelphia Soul prior to the 2011 season.

The Colts, meanwhile, were founded in 1979 by Ed Brosky, a practice player for the 1976 Pitt Panthers national championship team, and played for a minor league football national championship in 1981. Some notable players for the Colts include Darnell Dinkins, who used the team as a springboard to an eight-year NFL career that culminated with the 2009 world champion New Orleans Saints; Carlton Haselrig, who played for the Colts after his NFL career ended; Lisa Horton, who became the first female quarterback to throw a touchdown pass against male competition for the Colts in 2004, then led the Pittsburgh Passion to the National Women's Football Association championship three years later; Steve Moser, who kicked extra points for the Colts until the age of 70; and Tom Yewcik, who quarterbacked the Colts in their formative years after starting for the 1976 national champion Pitt Panthers and before being elected to the Pennsylvania state legislature. The Colts are named after Brosky's high school alma mater, the Chartiers Valley Colts.

The Steelers' 1970s Dynasty

They are a cultural icon, a sports franchise with a name as illustrious as any in pro football. They are a city's passion and, quite possibly, the entity that the metropolis is most associated with. And, depending on one's age and tastes, they may be the only thing on earth that can actually make polka music seem cool.

They are the Pittsburgh Steelers, and, in the 1970s, they constructed the greatest pro football dynasty of the Super Bowl era. In doing so, they completely changed not only the reputation of the franchise but perhaps of pro football as well.

The story of the Steelers' rise in the 1970s has been told many times and is referred to throughout this book, but here's a quick rundown. For 36 years, the Steelers had not won so much as a playoff game before Chuck Noll became the head coach in 1969. The team then invested in scouting with Bill Nunn, formerly a sportswriter for the *Pittsburgh Courier*, who helped bring forth a slew of talent from black colleges, paving the way for the likes of John Stallworth, Donnie Shell and Mel Blount. Three Rivers Stadium opened in 1970, and after the selection of running back Franco Harris in the first round of the 1972 draft, the Steelers "never lost," as team president Dan Rooney would say in his Hall of Fame induction speech.

The Steelers went on to draft nine Hall of Famers from 1969 to 1974—defensive lineman Joe Greene, quarterback Terry Bradshaw, cornerback Blount, linebacker Jack Ham, Harris, wide receiver Lynn Swann, linebacker Jack Lambert, wide receiver Stallworth, and center Mike Webster—including four in 1974 alone (Swann, Lambert, Stallworth and Webster), the year of their first Super Bowl triumph. But it was divine intervention that helped the Steelers win their very first playoff game.

Playing the Oakland Raiders on December 23, 1972, the Steelers hosted their first playoff game since 1947. The Steelers and the Raiders would go on to meet in the postseason for five straight years following the 1974, '75 and '76 seasons, including three straight in the AFC championship game, but no game would be as memorable as this one.

The Steelers led a defensive struggle, 6–0, before Ken Stabler scrambled 30 yards for a touchdown with a minute and a half to play to give Oakland a 7–6 lead. On the ensuing possession, the Steelers were faced with fourth and 10 with 22 seconds left when quarterback Terry Bradshaw escaped a fierce Oakland pass rush and threw to running back Frenchy Fuqua at mid-field, only to be savagely hit by defensive back Jack Tatum. The pass deflected, seemingly headed toward the ground to fall incomplete and eliminate the Steelers' chance of victory.

But on the ricochet, the ball actually went straight toward Harris, the NFL Rookie of the Year, who caught the ball in stride before it could fall to the turf and then raced for the winning 60-yard touchdown, giving Pittsburgh a 13–7 victory, their first ever in the postseason. Jubilant fans stormed the field. Steelers broadcaster Myron Cope, taking a tip from fans Sharon Levosky and Michael Ord, dubbed the play "immaculate," and the term "the Immaculate Reception" was coined. The Steelers had finally won, and their passionate fan base was born. Even today, a statue commemorating what has been called "the greatest play in football history" greets visitors to the Pittsburgh International Airport.

It took the Steelers two more years to win the Super Bowl. The AFC was strong, with legendary teams in Miami and Oakland, yet the Steelers not only held their own, but also surpassed their rivals. In 1974, they won the Super Bowl against the powerful Minnesota Vikings, 16–6, by allowing only 17 yards rushing and 102 yards passing, thanks to the "Steel Curtin" defense of Greene, L.C. Greenwood, Dwight "Mad Dog" White and Ernie Holmes. The next season, they stuffed 14 points in the fourth quarter to come from behind and beat the Dallas Cowboys, 21–17, in Super Bowl X, thanks in large part to a 64-yard touchdown reception by Lynn Swann from Terry Bradshaw on third and five late in the game. Two years later, the Steelers again bested the Cowboys, with

Bradshaw throwing for four touchdowns in a 35–31 victory, thus becoming the first team to win three Super Bowls. They became the first team to win four the very next season when Bradshaw connected with Stallworth for two long passes in the fourth quarter to come from behind and beat the upstart Los Angeles Rams, 31–19. No team in the Super Bowl era has ever won as many world championships in as short a period of time. But perhaps more importantly, the Steelers seemed to capture the nation's fancy. In addition to the ads, catch the reruns of the day and you'll see the Steelers mentioned throughout pop culture, from the episode of *Taxi* in which the cabbies befriend a fictional ex-Steeler (played by Bubba Smith) looking for another shot at the NFL to Dana Plato's Kimberly Drummond character on *Different Strokes* telling an audience that she might want to be the quarterback of the Steelers when she grows up, only to be met with cynicism from Gary Coleman's Arnold.

It was a legendary team at a legendary time. It has been speculated that the Steelers and other winning Pittsburgh teams of the era provided inspiration to western Pennsylvania mill workers who were being laid off to retrain themselves in other fields. Whether one chooses to believe that or not, it can easily be said that the 1970s Steelers helped reverse the fortunes of the franchise, from that of being the NFL's doormat to its most successful team since the 1970 AFL–NFL merger.

Pennsylvania Football Facts

- The Eagles fight song, "Fly, Eagles, Fly!" is heard after every Eagles touchdown at home and before the team is introduced prior to kickoff.

- The combined Steelers–Eagles team of 1943 finished the season with a record of 5–4–1. It was the first winning season for the Eagles franchise and just the second for the Steelers.

- The 1944 merger between the Chicago Cardinals and the Pittsburgh Steelers was referred to in the press as Card-Pitt, but because the team was so bad and failed to win a single game, they became known as Car-Pit because every other team simply walked all over them.

Pennsylvania Football Quotes

"You can't dodge them all...I got hammered plenty of times through the years. But you just get up and keep playing. I can tell you from experience, though, sometimes it hurts like hell."

—Former Steelers quarterback Terry Bradshaw

"Losing has nothing to do with geography."

—Former Steelers head coach Chuck Noll, upon being named to the position in 1969. Noll went on to win more Super Bowls than any other coach (four) with a franchise that had never won a playoff game prior to his being hired.

Chapter Three

College Football: Pitt, Penn State and a Little Bit More

What's a Nittany Lion?

The University of Pittsburgh sports teams adopted the nickname "Panthers" in large part because panthers roamed the area of campus prior to its development. Note, for instance, the Panther Hollow section of Oakland. But while mountain lions are certainly indigenous to central Pennsylvania, what is a "Nittany Lion"?

Penn State can thank native Pennsylvanian Harrison D. "Joe" Mason for their teams' nickname.

Mason, a Monongahela native, captained Penn State's baseball team during the first decade of the 20th century. Scheduled to play at Princeton on April 20, 1904, the Penn State baseball team was given a tour of the campus. Inside a gymnasium was Princeton's mascot, a stuffed and mounted Bengal tiger, which the Penn State nine were then told was "the fiercest beast of all!"

"Up at Penn State, we have Mount Nittany right on our campus where lives the Nittany mountain lion, who has never been beaten in a fair fight," Mason replied. "So, Princeton Tiger, look out!"

Penn State backed up Mason's bravado with an 8–1 victory against Princeton. The seed was planted.

It sprouted three years later. Mason, the anonymous editor of Penn State's first humor magazine, *The Lemon*, urged the university to adopt the Nittany Lion as a mascot and called for a vote. The Class of 1908 agreed, and the Nittany Lion replaced previous mascots, including a bulldog and a mule, as the symbol for Penn State's athletic teams.

What About the Panthers?

The University of Pittsburgh first started referring to themselves as the Panthers in 1909. The university had changed its name from the "Western University of Pennsylvania" the year before, and the informal nickname, pronounced "Whupps," no longer seemed appropriate. Following a meeting of students and alumni on November 16, 1909, the name Panthers was adopted, because, in the words of 1909 graduate George M.P. Baird:

1. *The panther was the most formidable creature once indigenous to the Pittsburgh region.*

2. *It had ancient, heraldic standing as a noble animal.*

3. *The happy accident of alliteration.*

4. *The close approximation of its hue to the old gold of the University's colors (old gold and blue), hence its easy adaptability in decoration.*

5. *The fact that no other college or university then employed it as a symbol.*

In the 1990s, fans often saw a costumed panther nicknamed "Roc" after Steve Petro, a longtime figure in Pitt athletics, who was nicknamed "Rock" while playing for Jock Sutherland.

Joe Paterno

In major college football history, Joe Paterno is the only head football coach to win 400 games. He led Penn State to five undefeated seasons and two national championships, improving the perception of college football in the Northeast in the process.

Paterno also revolutionized college football when Penn State joined the Big Ten Conference, which set in motion a chain of events that would lead to Super Conferences, and in 1986, he became the only college football coach ever to win *Sports Illustrated*'s prestigious Sportsman of the Year award.

Paterno's career bridges generations. When he became Penn State's head coach in 1966, the Southeastern Conference was still segregated. By 2002, female kicker Stephanie Weimer of Serra Catholic High School was trying out for the team.

Commitment to academics, preference given to upperclassmen for starting positions and helping Penn State go from a 30,000-seat stadium when he was an assistant to one that seats more than 100,000 all are part of his legacy, as is the decision not to play Pitt, thus ending one of college football's great rivalries and the premier showcase to the country for Pennsylvania football.

Pop Warner

Willie Stargell wasn't the only legendary Pittsburgh figure to be nicknamed "Pops." Glenn Scobey Warner was given the nickname, without the *s*, for his gentlemanly nature, sage fatherly advice and innovations, as well as for the fact that as a player at Cornell, he was somewhat older than his teammates. Warner is best remembered for what he did as a football coach throughout all three regions of Pennsylvania, at Carlisle, Pitt and Temple.

Warner came to Carlisle in 1899 after coaching stints at Cornell, Georgia and Iowa State. He taught the Indians many plays based on deception, as the Indians were often faster but not as strong as the opponents against which they played. Carlisle went 39–18–3 during his first tenure at the school, before departing for another three-year stint at Cornell. But by 1907, he was back at Carlisle, this time hesitantly allowing a brilliant track and field athlete named Jim Thorpe to play. Together, Thorpe and Warner would dominate college football through 1912 as Carlisle put up records of 10–1, 11–2–1, 8–3–1, 8–6, 11–1, and finally 12–1–1, as well as a mythical national championship in 1912. Warner also compiled a 10–1–1 mark at Carlisle in 1913, but a de-emphasis on the program and the school, which closed in 1917, led to a losing record in 1914. It has been theorized that the Carlisle Indians, representing a school designed to "Americanize" Native Americans, was a major factor in dispelling the racist image of American Indians as savages.

When Warner came to Pitt, the Panthers were already a good football team, finishing 1910 undefeated and unscored upon. But Warner, with his use of the single wing and double wing offense, took what was good and made it great, winning his first 30 games and only losing the 31st by one point. The Panthers won national championships in 1915, 1916 and 1918, and two of his protégés, Jock Sutherland and Doc Carlson, won national championships at Pitt as coaches of the football and basketball teams, respectively.

Warner left Pitt for Stanford after the 1923 season but returned to Pennsylvania as the head coach of the Temple Owls 10 years later. There, he guided the normally woeful Owls to a 31–18–9 record. In 1934, Temple went undefeated and played in the first Sugar Bowl.

The term "Pop Warner Football," a nationwide league of 5- to 16-year-old football players and cheerleaders similar to Little League Baseball, was bestowed to honor Warner after he spoke to the organization in its infancy during a banquet in Philadelphia in 1934.

Jock Sutherland

Jock Sutherland is the greatest football figure in the history of Pittsburgh, a city that may have more of a football legacy than any other in the world. In 24 seasons as a college football coach at Pitt and Lafayette, Sutherland never had a losing record, won six national championships while insisting on playing tough schedules and took Pitt to the Rose Bowl four times.

As a player, Sutherland played guard for Pop Warner at Pitt, leading his team to national championships in 1915 and 1916. He never lost to Penn State either as a player or as a coach, and he even helped fund the construction of Pitt Stadium.

In the 1930s, Pitt football was a dynasty. The Panthers won the national championship four times, and during a nine-year period, from 1929 to 1937, they only once lost more than one game in a season—1930. That year they lost two.

It wasn't just that Sutherland's coaching record at Pitt was 111–20–12, but the Panthers shut out their opponents 78 times. At various points in the 1930s, both Penn State and Notre Dame refused to play Pitt because the Panthers were so dominant, and the 1937 national championship squad with the "Dream Backfield" of Heisman runner-up Marshall Goldberg, Harold Stebbins, John Chickerneo and Dick Cassiano was often described as the best backfield in football history to that point.

Unfortunately, what Sutherland built was dismantled by Pitt chancellor James Bowman, who feuded with Sutherland and is said to have been envious of the coach's fame. When Pitt cut a $48 monthly housing stipend given to football players (the university did not have athletic dormitories at the time), Sutherland resigned after the 1938 season, leaving Pitt with such a reputation that when the Panthers started the 1939 season 3–0, they were ranked number one in the country by the Associated Press, but they lost four of their final six games that season and would not be ranked first again until 1976.

After leaving Pitt, Sutherland became one of the first college coaches to try his hand with the professionals, coaching the Brooklyn football Dodgers to a 15–7 record in the 1940 and 1941 seasons and helping launch Clarence "Ace" Parker into the Pro Football Hall of Fame. He then joined the navy as a lieutenant commander in World War II. After the war, he became the head coach of the Steelers and led them to their first-ever playoff appearance. Sutherland died after the 1946–47 season following surgery to remove a brain tumor.

An interesting side note is that while Warner often used deception in his strategies, Sutherland was much more "smash mouth" and brutal, though both coaches were known to have extremely physical practices.

Jim Thorpe

In 1950, Jim Thorpe was named as the top athlete for the first half of the 20th century by the Associated Press. And although Thorpe was well known as a Major League Baseball player, pro football player and Olympic decathlete, it is perhaps as a football player for the Carlisle Indians that his legacy is best remembered.

Thorpe did more than just lead the Indians to national prominence at the beginning of the 20th century. In an era when many people were led to believe that Indians, or Native Americans, were savages in need of "Americanization," Thorpe's athletic exploits gave many Americans the chance to idolize a Native American for the first time and see through the false barriers of prejudice.

It is said that his coach, Pop Warner, did not want the 5-foot-9½, 144-pound Thorpe to join his football team, theorizing that the game would be too rough for him. But when Thorpe could not be tackled during a practice, Warner relented. As a result, in 1908, Thorpe made the third team All-American status and was selected as a first teamer for the next four years.

In 1911, he kicked four field goals and dominated Carlisle's ground attack in an 18–15 triumph at Harvard in front of 30,000 fans. In 1912, against the Army team and future President Dwight Eisenhower, Thorpe had one touchdown run of 92 yards called back by penalty, so he merely took the next carry 97 yards for a score in a 27–6 victory that led the Indians to the national championship.

It was this victory against Army that proved to be culturally significant. Native Americans, realizing what such a triumph for Carlisle meant, were thrilled at the exploits of Thorpe and his team.

Thorpe would play professional sports in Ohio and New York City, including the baseball and football Giants. After his athletic career ended, he struggled financially, working as, among other things, a movie extra. He died in 1953 and was buried in Pennsylvania after the State of Oklahoma denied his family's request to build a memorial to him. Instead, Thorpe's widow Patricia found a small town named Mauch Chunk between Allentown and Wilkes-Barre that offered to rename their borough after Thorpe and give him a proper memorial, with a grave marker reading: "Sir, you are the greatest athlete in the world."

Pitt Does the Right Thing, and May Have Paid for It

Pitt's Bobby Grier was the first African American to play in the Sugar Bowl when he suited up for the Panthers in their 1955 game against Georgia Tech. Grier received a ton of positive support from the public when Georgia governor Marvin Griffins first recommended that the Yellow Jackets boycott the game. But Ramblin' Wreck (Georgia Tech) head coach Bobby Dodd would have no part of any boycott.

Griffins eventually watched Georgia Tech's 7–0 victory at Tulane Stadium on the Jackets' sideline after Tech fans burned him in effigy, and Grier received bags of supportive fan mail. Incredibly, after the game, the Louisiana state legislature passed legislation making the Sugar Bowl a segregated bowl game once again. This lasted until 1964 and was a large factor as to why the 1963 Panthers, who had a 9–1 record and were ranked third by United Press International (UPI), did not play in a bowl game that season. One wonders if a bowl payout might have helped Pitt avoid the rough years that the program endured for the rest of the 1960s.

Washington and Jefferson Play in the Rose Bowl

The 1921 Washington and Jefferson Presidents, now a Division III program, played in the Rose Bowl, battling California in a scoreless game on January 1, 1922. The Presidents were coached by Hall of Famer Greasy Neale and featured quarterback Charles "Pruner" West, the first African American quarterback to play in the Rose Bowl. W & J could only afford to take 11 men with them to Pasadena, yet they still outplayed the Golden Bears, holding them to just two first downs for the entire game and missing victory when their own touchdown was called back on an offside penalty. Pruner briefly played pro football for the Akron Pros before becoming a successful physician.

Tony Dorsett Helps Revive Pitt

When Aliquippa running back Tony Dorsett came to the University of Pittsburgh in 1973 from Hopewell High School to play for new head coach John Majors after being heavily recruited by assistant Jackie Sherrill, the Panthers were in the doldrums. Pitt had just finished 1–10 and had not had a winning season since 1963. But Dorsett led a large recruiting class and, along with an upgrade in facilities, started a winning era for Pitt football. In his very first game, Dorsett ran for 100 yards in Athens as the upstart Panthers tied Georgia, 7–7, paving the way for a 1686-yard rushing season, a 6–4–1 record and Fiesta Bowl berth for the Panthers, and perhaps the greatest playing career in college football history.

In 1974, Dorsett broke Marshall Goldberg's school record for rushing yards. In 1975, he rushed for a school-record 303 yards to beat Notre Dame, and in 1976, he won the Heisman Trophy and became the first player in NCAA history to rush for 6000 yards as Pitt went 12–0 to win their first national championship since 1937. All of the Panthers' victories in 1976 came by eight points or greater, and Dorsett's 6082 career rushing yards stood as the NCAA Division I-A record for 22 years.

Sherrill, Green and Marino Keep It Goin'

As dominant as the 1976 Panthers were, the 1980 squad may have been even better. The 1980 Pitt squad has been called the greatest-ever collection of college football players by luminaries ranging from their head coach, Jackie Sherrill, to Florida State head coach Bobby Bowden. The Panthers' defensive line of ends Hugh Green and Ricky Jackson, nose guard Jerry Boyarsky and tackles Greg Meisner and Bill Neill all became starters in the NFL as rookies. Behind this front was All-American linebacker Sal Sunseri and safety Carlton Williamson, who would start the next season on the Super

Bowl–champion San Francisco 49ers. An incredible offensive line featured Outland Trophy–winner Mark May and Jim Covert at tackle, center Russ Grimm, and Emil Boures, Rob Fada and Ron Sams rotating at guard. All became starters in the NFL, with May and Covert enshrined in the College Football Hall of Fame and Grimm inducted into the Pro Hall. They blocked for future NFL running back Randy McMillan and gave time for receiver Julius Dawkins to break free for passes from legendary quarterback Dan Marino.

The Panthers limited opponents to fewer than 10 points nine times in the 12 games they played, outscoring their opposition 380–130. When sophomore Marino was injured in mid-season, Rick Trocano, a future NFL player in his own right, stepped in, and Pitt didn't miss a beat. Green finished second in the Heisman Trophy balloting after leading the number one ranked defense in the country that limited opposing rushers to just 1.5 yards per carry. It was the strongest showing a defensive player had ever received in the Heisman balloting at the time.

The 1980 Panthers finished 11–1, the second season of a three-year period in which Pitt produced a 33–3 record and a 42–6 mark during the Marino era. The only setback for the Panthers was a 36–22 loss to Florida State in which Pitt committed seven turnovers and had five field goals kicked against them. Green and the Panthers redeemed themselves when they stuffed South Carolina, led by Heisman Trophy–winner George Rodgers, 37–9, in the Gator Bowl but finished second in the polls behind 12–0 Georgia led by Herschel Walker.

The following season, Marino threw a fourth-down, 33-yard touchdown pass to John Brown in the Sugar Bowl, with 35 seconds left in the game to beat Georgia, 24–20, further adding to the Panthers' legacy. Though they may have only the 1980 *New York Times* computer poll to show for it, Pitt was almost unquestionably the best college football program of the era.

Penn State Wins Two National Titles in the 1980s

For years, the rap on Penn State football has been that they have played a soft schedule. As a result, the 1968, 1969 and 1973 Nittany Lions remained undefeated, but each time finished short of a national championship.

But in 1982, the team finally caught some breaks. First, they handed second-ranked Nebraska their only loss of the campaign, in large part because of a phantom catch by Mike McCloskey late in the game. After suffering a 42–21 loss to old nemesis Bear Bryant in Alabama, the Lions put up six straight victories of nine points or greater against a schedule that featured three ranked foes. Then, when Southern Methodist tied Arkansas late in the season to drop their record to 10–0–1, it was enough to earn second-ranked Penn State a shot at the national championship against top-ranked Georgia and Herschel Walker in the Sugar Bowl, just the sixth time the number one and number two ranked football teams in the country had met in the postseason at that point.

In the championship game, Penn State running back Curt Warner outgained Walker 117 yards to 107, and the Nittany Lions jumped out to a commanding 20–3 lead. When the Bulldogs attempted a comeback, quarterback Todd Blackledge connected with Greg Garrity for a 48-yard touchdown strike early in the fourth quarter that proved to be the winning margin in a 27–23 victory.

Three years later, the Nittany Lions played for the national championship again, but fell to Oklahoma 25–10 in the Orange Bowl. The following season, 1986, the Lions finished the regular season 11–0 again, but were heavy underdogs to the top-ranked Miami Hurricanes in the Fiesta Bowl.

Penn State intercepted five Vinny Testaverde passes, most notably when linebacker Pete Giftopoulos picked off the 1986 Heisman Trophy winner at the goal line on the final play of the game. Punter John Bruno consistently pinned the Hurricanes deep, helping the cause of the Nittany Lions, who were outgained 445 yards to 162 yards in the game and achieved just eight first downs. Still, with the turnovers, long drives weren't necessary. This was proven when linebacker Shane Conlan intercepted his second pass of the game to give Penn State possession at the Miami five-yard line midway through the fourth quarter. D.J. Dozier scored on a six-yard run immediately afterward, and it proved to be the winning margin in a 14–10 victory that gave the Lions their second national championship in four years.

Penn State made one more bid at a national title. They went undefeated in 1994, but, after deciding to join the Big Ten, were forced to play in the Rose Bowl against 9–3 Oregon, whom the Lions easily defeated, 38–20. Nebraska, who had also finished with an 11–0 record in 1994, played in the Orange Bowl against third-ranked Miami, and with a 24–17 victory against a superior opponent, won the national championship.

John Cappelletti

Cappelletti is Penn State's only Heisman Trophy winner. A graduate of Monsignor Bonner High in Drexel Hill, Cappelletti is most remembered not for rushing for 1522 yards and 17 touchdowns in the Nittany Lions' undefeated 1973 campaign, but for his inspiring Heisman Trophy speech in which he dedicated his award to his brother Joey, who would die of leukemia three years later.

Chapter Four

Hockey Night in PA

The First Professional League

For the longest time, hockey historians pointed to the International Hockey League, which was formed in 1904, as the first fully professional league in the history of the sport. Based in northern Michigan, the league had five teams and attracted some of the best players in the game at the time. But, in fact, another league out of the U.S. claims the prize as the first pro hockey league. The Western Pennsylvania Hockey League (WPHL) began as an amateur league in 1890 but made the switch to a fully professional league in 1902. "Professional" meant that the league was formally organized with rules, a board of governors and, most importantly, paid players on a regular basis. The WPHL folded just two seasons later but eventually returned in 1907.

The Pittsburgh Pirates

When the NHL began operation in 1917, it was strictly composed of Canadian teams. Hockey was founded in Canada, and it was relatively easy to find the fans to support an NHL franchise there. The United States, however, proved to be a more difficult nut to crack. It wasn't that hockey was an unknown entity in the U.S., as several leagues and teams had existed for many years, even prior to the creation of the NHL. The problem for U.S.-based hockey was the ability to sustain a professional team long term. Professional-level hockey had succeeded in the U.S. before—in fact, the Seattle Metropolitans of the Pacific Coast Hockey Association won the Stanley Cup in 1917—but ultimately, the PCHA folded in the early 1920s.

The NHL's first foray into the United States came in the 1924–25 season with the addition of the Boston Bruins, and though the Bruins had a horrible record, winning just six games, the people of the city seemed to embrace the new team. With the NHL board of governors feeling much more secure about their push into the States, the league decided to allow the addition of two more American teams. The two cities to receive franchises were New York and Pittsburgh.

New York City seemed the obvious choice for the NHL to expand into, given its large population and future potential. The decision was made to grant Pittsburgh a team because former Toronto National Hockey Association (NHA) owner Eddie Livingstone had been threatening to establish a rival league of his own in the United States and had mentioned Pittsburgh as a possible location. In order to stop Livingstone, the NHL granted the already-existing semipro team, the Pittsburgh Yellow Jackets, a franchise, and they became the seventh club to join the league. The new Pittsburgh Pirates would welcome in some NHL-level players but would keep 10 former Yellow Jackets players.

The Pirates were placed in the newly created American Division along with the New York Americans and the Boston Bruins, and would play their season in Duquesne Gardens in Pittsburgh's Oakland neighborhood. Along with the former Yellow Jackets, the Pirates were joined by several high-profile NHL players, including former Montreal Canadiens goaltender

Roy Worters, right winger Alf Skinner and their coach, former Canadiens defenseman Odie Cleghorn. The Pirates had a solid lineup of players and came into the 1925–26 NHL season with high hopes, even though they were an expansion team.

The Pirates played their first game on Thanksgiving night in Boston against the Bruins, winning the contest by a final score of 2–1. The Pirates continued to surprise their doubters as the season progressed, pushing into the lead of the American Division and finishing the season with enough points to move into the playoffs. The good feelings brought on by the successful season were quickly dashed in the playoffs as the Pirates met the Montreal Maroons in the opening round of a best-of-three series. The Pirates knew they were in tough against the Maroons, who had the league's top scorer, Nels Stewart, and the best goaltender in Alex Connell. The Pirates fell in two straight games before a disappointed home crowd at Dusquene Gardens, while the Maroons went on to win the Stanley Cup.

After such a good start for an expansion franchise, great things were expected of the Pirates in their sophomore year, but they finished the 1926–27 season in fourth place in the league and were out of the playoffs. The following season proved that the club was not simply a one-hit wonder, as they finished with a record of 19 wins, 17 losses and eight ties, and with enough points to push them into the playoffs. They faced the New York Rangers in the opening round in a two-game, total-goal series played in New York. The Rangers blanked the Pirates in the opening game 4–0, giving the Pirates a difficult task in the second and final game of the series, but the Pirates managed to win the second game by a score of 4–2. However, because it was a total-goal series, the Pirates lost 6–4. The Rangers, meanwhile, went on to win the Stanley Cup. This was Pittsburgh's last taste of the Stanley Cup playoffs until the 1970 Pittsburgh Penguins.

The next two seasons were simply awful for the Pirates. In 1928, financial problems forced the original owner of the franchise, James Callahan, to sell the team to an ownership group that included mobster Bill Dwyer. Despite the extra muscle in the boardroom, the product on the ice floundered. The 1928–29 Pirates won only nine of 44 games that season, and the following season, they managed only five wins. With the onset of the Great Depression and a significant drop in attendance, the end of the 1929–30 season also marked the end of the Pittsburgh Pirates.

The Philadelphia Quakers

With the Duquesne Gardens' seating capacity at just 5000, it was decided at the NHL board of governors meeting in association with the Pittsburgh Pirates ownership group that the team would be relocated. It was hoped that the move would be temporary while the world waited for the end of the Depression and for Pittsburgh to build a suitable new arena. So as to not make the franchise move too dramatic, the team went to the other side of Pennsylvania, and, in 1930, the Pittsburgh Pirates became the Philadelphia Quakers.

Fans of hockey in the state had hoped that a change of venue and a new name would change the fortunes of the team, but turning around a team that had won only 14 games in the two previous seasons proved to be too difficult.

In the Quakers' first three games, they only managed to score one goal. Their defense was practically nonexistent, their goaltending was filled with holes, and they did not have one decent scoring forward. As a result, fans stayed away, and the team plunged further into debt. The Quakers finished the season at the bottom of the league with a horrendous record of 4–36–4, for a winning percentage of .136, the lowest in NHL history until the Washington Capitals of the 1974–75 season finished with a percentage of .131.

At the merciful end of the season, the Quakers announced they would not ice a team the following year, planning to return when the economy stabilized. However, the Depression left the owners without any cash to risk on another startup team in the NHL, and both Pittsburgh and Philadelphia would not return to the league until 1967, with the arrival of the Penguins and Flyers.

Remember the Cooperalls?

At the beginning of the 1981–82 NHL season, the Philadelphia Flyers experimented with one-piece pants called Cooperalls instead of the normal half-pants that had been worn in hockey since the beginning of the sport. To be fair, the Flyers were not the only team to try the new look, as the Hartford Whalers also thought it might be a good idea to add the new pants to their uniforms for the 1982–83 season. It was management's thinking that the ankle-length pants that slipped over the players' protective gear would look far better and be more practical on the ice. They were very wrong. Players on the two teams reluctantly put on the new uniform and started the season. From the first game, complaints from the players and the fans began to roll in. Players thought the long pants limited their mobility, and fans thought they looked stupid. Management had hoped that the pants would be well received by the players and perhaps help them in their game as the pants provided a tighter fit, but the statistics tell a different story. In the 1980–81 "pant-less" season, the Flyers had a winning record of 41 wins, 24 losses and 15 ties. During the Cooperalls season of 1981–82, the Flyers' record fell to 38 wins, 31 losses and 11 ties. To prove that this was not simply a bad season for the Flyers, the next year, when the organization returned to the regular half-pants, their record jumped back up to 49 wins, 23 losses and 8 ties.

The Hartford Whalers did not learn from the Flyers' mistake and wore their green long pants for the 1981–82 season, but after that, the NHL decided to ban the Cooperalls league-wide. Fans and especially players could not thank them enough.

No Brotherly Love in This Bunch

The Broad Street Bullies of the 1970s were a force to be reckoned with on the ice. Through sheer physical intimidation and scoring talent, the Philadelphia Flyers of the mid-1970s were one of the only teams in the NHL able to compete with the juggernaut teams of Montreal and Boston. Led by their toothless captain Bobby Clarke, the Flyers bashed, crashed and hacked their way to the top of the league, capturing the hearts of the Flyers faithful and bringing home the Stanley Cup two years in a row.

When the Philadelphia Flyers entered the NHL during the expansion season of 1967–68, they were decent but still needed a few years to coalesce into a club that was able to compete against the powerhouses of Toronto, Montreal and Boston. The Flyers flirted with different systems and players but could not find success in the postseason. They had their worst season in 1969–70, winning only 17 games, but the team ensured their future success in the 1969 draft by selecting Bobby Clarke 17th overall and future enforcer Dave Schultz 52nd overall.

Through drafting and trading, the Flyers were finally developing into a group that could compete with the top teams in the league, adding players like goaltender Bernie Parent, Rick MacLeish and Reggie Leach, but it was the hiring of head coach Fred Shero in 1971 that completely turned around the team and established a style of play that would earn them the nickname "The Broad Street Bullies."

The nickname was coined by *Philadelphia Bulletin* sportswriters Jack Chevalier and Pete Cafone in a January 3, 1973, article written after a particularly brutal 3–1 victory over the Atlanta Flames that involved fights, blood and a lot of penalties. They wrote: "The image of the fightin' Flyers is spreading gradually around the NHL, and people are dreaming up wild nicknames. They're the Mean Machine, the Bullies of Broad Street and Freddy's Philistines." The article was accompanied by the headline, "Broad Street Bullies Muscle Atlanta."

Fred Shero had established a system of hard forechecking, grinding and puck possession that saw the Flyers move from fifth place in the division in the 1971–72 season to Stanley Cup champions in 1974. Shero summed up his team's philosophy with one simple phrase that he had posted in the dressing room: "Take the shortest route to the puck carrier and arrive in ill humor."

The Flyers' game was one of intimidation and skill. Players such as Bobby Clarke and Reggie Leach could deliver devastating checks as well as score skillful goals, backed up by the stellar goaltending of Bernie Parent. By 1974, the remaining teams in the NHL had figured out the Flyers' crash-and-bash system of hockey and implemented ways to get around it. The only problem was that the Flyers were just too good at it. Playing against highly offensive-minded teams like the Boston Bruins, the Flyers used their size and strength to defeat them in the 1974 Stanley Cup finals, and used the same tactics in 1975 to conquer the high-scoring Buffalo Sabres. The victories did not come easy, as every game and every shift required a complete team effort, but the Flyers made it work. By the mid-1970s, the Spectrum had become one of the most intimidating buildings for opponents to venture into. Most notably, the Pittsburgh Penguins visited

Philadelphia 42 times from 1974 to 1989 without a single victory, as the Flyers registered a 39–0–3 mark against the Pens during that time.

The era of the Broad Street Bullies began to fade after the 1976 playoffs, when they again bullied their way into the Stanley Cup finals but were defeated easily in four straight games by the Montreal Canadiens. Two seasons later, the architect of the Flyers' crash-and-bash style, Fred Shero, left the team to become the general manager and coach of the New York Rangers. The era of the "Bullies" passed into history, but the atmosphere that they brought to Philadelphia remains to this day.

The Bullies Force the Russians to Flee

The last great victory for the Broad Street Bullies came not in a regular NHL season or the playoffs, but in a special series game played against the Soviet Union's mighty Central Red Army. Called the "Super Series," the games were simply exhibition matches pitting NHL teams against the Soviets' best teams and were held from 1975 to 1991.

The most powerful of the Russian teams was the Central Red Army, the Soviets' premiere elite squad of players. In the three games that the Red Army played before facing off against the Flyers, they did not lose once. Only the Montreal Canadiens, considered the NHL's most well-rounded team, managed to tie the Red Army 3–3. So when the Russians rolled into the Spectrum on January 11, 1976, they were expected to have a relatively easy time with the undisciplined Flyers. However, this was not the case. The Flyers were not intimidated by the Red Army and continued their rough and rugged style of play. They so caught the Russians off guard with a series of vicious checks and slashing that the entire Soviet bench left the ice midway through the first period in protest. After a delay, the Red Army returned when NHL officials warned them that they would lose their salary for the series if they did not play the entire game. The Soviets returned to the ice accompanied by the mocking boos of the Flyers faithful and managed to muster up just enough energy to finish the game. The Flyers won, 4–1. After the game, Fred Shero commented in his typical fashion, "Yes, we are world champions. If they had won, they would have been world champions. We beat the hell out of a machine."

Although the victory was just in an exhibition series, this was serious hockey. The two teams were playing for hockey supremacy and the right to be known as the best in the sport.

The Hammer

As an integral member of the Broad Street Bullies, Dave "The Hammer" Schultz had quite the reputation around the league for his habit of dropping his gloves and fighting anyone who got in his way. Although his penalty minutes did not match those of other fighting greats such as Tiger Williams and Tie Domi, Schultz was well known as one of the toughest fighters ever to play the game, hence his nickname.

Bobby Clarke

Bobby Clarke was the leader of the Broad Street Bullies, the captain of the Philadelphia Flyers team that became the first of the six 1967 expansion teams to win the Stanley Cup. Additionally, he was an inspiration to anyone who was a diabetic or preferred aggressive hockey.

Clarke came to the Flyers in 1969, and, as a rookie, he was named to the All-Star team. In his third year in the NHL, he scored 35 goals and won the Bill Masterson Memorial Trophy for overcoming diabetes to play in the league. At the time, he was the youngest team captain in NHL history at 23.

Clarke became the first player from an expansion team to score 100 points when he tallied 104 in 1972–73, winning his first Hart Trophy as NHL MVP along the way. The next season was the Flyers' first Cup year, with Clarke scoring the game winner in game two of the finals when he put in a rebound in overtime against Boston's Gilles Gilbert. The Flyers repeated in 1974–75 behind Clarke's 89 assists, a record for a center, and, in 1975–76, he, along with Reggie Leach and Bill Barber, scored 141 goals, the most ever for a single line. Although the team was weakened by the loss of goaltender Bernie Parent to injury, the Flyers still made it to the Stanley Cup finals before bowing to Montreal, and Clarke was awarded his third Hart Trophy. That season marked the peak of Clarke's career, but there were still many highlights to come, including becoming a player–assistant coach in 1979– 80 and seeing the Flyers go 35 games without a loss that season to reach the Cup finals again. He finished with 1210 points in a 15-year career that never saw him play fewer than 62 games in a season, and he was named the Flyers' general manager in 1984.

Clarke was the Flyers' GM on and off for 19 seasons and three Stanley Cup finals appearances. He also was the GM of the Minnesota North Stars when they made their miracle run to the Stanley Cup finals before losing to Mario Lemieux and the Pittsburgh Penguins. But Clarke's tenure as Flyers GM is most remembered for his feud with star center Eric Lindros, who, despite much fanfare upon joining the Flyers, never met Clarke's career high of 119 points scored in a season. Clarke and Lindros' father, who served as Eric's agent, often squabbled, resulting in Lindros sitting out a season until he left for the New York Rangers in 2001–02. Toward the end of Clarke's reign as GM, he was criticized for putting big defensemen on the ice to try to stop smaller, more agile opposing forwards, a philosophy that likely came from his days with the Broad Street Bullies.

"Only the Lord Saves More than Bernie Parent"

Or so read a bumper sticker on a Pennsylvania-registered car during the French Canadian goaltender's reign as the number-one netminder with the Flyers during their golden years in the mid-1970s.

Parent described goaltending as playing "three periods of hell," but he relished every moment of that pressure. Often the joker in the locker room, he made everyone feel comfortable around him, but when it was time to hit the ice, he was all business. As a kid growing up in Montreal in the glory days of Jacques Plante, Parent studied the legendary Canadiens goaltender's every move on the ice—the way Plante played the angles, how he came out to meet shooters and how he played the puck. Parent even had the same odd demeanor that drove his coaches crazy, just like Plante, who was known to knit before a hockey game in order to stay focused.

"You don't have to be crazy to be a goalie," Parent would often say, "but it helps."

Parent got his start in the NHL with the Boston Bruins. He had hoped to make it into the starting job, but the Bruins decided to play Gerry Cheevers instead. It didn't matter much because when the league expanded in 1967, Parent was picked up in the expansion draft by the Flyers. But the Flyers were far from being the physical powerhouse they would become in the mid-'70s, and as a result, Parent's numbers suffered, along with those of the rest of the team. Hoping to find a solution, Parent was then traded to the Maple Leafs, where he was mentored by Jacques Plante, who was then the Toronto goaltender. But despite the presence of his hero, Parent's time with the Leafs left him unhappy, and in 1972, he left the NHL to try his luck with the newly formed World Hockey Association.

Playing in the uniform of the Philadelphia Blazers, Parent only managed to play 63 games before the franchise was forced to shut down because of financial difficulties. Without a team to play for, he faced the prospect of returning to the Maple Leafs organization, as he was still under contract with them, but instead, he demanded a trade back to the Flyers. The Flyers were more than happy to oblige, as their experiments with other goaltenders had failed. Parent returned to Philadelphia for the 1973–74 season and backstopped the Flyers to glory.

With Parent posting a 1.89 goals-against average during the regular season, the Flyers finished second overall in the league, one point behind the first-place Boston Bruins. After disposing of the Atlanta Flames in the opening round of the playoffs in four straight games, the Flyers needed Parent as they faced the tenacious New York Rangers. The series went to seven games, but it was Parent and the Flyers that would come out the winners and take Philly into its first-ever Stanley Cup final.

Up against the Boston Bruins, Parent was facing the most potent offense in the history of the game to that time. During the regular season, Phil Esposito, Bobby Orr, Ken Hodge and Wayne Cashman had finished at the top of the league in scoring. The Bruins had potted an incredible 364 total goals that season, while the Flyers had managed only 273. However, the more telling statistic was that the Bruins had allowed 221 goals, while Parent and the Flyers had allowed just 164.

It was a tough challenge, but as the series got underway, Parent proved more than equal to the task. The Bruins could not figure out Parent, and only once in the series did they manage to score more than three goals in a game. Parent topped off the six-game defeat of the Bruins with a 1–0 shutout to win the Stanley Cup. For his efforts, he received the Conn Smythe Trophy as the playoffs' most valuable player.

Parent followed up that incredible season with a repeat Stanley Cup performance in 1975, and again took his team to the finals in 1976. This time, however, it was the Montreal Canadiens that got the best of the Flyers, winning the Cup in a four-game sweep. Parent remained the Flyers number-one goaltender up until a freak accident during the 1978–79 season, when a player's stick caught him in the eye and forced him to retire at the age of 34. For his brief but spectacular career, Parent was inducted into the Hockey Hall of Fame in 1984.

Mario Lemieux and the Pens Dynasty

In the history of American sports, perhaps only Jackie Robinson was asked to do more and delivered. When Canadian Mario Lemieux was drafted by the Pittsburgh Penguins in 1984, he was asked not only to make the laughing stock franchise into a winning team, but also to play at the same level as Wayne Gretzky. Lemieux did that and more, revitalizing Pittsburgh into a tremendous hockey market and leading the Penguins to Stanley Cup championships both as a player and as an owner. Along the way, he dominated the sport despite suffering from cancer, then saved the franchise yet again by purchasing it. In 2002, he also led the Canadian Olympic men's hockey team to their first gold medal in a half-century.

In Lemieux's rookie season with the Penguins, surrounded by "talent" that had finished 16–58–6 the year before, he scored 100 points and was named the MVP of the All-Star Game. In his second season, he scored 141 points; in his third, 50 goals; and in his fourth, 70, including a memorable break-away game winner late in the season against Washington, with the goalie pulled in sudden-death overtime, a game the Pens had to win to stay alive in the playoff hunt.

Then, in his fifth season, Lemieux finished with 199 points, the most that any player not named Gretzky has ever scored (but truth be told, Gretzky had much more talent around him in Edmonton than Lemieux did in his early years in Pittsburgh). Lemieux's 199-point, 85-goal season set two NHL records: he scored 57.3 percent of the Pens' goals that season, and he tallied 13 goals shorthanded. It was the first time in Lemieux's career that the Pens had made the playoffs, and it was only the beginning.

The next year, Lemieux's star status brought the All-Star Game to Pittsburgh. In the first nationally televised meeting between Lemieux and Gretzky, it was Mario who dominated, tying an All-Star record with four goals and winning MVP honors in a 12–7 Wales Conference victory. The game was held in the midst of Lemieux's 46-game scoring streak, the second longest in NHL history, stopped only because of a back injury.

Injuries seemed to be the only thing that could halt Lemieux. At the start of the 1990–91 season, he missed the first 50 games because he required back surgery, but he returned in time to help the Pens win their first division crown. Penguins general manager Craig Patrick, Herb Brooks' assistant on the 1980 U.S. Olympic men's hockey team that won the gold medal, acquired veterans such as future Hall of Famers Joey Mullen, Ron Francis, Bryan Trottier and Larry Murphy, as well as hard-hitting defenseman Ulf Sammuelsen to complement Lemieux. Now, with Mario centering a line with Kevin Stevens and Mark Recchi, the Pens were about to start a dynasty behind Hall of Fame head coach "Badger" Bob Johnson.

The Penguins would win their first Stanley Cup in 1991 despite losing the first playoff game they played in every series. But led by Lemieux's 44 points, the second-most in postseason history, the Pens were able to overcome any deficit, be it the

2–0 hole they trailed Boston with in the Wales Conference finals or the 2–1 deficit they faced while playing upstart Minnesota. For these efforts, Lemieux won the Conn Smythe Award as playoff MVP.

Despite Johnson's death in the off-season, Pittsburgh repeated in 1992 under Hall of Fame coach Scotty Bowman. Although the team was sluggish in the regular season, finishing third in the Patrick Division, they came on in the postseason. First the Pens rebounded from a deficit of three games to one in the first round of the playoffs to win in seven games, then they defeated the Rangers in six games despite Rangers forward Adam Graves' vicious, hand-breaking chop of Lemieux's forearm in the series' second game. But Francis' hat trick and Troy Loney's strong play in game four, as well as contributions from two newcomers—1990 first-round draft choice Jaromir Jagr and newly acquired Rick Tocchet—led the Pens to victory in games five and six.

It turned out to be the first of 11 straight victories for the Pens. Lemieux was able to return for the Wales Conference finals against Boston and the Stanley Cup finals against Chicago, both Penguin sweeps. Memorable moments against the Blackhawks included a comeback from a 4–1 deficit in game one, thanks to Jagr's game-tying backhanded goal after skating around three defenders late in the third period, then Lemieux's game winner off a faceoff with 13 seconds remaining, and Hall of Fame goalie Tom Barrasso's 27 saves in a 1–0 Pittsburgh triumph in game three. Despite missing four games, Lemieux still led all goal scorers with 14, earning him a second Conn Smythe Award, as well as his third Art Ross Trophy for leading the NHL in scoring during the regular season.

In 1992–93, the Penguins won the Presidents' Trophy for having the best record in the NHL. But Lemieux's biggest triumph that year was his battle against Hodgkin's lymphoma, a form of cancer. Diagnosed on Janurary 12, 1993, as he was on pace to set a new NHL scoring record, Lemieux missed two months of the season while undergoing radiation treatments. On the day of his final treatment, he flew to Philadelphia and scored a goal and an assist against the Flyers. Upon Lemieux's return, the Pens set an NHL record by winning 17 consecutive games, and even when they were upset in the playoffs by the New York Islanders in the second round, they did it with style, overcoming a 3–1 deficit with two minutes remaining in the seventh game to send the match into overtime. Incredibly, Lemieux won the scoring title again despite missing a quarter of the season and was also awarded the Bill Masterson Memorial Trophy for his perseverance and inspiring story. He also started the Mario Lemieux Foundation, which helps fund medical research projects.

Still, all the hits he took early in his career when the Pens were building around him took their toll. Although the Pens and Lemieux continued to play at a high level, he sat out the strike-shortened 1995 season, only to come back with another outstanding season in 1995–96, leading the NHL in scoring again with a five-goal, seven-point game in an 8–4 victory against Wayne Gretzky and the St. Louis Blues at the Civic Arena, a key highlight. The Pens advanced to the Stanley Cup semifinals before bowing to upstart Florida in the finals, but Lemieux still won his third Hart Trophy as league MVP.

Lemieux announced his retirement the following season, one in which he tied an NHL record with four goals in a single period while playing against Montreal. At the time, he was the only player in NHL history to average more than two points per game over a career, and he was named to the Hockey Hall of Fame without having to endure the three-year waiting period for consideration that most players do. However, when the Penguins were forced to declare bankruptcy two years later, Lemieux stepped in and bought the team to keep it in Pittsburgh, then suited up again to lead the team to the Stanley Cup semifinals once more. It was the Penguins' 11th straight postseason appearance.

While the team was in a period of rebuilding early in the 21st century, Lemieux had one more moment of greatness. He captained the 2002 Canadian men's hockey team in the Salt Lake City Olympics, earning Canada its first gold medal in the sport since 1952, and he was the team's second leading scorer in the medal rounds.

Lemieux retired as a player a second time during the 2005–06 season, holder of the record for the highest goals-per-game average combining regular season and playoff games. He has since been instrumental in building a second Stanley Cup contender and overseeing the Consol Energy Center. He was made a knight in the National Order of Quebec by premier Jean Charest in 2009 and has been known to house young up-and-coming Pens stars such as Sidney Crosby and Marc-Andre Fleury in their formative years in the NHL.

Sidney Crosby and Evgeni Malkin

In Montreal, Guy Lafleur succeeded Maurice Richard. In Detroit, Steve Yzerman succeeded Gordie Howe and Ted Lindsay. And in Pittsburgh, "Sid the Kid" and "Geno" have carried the torch originally lit by Mario Lemieux.

The Pittsburgh Penguins had fallen on hard times at the beginning of the 21st century. Although Lemieux returned from retirement to lead his team to the Stanley Cup semifinals in 2001, the Pens' streak of 11 straight playoff berths ended the following season, and the team soon fell to the bottom of the standings. But things began to look up when they were able to draft goaltender Marc-Andre Fleury in 2003, Evgeni Malkin in 2004 and Sidney Crosby in 2005. Playing alongside

Lemieux briefly in his rookie campaign, Crosby broke the Pens' rookie scoring record set by the "Big Guy" with 102 points. The next year, Crosby led the NHL in scoring with 120 points to take the Pens to their first playoff berth in five seasons. Then, as the youngest captain in the team's history, Crosby went to the Stanley Cup finals with the Pens the following year. In 2009, the Pens won the Cup, and, just for good measure, in 2010, Crosby scored the game-winning goal in overtime of the Olympic finals to give Canada's men's team the gold medal in a 3–2 victory against the United States.

Evgeni Malkin is Crosby's sidekick. The NHL's leading scorer in the Pens' Cup season of 2009, Malkin also won the Conn Smythe Award for playoff MVP, joining Lemieux as the only other Pittsburgh player to do so. Malkin was also Rookie of the Year for the Pens during this era's first playoff season of 2007, and, after Crosby took the award in both 2006 and 2007, Malkin won Pittsburgh's prestigious Dapper Dan Sportsman of the Year Award in 2009.

Mario Scores for the Cycle

In the history of hockey, there have been many records established by great players. Joe Malone's seven goals in one game, Rocket Richard's 50 goals in 50 games, goaltender George Hainsworth's 22 shutouts in 44 games during the 1928–29 season, Darryl Sittler's 10 points in one game on February 7, 1976, and—one of the last great records to be established—Wayne Gretzky's 92 goals during the 1981–82 season. By the mid-1980s, it seemed as if all the incredible records and feats of individual prowess had been accomplished. The Richards, Gretzkys and Mike Bossys of the NHL had seemingly done it all and left no magic for future generations. But then came along "Mario the Magnificent."

By the 1988–89 season, fans of the Pittsburgh Penguins already knew that Mario Lemieux was one of the greatest players ever to play the game. Every time he stepped onto the ice, he was considered a threat, but despite his incredible scoring statistics and value to his team, Lemieux had never set one of those memorable records that would be repeated on Sports-center for years into the future. Then, on December 30, 1988, Lemieux scored five goals against the New Jersey Devils. As amazing as a five-goal game is, scoring each goal in a different manner is one of those feats that can be put in the same category as Gretzky's 92 goals and Sittler's 10-point game. Lemieux somehow was able to score a power-play goal, a shorthanded goal, an even strength goal, an empty net goal and a goal on a penalty shot.

After the game, which the Penguins won 8–6, Lemieux spoke to reporters about his accomplishment: "It was a good game. It seems everything I did went the right way. I felt pretty good before the game. I had the day off yesterday and that helps me, especially at this time of year."

He remained modest about his incredible accomplishment, but in the history of the game, no one has ever accomplished a scoring feat so incredible. That's why he was nicknamed "The Magnificent."

The Short But Amazing Life of Pelle Lindbergh

Long considered one of the greatest netminders to come out of Sweden, Pelle Lindbergh started his NHL career with the Philadelphia Flyers in 1982. The future looked very bright for the young phenom. The Flyers first noticed Lindbergh playing for Sweden in a game against Czechoslovakia during the 1980 Olympic hockey tournament. The Czechs were by far the better team, constantly on the puck and firing shots on Lindbergh from all angles. The Swedes were outshot

36 to 16, but Lindbergh's goaltending made the difference in a 4–2 victory for Sweden.

Blessed with lightning-quick reflexes and excellent technical skills, Lindbergh played the game like Grant Fuhr. The Swedish goalie impressed wherever he played. "I've never seen a goalie with such fast legs," said goaltending legend Jacques Plante.

The Philadelphia Flyers signed him to his first professional contract in 1980. After playing for a full season with the Flyers' farm team in Portland, Maine, Lindbergh finally realized his dream when he played eight games during the 1981–82 regular NHL season. He impressed the Philadelphia brass enough to earn a spot on the team and played 40 games during the 1982–83 regular season, earning a respectable 2.98 goals-against average.

Lindbergh's career peaked during the 1984–85 season, when he played in 65 games and led the Flyers to the top spot in the league. For his amazing efforts, he received the Vezina Trophy, the highest honor a goaltender can receive and a first for a European player. Lindbergh helped the Flyers in the 1985 playoffs by getting them past their first-round opponents, the New York Rangers. Next, Philadelphia defeated the New York Islanders, with Lindbergh registering two shutouts. The Quebec Nordiques fell in six games, but Lindbergh's luck ran out when he met Wayne Gretzky and the Edmonton Oilers, who eliminated the Flyers in five games.

Lindbergh signed a six-year deal with the Flyers during the off-season and immediately went out and bought himself the car of his dreams, a Porsche. Just eight games into the 1985–86 season, Lindbergh hit a concrete wall while driving in New Jersey. Although he initially survived the crash, he was left in a vegetative state with little hope of recovery. His parents made the difficult decision to disconnect the artificial life support on November 11, 1985, ending Pelle's promise of an illustrious career as one of the league's top goaltenders. He was just 26 years old.

Hextall Scores a Goal

When Ron Hextall entered the NHL as a rookie, he proudly declared that one day he would score a goal. "I've worked on my shot a lot. I can hit the net from our zone. I've even practiced a bank shot. I'm just waiting for the right situation," said the confident young rookie. Just one year later, he would achieve his dream of becoming the first goaltender in NHL history to shoot a puck into the opposition's net.

On December 8, 1987, the Flyers were up by two goals against the Chicago Blackhawks with one minute remaining in the game. The Hawks pulled their goalie in favor of an extra attacker. Then came the mistake Hextall had been waiting for. He got the puck on a bad dump-in by the Hawks, dropped his hands to the shooting position, took one last look at the empty net and fired the puck down the ice to score. "I don't mean to sound cocky," Hextall said after the game. "But I knew it was just a matter of time before I flipped one in."

One goal wasn't enough for Hextall, who repeated his amazing achievement the following year in the playoffs against the Washington Capitals.

Kate Smith Blesses the Flyers

The Broad Street Bullies had a plethora of hockey skills at their disposal to help them win games: large, bruising defensemen, skilled scoring forwards, Vezina Trophy–winning goaltending—and the sweet vocals of Kate Smith.

It seemed that whenever she sang "God Bless America" before a Flyers home game, they won. The Flyers' record in the seven years when they occasionally substituted the national anthem for Smith's "God Bless America" was an incredible 36–3–1. Whether it was the inspirational words of the song or the tone of her voice, something about Smith's singing propelled the team to victory, and they carried those winning ways into the 1974 Stanley Cup playoffs.

In the first round against the Atlanta Flames, the Flyers won in four straight with the assistance of Smith in both home games. Then they faced off against the New York Rangers and jumped out to a 2–0 series lead, but New York bounced back with two wins at home to tie the series. Both teams then traded wins to force a deciding seventh game in Philadelphia. The Flyers were taking no chances this time. Before the game started, Smith came out onto the ice and belted out "God Bless America" to the delight of the sold-out arena. With Lady Luck Kate Smith on their side, the Flyers took an early lead and finished off the Rangers to move into the Stanley Cup finals to play the Bruins. Kate Smith had come through again.

In the finals, the Flyers had a 3–1 series lead and traveled to Boston to try to finish the Bruins on their home turf. The game was a bloody affair filled with spearing, crosschecking, fighting and slashing. The Bruins won the game 5–1, and as the Flyers made their way off the ice at the end of the game, the Boston fans began singing their own version of "God Bless America" in a sarcastic tone.

In response to the taunts by Bruins fans, Kate Smith belted out her most powerful and inspiring version of the song at the start of the next game, hoping to impart some luck to the Flyers so that the series would not have to return to Boston. The song, however, seemed to inspire both teams. The pace of the game was fast, and both the Bruins and the Flyers had their fair share of chances, but it was the Flyers that got on the board first, and Bernie Parent kept the Bruins from scoring a single goal. The Flyers and Kate Smith had won the Stanley Cup.

Even though Smith passed away in 1986, to this day, the Flyers still play the song before major playoff games. Another singer will begin the song, and then halfway through, a video recording of Smith singing is put on screen as she belts out the final notes of "God Bless America."

Stanley Cup Fog

Game three of the 1975 Stanley Cup finals between the Buffalo Sabres and the Philadelphia Flyers was one of the strangest in playoff history. Ever since hockey became an indoor sport, weather was never really a factor in what happened on the ice. Ice surface quality had improved over the years, and by the mid-1970s, you could have a near-perfect sheet of ice inside, while the sun blared down outside. There were occasional malfunctions in equipment that resulted in poor ice conditions, but on May 20, 1975, a heat wave swept across New York State and, for one of the first times, affected an NHL game inside an arena.

Memorial Auditorium in Buffalo had no air-conditioning, and when 20,000 excited fans added their own heat to an already warm interior, the temperature at rinkside rose to an incredible 87°F. The heat made the ice surface soft and watery, and created a thick layer of fog that spread eerily across the rink. Since this was the playoffs, the game was allowed to proceed, but as time went on, the fog just got thicker. Several times during the first period, the referees had to stop play and ask the players to skate around the ice in order to disperse the fog so they could see. When that failed, maintenance crews had to be called out to wave large sheets to get rid of the troublesome fog. On top of the visibility issues, as the ice melted and turned into vapor, noxious chlorine fumes were released into the air, making players light-headed and forcing the coaches to run short shifts. Because visibility was so poor, the game became a bonus for shooters and a bust for goaltenders.

On the first five Flyers shots, Buffalo goaltender Gerry Desjardins let in three goals, unable to see the puck until the last second. The Sabres managed to rally from behind with a few mist-shrouded goals of their own to send the game into overtime, tied 4–4. The game ended in Buffalo's favor when Rene Robert managed to sneak in a bad-angle shot that Bernie Parent lost sight of in the fog.

An Example of Hockey Gamesmanship

There is definitely no love lost between the Montreal Canadiens and the Philadelphia Flyers, and that mutual hatred came spilling out onto the ice during the 1987 playoffs when the two teams met in the Conference finals.

Canadiens Shayne Corson and Claude Lemieux had developed a ritual before every game of waiting until all the opposing players had left the ice after the pre-game skate so that they could shoot a few pucks into the other team's net. After several games of watching the two Canadiens players throw pucks at their net, Flyers tough guy Ed Hospodar enlisted the services of goaltender Chico Resch to put an end to this insulting ceremony. When the horn sounded at the end of the pre-game skate, Corson and Lemieux waited for the Flyers to leave the ice, but when they saw that Resch and Hospodar were determined to be the last players to do so they eventually retreated to the Canadiens dressing room.

Feeling like they had accomplished their mission in disrupting the Canadiens' ritual, Hospodar and Resch made their way to their dressing room. But just as they were about to move out of sight, they looked back and noticed that Corson and Lemieux had popped back onto the ice and were rushing toward the Flyers net with a puck. Resch was the first to react, whipping his stick at the puck, but he missed, and Lemieux scored his ritual goal. Two seconds later, Hospodar was out on the ice, raining down punches on Lemieux's head. It didn't take long for both dressing rooms to get wind of the fight, and the ice of the Montreal Forum quickly became the scene of a brawl. As there were no referees on the ice at the time, the battle raged for over 10 minutes, much to the delight of the crowd. The only one to receive a punishment from the league in the whole affair was Hospodar, who was suspended for the remainder of the playoffs. The Flyers ended up winning that game and clinching the series to move on to the finals—where they would lose to the Edmonton Oilers.

Longest Winning Streak(s)

The Philadelphia Flyers were just beginning to shake off the Broad Street Bullies image they had expertly cultivated during the '70s and were transitioning their team to the faster style of hockey that had been pioneered by the New York Islanders and the Edmonton Oilers. The Flyers were a team of aging veterans and young talent, not expected to go very far when the 1979–80 season got underway. Pat Quinn was just entering his first full year as head coach of the team, having taken over halfway into the previous season. Pete Peeters was in goal in place of the popular Bernie Parent but had yet to show that he could take over as the number-one goaltender. However, the Flyers started off the season with confidence, winning their season opener on October 14, 1979, against the Toronto Maple Leafs by 4–3, and in mid-December, they had yet to lose. By January 7, 1980, they had compiled an amazing record of 25 wins and 10 ties. That January night, they played the Minnesota North Stars and tried to extend their streak to 36 games but were defeated 7–2. The 35 games

are a record for the longest unbeaten string (wins plus ties) in
NHL history.

Not to be outdone, the Pittsburgh Penguins have the longest
winning streak in NHL history, 17 games in 1993. This amazing
string of victories coincided with the return of Mario Lemieux,
who missed 24 games after being diagnosed with Hodgkin's
lymphoma and receiving radiation treatments to cure it. Just
two games after returning, having scored a goal and an assist
against the Flyers on the same day he received his final treatment, the Pens beat the Boston Bruins at the Civic Arena,
3–2, on March 9. Pittsburgh would not lose again for the rest
of the regular season.

The first three games of their streak were decided by one
goal, including a 4–3 overtime victory against Wayne Gretzky's
Los Angeles Kings won on a Jaromir Jagr power-play goal
after future Pens assistant coach Tony Granato was called for
slashing in the extra period. In both the fourth and fifth
games of the streak, Lemieux scored four goals. In the sixth,
Kevin Stevens got his 50th goal of the season, and in the
ninth, goalie Tom Barrasso stopped 36 Boston shots. The 13th
game of the streak saw Pittsburgh overcome a 2–0 Quebec
lead to win, 5–3, at the Colisée de Québec to clinch the
Presidents' Trophy. The 14th straight victory saw the Pens
win without defensemen Ulf Samuelsson and Kevin Stevens,
and the 15th win on April 7, which tied the NHL record set by
the New York Islanders in 1982, saw the Pens beat Montreal,
4–3, on Samuelsson's game-winning slap shot in overtime.
Ironically, it was the Pens who had stopped the Islanders'
streak 11 years before.

The 16th game was never in doubt. On April 9, 1993,
Lemieux scored five goals to lead the Pens to a 10–4 victory
at Madison Square Garden against the Rangers, then added
one more victory the next day against the Blue Shirts in

Pittsburgh, 4–2. The streak ended with a 6–6 tie against New Jersey in the final game of the regular season.

All in all, Lemieux scored 27 goals and registered 23 assists during the streak. His time off had put him 12 points behind Pat LaFontaine for the NHL scoring lead, but when the streak ended, he had won the Art Ross Trophy by 12 points, 160–148.

Superstar City

The Pittsburgh Penguins have had eight players who scored 50 goals in a season since the team joined the NHL in 1967. No other team in the NHL has had more 50-goal scorers, not even the 100-year-old Montreal Canadiens or the high-scoring Edmonton Oilers. Embracing an open, offensive style of hockey has allowed the Penguins to ice some of the most skilled and creative goal scorers in the history of the game. They are Pierre Larouche (53 goals), Jean Pronovost (52), Rick Kehoe (55), Mike Bullard (51), Mario Lemieux (54, 70, 85, 69, 69, 50), Jaromir Jagr (62, 52) and, finally, Sidney Crosby (51).

Pennsylvania Hockey Facts

- On November 28, 1925, legendary Montreal Canadiens goaltender Georges Vezina played his final game. He keeled over in pain after two periods of play and passed away a few months later from tuberculosis.

- Forward Hib Milks was the Philadelphia Quakers top scorer, recording 17 goals during the 1930–31 season.

- Only one of the Philadelphia Quakers' 22 players was American born: Cliff Barton, born in Sault Ste. Marie, Michigan.

- The NHL record holder for most penalty minutes (career) for a goalie is Ron Hextall, with 584. The Flyers goaltender wielded his goalie stick like an ax and picked up his fair share of penalties along the way.

- The record for the most penalty minutes (season) for a goalie, 113, is held by Ron Hextall (Philadelphia), 1988–89. Maybe if he'd had to sit in the penalty box, he would have learned his lesson.

- Hextall also holds the record for the most penalty minutes (playoffs, career) for a goalie—115. Hextall did not help his team's hunt for the Stanley Cup at all because he gave his opponents so many power-play chances. This is probably one of the reasons why he finished his career without a Cup to his name.

- The record for the most playoff losses in a season, 11, is shared by Ron Hextall (Philadelphia), 1986–87, and Miikka Kiprusoff (Calgary), 2003–04. When almost every series goes to seven games and you make it to the Stanley Cup final, you accumulate a few losses.

- Despite being diagnosed with diabetes at the age of 15, Bobby Clarke went on to have an incredible NHL career and earned a spot in the Hockey Hall of Fame.

- At the end of the 1972–73 season, Philadelphia Flyers forward Rick MacLeish became the first expansion team player to score 50 goals when he compiled a total of 50 goals and 50 assists that season.

- The 1975 Philadelphia Flyers were the last team in NHL history to win a Stanley Cup with an all-Canadian lineup.

- Sidney Crosby became the youngest player to wear the captain's "C" on his jersey at the tender age of 19 years and 297 days. The previous record holder was Vincent Lecavalier of the Tampa Bay Lightning at 19 years and 324 days.

- Sidney Crosby wears the number 87 because he was born on August 7, 1987 (08/07/87).

- NHL players born in Pennsylvania:

Bob Beers (Pittsburgh)

Pete Babando (Braeburn)

Irwin Boyd (Ardmore)

Tom Brennan (Philadelphia)

Jay Caufield (Philadelphia)

Nate Guenin (Sewickley)

Christian Hanson (Venetia)

Chad Kolarik (Abington)

Grant Lewis (Pittsburgh)

Ryan Malone (Upper St. Clair)

Justin Mercier (Erie)

Ryan Mulhern (Philadelphia)

Gerry O'Flaherty (Pittsburgh)

George Parros (Washington)

Dylan Reese (Pittsburgh)

Mike Richter (Abington)

David Sloan (Philadelphia)

Jesse Spring (Alba)

Ray Staszak (Philadelphia)

Eric Tangradi (Philadelphia)

Bill Thomas (Pittsburgh)

R.J. Umberger (Pittsburgh)

Mike Weber (Pittsburgh)

John Zeiler (Jefferson Hills)

Pennsylvania Hockey Quotes

"Success is not the result of spontaneous combustion. You must first set yourself on fire."

—Flyers coach Fred Shero

"Win today and we walk together forever."

—Fred Shero

Chapter Five

Talkin' Baseball

Major League Baseball in Altoona

Pittsburgh and Philadelphia aren't the only cities in Pennsylvania to have a Major League Baseball team. For a month and a half in 1884, Altoona had one as well.

Ninety-one years before Andy Messersmith sued for free agency in baseball, the Union Association (UA) was an upstart league that offered players an escape from the reserve clause that bound a player to the organization that signed him until he was traded, sold or released.

In 1883, an independent baseball club was formed in Altoona that averaged 1600 patrons a game. The team searched for a minor league to join in 1884 but was rebuffed, so they decided to make a bold attempt at applying to the newly formed Union Association, which was trying to be a major league alongside the National League and the American Association.

The UA, meanwhile, needed a western Pennsylvania city to host a franchise and was unable to place one at the beginning of the season in Pittsburgh. Although Altoona may have been significantly smaller than the other seven cities in the league—Baltimore, Boston, Chicago, Cincinnati, Philadelphia, St. Louis and Washington—it was a major railroad hub and therefore made sense geographically, especially with the placement of the other franchises.

Unfortunately, the Pride, or "the Famous Altoonas" as they were billed when they visited Cincinnati, were not of major-league caliber. They lost their first 11 games, including one played in St. Louis on a Sunday, which angered their fans back in Pennsylvania who adhered to blue laws.

Although the Pride drew more than 6000 fans for their first three home games, the fad wore off quickly. By the end of May 1884, Altoona was just 6–19 and drawing only 200 fans a game. The team was forced to disband, as was the UA after the season ended.

The Pride had one lasting legacy—rookie shortstop Germany Smith, Altoona's leading hitter with a .315 average. Although he made Altoona his home for the rest of his life, Smith landed with a National League team in Cleveland later in 1884 and went on to play 15 years of Major League Baseball, mostly with Brooklyn and Cincinnati.

How the Pirates Got Their Name

Upon their inception in the late 19th century, the Pittsburgh Pirates were originally known as the Alleghenys. This name came from the fact that they played in Allegheny City, now referred to as Pittsburgh's North Side neighborhood, which was incorporated into Pittsburgh in 1907. The Alleghenys became the Pirates not so much because of the phonetic alliteration or an early attempt at marketing, but because of an 1891 player transaction.

Although the battles that Curt Flood and Andy Messersmith engaged in during the 1960s and '70s brought free agency to Major League Baseball for good, baseball players' desire to break the reserve clause that bound a player to his team until he was traded, sold or released was hardly a new concept. In 1890, major league players created their own league, the Players League, and many of the top players of the day flocked to the new organization. No team was harder hit by player defection than the Alleghenys. They filled in their roster with local amateurs and struggled to a franchise worst 23–113 record.

The Players League lasted for only a year, and upon its demise, players were ordered back to their old teams. However, one man did not comply with the order. Louis Beirbauer, a .300-hitting second baseman and a member of Philadelphia's American Association franchise in 1889, signed with Pittsburgh instead of returning to his former team. The act was referred to as "an act of piracy on the high seas" by a Philadelphia newspaper, and the name "Pirates" stuck.

Today, one of the private clubs in Pittsburgh's PNC Park is named "Bierbauer's" after the player who could be called the original Pittsburgh Pirate.

The Urban Legend of the Bucs' 1908 Pennant Race

The 1908 baseball season is best remembered for "Merkle's Boner," when the New York Giants lost a pennant to the Chicago Cubs after Fred Merkle failed to touch second base while running from first on what appeared to be a game-winning hit by Al Bridwell, resulting in a tie game late in the season. When the two teams tied for first place at the end of the season, the Cubs won the extra game and took the pennant. What isn't well known is how close the Pittsburgh Pirates came to winning the pennant that year, which would have given them five pennants in the 1900 to 1909 decade.

The Pirates finished one game out of first place in 1908 but led the National League by a half-game heading into the last game of the season at West Side Grounds in Chicago on October 4.

In front of what was believed to be the largest crowd ever to see a baseball game at that point, Hall of Famer Vic Willis and the Pirates lost, 5–2, to Mordecai "Three Finger" Brown and the Cubs. Had the Pirates won the game, they would have taken the pennant, and Merkle's infamous error would have gone unnoticed.

Interestingly enough, Hank O'Day, the same umpire who called Merkle out, also arbitrated this game. And at the top of the ninth with a man on base, Pirates batter Ed Abbaticchio hit a long drive down the right field line that was ruled just foul. The play was so close that O'Day consulted with a colleague to back him up, but the ruling stood.

This play gave rise to a long-standing urban legend. Supposedly, a fan brought a lawsuit to court in the months that followed, stating that she had been injured when struck by Abbaticchio's drive, but the court ruled against her since it was determined she was sitting in fair territory, not foul. Those Pirates fans who believe the story have been left wondering what might have been.

However, the incident never happened. In 1965, Herbert Simons and the staff of *Baseball Digest* checked through the records of every Chicago court and newspaper dated up to two years after the game and found no record of such a trial.

The Pirates had to be content with winning the World Series the following year instead.

What's a Philly?

The original name for the Philadelphia baseball club, the Phillies, stuck when three-year-old filly Regret won the 1915 Kentucky Derby, the first years that Philadelphia took the National League pennant. The Phils were briefly called the Bluejays when the Carpenter family took over the team during World War II, but the new name was unpopular, and the team switched back to the original name.

D'oh!

There are legends for every position in baseball, and umpire Bill Klem was one of the most memorable men ever to call the game. He never took his job lightly and remained passionate throughout his career. His dedication to and respect for the game can be summed up in his most famous quotation: "Baseball is more than a game, it's a religion." Because baseball was so important to him, Klem expected those around him to conduct themselves with the same dignity and professionalism that he brought to the game. But, sometimes, his stubborn passion for the game could blind him to the reality of what was happening in it.

During one game in 1913, Klem was the recipient of numerous boos and jeers from the Pittsburgh Pirates dugout. After several innings of constant booing, Klem walked over and told the manager and players in a loud and convincing voice that he would toss out the next player who spoke out of turn to him.

When play resumed, the next Pirates batter stepped into the box, and Klem asked him for his name. After just getting yelled at by the umpire, the player sheepishly mumbled his name. But Klem could not hear over the noise of the crowd and shouted in a no-nonsense tone for the player to speak up. The Pirates batter looked the umpire in the eye and said, "Booe!"

Suddenly, Klem went beet red in the face and tossed the young batter out of the game. Pirates manager Fred Clarke ran out of the dugout to demand why his player had been kicked out of the game. Klem, confident in his decision, explained to Clarke that when he asked him his name, the kid answered, "Boo." There was no way the young man was going to get away with a smart answer like that under his watch.

With a huge smile on his face, Clarke informed the umpire of the batter's name: Everitt Booe. Play eventually resumed after Klem removed his foot from his mouth.

It's in the Cards

"T206" refers to the baseball cards produced by the American Tobacco Company from 1909 to 1911. The cards were added to packs of loose tobacco, and, at that time, baseball cards were quite common. However, it was the size, rarity and quality of the color lithographs that made this series of cards so collectable and so expensive today. In among the 523 cards of the T206 set is one card in particular that stands out, that of Pittsburgh Pirates legend Honus Wagner.

At the time of the card's printing, Wagner was one of the top players in the game and the most recognizable face to the wider public. He had already given the rights to various companies to use his image to advertise products such as chewing gum, gunpowder and soft drinks. (Times have changed. Imagine the slogan: "Sidney Crosby Brand Gunpowder: Explodes with the Same Force as Crosby's Shot.") However, Wagner had never given his consent for the American Tobacco Company to use his picture, and in 1912, he threatened legal action if they did not remove his image from the card.

The reason for Wagner wanting to have his image taken off the card has been the subject of much speculation, but the most commonly held belief was that he did not want his name and face associated with tobacco, as many young fans might purchase the packets just to get his picture. Having his card removed from the series increased both its rarity and its historical value. So from the time of the first issue in 1909 until 1911, only 50 to 200 cards were ever released to the public, and in among those, Wagner's would become the most expensive baseball card in history.

First listed in 1933 in Jefferson Burdick's *The American Card Catalog* as having a value of $50, the Honus Wagner card would far exceed its initial valuation. One card in particular began its journey in the hands of a collector named Alan Ray from Hicksville, New York, who sold his T206 Honus Wagner for $25,000 in 1985 to a sports memorabilia dealer. The dealer held onto the card until 1987, when he sold it to a California businessman for $110,000. Then, in a 1991 auction, the card was put up for $114,000, but interest was high, and by the time the auctioneer closed the sale, the card had fetched $451,000.

The new owners of the card were none other than Wayne Gretzky and Los Angeles Kings owner Bruce McNall. Soon thereafter, the card became known as the Gretzky T206 Honus Wagner. Gretzky sold the card in 1995 for $641,500, and in 2000, it was sold again for $1.265 million, then once more in 2007 for $2.35 million, before an anonymous collector from California finally bought it for the enormous sum of $2.8 million.

Just how good a player was Wagner? It is difficult to compare eras in sports history. Athletes are bigger and stronger today, and also use superior equipment. Fans of the historical aspect often argue that the athletes of yesterday were not as corrupted by money and had a better sense of the fundamentals. However, nearly a century after playing his last game with the Pirates, one thing that can be said about Honus Wagner is that he is still listed as the greatest shortstop of all time on most historians' lists. It is likely that no other athlete of the dead-ball era is consistently ranked as high as he is.

Wagner led the National League in a statistical category 38 times in his career, including eight batting titles. After spending three years with the Louisville Colonels in the

19th century, he played entirely for Pittsburgh from 1900 to 1917. The Colonels and the Pirates merged in 1900 after Louisville owner Barney Dreyfuss purchased the Pittsburgh franchise. And when Wagner's career is recalled, historians find he was a .328 lifetime hitter, stole 722 bases and retired as the sixth leading home run hitter in the history of the major leagues with 101.

The 1909 World Series has historically been viewed as a showdown between the two greatest players of the day, Honus Wagner and Ty Cobb. Wagner and rookie pitcher Babe Adams, who won three games in the series, led the Bucs to a seven-game victory, with Wagner hitting .333 to Cobb's .231.

Art McKennan, the Pirates' longtime public-address announcer who worked for the team from 1919 to 1993, as a boy had the privilege of seeing Wagner play. He ranked Wagner's range at shortstop as the second greatest he'd ever seen, behind only Ozzie Smith. But when one considers that McKennan only saw Wagner at the end of his career, and that in his prime, Wagner's total chances per game actually exceeded those of Smith, a legitimate argument can then be made for the potential greatness for Wagner if he was playing today.

After his playing career ended, Wagner served as a coach for the Pirates for 21 years. He also owned a sporting goods store that remained in operation in Pittsburgh until 2011. He was elected to the first class of the Baseball Hall of Fame in 1936, and legendary New York Giants manager John McGraw called Wagner the greatest player ever.

Willie Stargell

Willie Stargell, who played for the Pirates from 1962 to 1982, was not only the most feared slugger of his day, but also the most universally beloved. The Pirates slugger had, perhaps, more raw power than any baseball player who ever lived. In an era before steroids and one in which speed and pitching were the dominant forces in the game, Stargell hit more home runs than any other player in the 1970s—296—and hit them longer than almost anyone who has ever played baseball.

Until Mark McGuire, Stargell was the only player to hit a home run completely out of Dodger Stadium. As of 2010, he is still the only player to have done it twice. He hit the longest home run in the history of Veterans Stadium in Philadelphia and Olympic Stadium in Montreal, and he hit twice as many upper-deck home runs at Three Rivers Stadium—four—than any other player in history. He also hit more home runs at Shea Stadium than any visitor, hit seven of the 18 blasts that reached or cleared the right field roof at Forbes Field despite playing at the park for only seven full seasons, and in 1970, he hit home runs at all 14 ballparks he played in, including the somewhat exacting task of hitting homers at both Crosley Field and Riverfront Stadium in Cincinnati despite playing only three games in those parks.

Stargell also is perhaps the only man in baseball history to hit a home run into a swimming pool (at Jarry Park in Montreal) and a tuba (in the 1965 All-Star Game, his blast went into the bullpen at Minneapolis' Metropolitan Stadium and landed in the instrument of a marching band that was there at the time).

But Stargell's legacy is so much more than his home runs. He is remembered for his gentlemanly nature and community service, most notably raising money to find a cure for sickle-cell anemia. His love of Pittsburgh was infectious—the city's nickname "City of Champions" is often attributed to Stargell from when he told Pittsburgh fans at the Pirates' 1979 World Series championship celebration, "We come from a city that has nothing but champions!"

"If you took a poll of all 650 major league players, there wouldn't be a guy who wouldn't like him," Joe Morgan said.

Stargell will best be remembered for his 1979 season. He may have only led the National League in one statistical category—fielding percentage (setting a Pirates record of .997 that stood for 15 years)—but his contributions went beyond hitting .281 with 32 home runs and 82 runs batted in.

He was the captain of the team, offering guidance and leadership to his teammates like few other players have in baseball history. Few remember the nickname Pirates broadcaster Bob Prince gave Stargell early in his career, "Willie the Starge." No, Stargell will forever be remembered as "Pops," the calming father figure and team patriarch of a wild and crazy collection of talent. After hearing Sister Sledge's hit "We Are Family" during a rain delay, Stargell immediately proclaimed it as the Pirates' official team song to demonstrate the closeness the team felt toward one another, and the idea took off, forever earning the team the nickname "The Family." He also gave out small gold stars, known as "Stargell Stars," to his teammates for key contributions, which the players placed on their unique "pillbox-style" caps.

Furthermore, in 1979, Stargell became the only player in baseball history to be named Most Valuable Player of the regular season, League Championship Series and World Series in the same year. His home runs in the NLCS helped Pittsburgh beat the Reds in the playoffs for the first time after three NLCS defeats earlier in the decade, and his seven long hits against Baltimore set a World Series record, including a two-run home run in the sixth inning of the seventh game to gave "The Family" the world championship.

That season, he was also named *Sports Illustrated*'s "Sportsman of the Year" with Terry Bradshaw, as well as earning a slew of other similar awards from sources such as *The Sporting News* and *ABC's Wide World of Sports*. His popularity was such that it seemed the public at large couldn't get enough of this great man who, after his playing career ended, would narrate speeches from the likes of Martin Luther King Jr. or Abraham Lincoln to the accompaniment of a symphony orchestra and sit on a board of Pennsylvania wine tasters. Sitcoms would drop his name into dialogue, interview requests soared and endorsements popped up from everyone from Burger King to People's Gas.

Stargell retired in 1982 after playing 21 seasons with the Pirates, having set many team records, including most home runs, with 475, and no other player in the history of the Pirates played on more first-place teams. Stargell was elected to the Hall of Fame on the first ballot in 1988, and he worked as a coach and front-office staff of the Pirates and Atlanta Braves until his passing in April 2001 at the age of 61.

Roberto Clemente

Like Willie Stargell, Roberto Clemente played his entire career for the Pirates from 1955 to 1972. He was a fiercely proud individual, beloved in both his native Puerto Rico and in Pittsburgh, and he died a hero's death on December 31, 1972, trying to help others.

Clemente was the leading hitter of the 1960s, belting a .328 average for the decade and winning batting titles in 1961, 1964, 1965 and 1967. He also won the National League's Most Valuable Player Award in 1966, when he hit .317 with 29 home runs and 119 RBIs as the Bucs just missed beating out the Dodgers for the National League pennant, finishing three games back. His .317 lifetime average was the highest in the NL among right-handed hitters in the second half of the 20th century. Aside from his batting success, Clemente's throwing arm from right field was legendary, he played through an incredible assortment of injuries, and he broke through the cultural barrier of being one of the first Latino players in America with equal parts pride and dignity.

After leading the Bucs to three straight first-place finishes from 1970 to 1972 and collecting his 3000th hit in his last at bat of the '72 season, Clemente was motivated to help Nicaraguan earthquake victims late that year. He saw that donations to help the needy were being stolen or misdirected, so he decided to gather supplies, charter an airplane and conduct a humanitarian mission, theorizing that no one would steal from him. Sadly, the plane was old and the cargo was loaded improperly, and Clemente perished when his plane crashed into the sea on December 31, 1972. His body was never found.

As Major League Baseball's first Puerto Rican superstar, and because of his humanitarianism, Clemente has become a true baseball hero, especially in Latin America. There is a movement afoot to retire his uniform number, 21, throughout baseball— similar to how Jackie Robinson's number 42 has been retired.

Mike Schmidt

Before Mike Schmidt, the Philadelphia Phillies were looked upon as, perhaps, the Major League Baseball franchise most associated with losing. After acquiring Schmidt, however, the Phils became known as one of the dominant teams in baseball.

Most historians rank Schmidt as the greatest third baseman of all time. Adept at both slugging and fielding, he hit 548 home runs and won 10 Gold Gloves in an 18-year career spent entirely with the Phillies. The most prolific home run hitter of the 1980s with 313, Schmidt also holds the major league record for most assists by a third baseman in a single season, with 404 in 1974. But these numbers don't necessarily reflect his greatness.

When Schmidt joined the Phillies in 1972, Philadelphia was a hopelessly forlorn franchise that had only won two pennants in its entire history and no world titles. But after a rough rookie campaign, Schmidt blossomed to lead the NL in home runs for three straight seasons, thus putting the Phils into contention until they won their first division crown in 1976. It would be the start of three straight division titles for the Phillies, though they still couldn't shake their losing reputation, self-destructing in the playoffs every year.

That all ended in 1980, when Schmidt set the franchise record for the most home runs in a season, 48, including two game winners in the Phillies' season-ending series with the Montreal Expos that clinched the division championship. Then, in the fifth game of the World Series, with both the Phils and Kansas City Royals having won two games, Schmidt led off the ninth inning with a single to begin the two-run rally that gave Philadelphia a 4–3 victory. He also hit a two-run homer earlier in the game, and the Phillies went on to win their first World Series in six games. Schmidt was named the series and season MVP. He went on to win three National League MVP awards, and in 1983, a season in which the Phils took the pennant again, Schmidt was voted by the fans as the franchise's greatest player ever.

Ryan Howard

If Mike Schmidt ended the losing reputation of the Phillies, Howard improved it even more in the next generation. Both players led the Phils to a world championship and consecutive postseason appearances, something unheard of prior to their joining the club. Only Howard managed to shatter Schmidt's Phillies' record number of homers in a season when he hit 58 in 2006, the most ever for a second-year player. As of

2010, no player had ever reached 200 total home runs in his career faster than Howard.

What has made this young player so exciting is not just his promising future after belting more than 40 home runs in his first six major league seasons, his MVP Award in 2006 or his signature batting stance. It's that while many of his contemporaries' reputations have taken hits in the steroid age, Howard's reputation shines above it, be it with his extraordinary play or his sandwich shop television ads.

Grover Cleveland "Pete" Alexander

Grover "Pete" Alexander was the hero of the Phillies' first pennant-winning team in 1915, posting an incredible 31–10 record with a 1.22 earned run average, the first of six straight seasons in which he posted an ERA under 2.00. He followed this by registering 16 shutouts the following season, a major league record that likely will never be broken in the age of relief pitching.

Although Alexander's pitching feats rank with any pitcher in any era, he was sold to the Chicago Cubs following the 1917 season. Similar to the fortunes of the Pittsburgh Pirates when Barry Bonds left as a free agent or when Babe Ruth was sold from the Red Sox to the Yankees, Pete's departure started a streak of 14 straight losing seasons for the Phillies and 30 losing seasons in 31 years.

Alexander's career was immortalized in the 1952 film *The Winning Team*, in which he was played by Ronald Reagan.

Chuck Klein

Klein is a forgotten slugger in baseball annals, perhaps because the Phils were so bad during the time he played.

Some of his accomplishments have even been criticized; for instance, he led the NL in home runs in 1929 with 43, but it was only one more than Mel Ott, who the Phillies walked five times in the last game of the season. Klein played in a hitter-friendly era, so some of his totals are likely to be inflated. And after he was traded to the Cubs following his Triple Crown–winning season of 1933 (leading the league in home runs, batting average and runs batted in), he never hit 30 homers in a season again, leading to criticisms that his stats in Philadelphia were largely padded by the short right field at the Baker Bowl.

But without Klein, the Phils would not have posted a winning record in 1932, their high-water mark between 1918 and 1947. That one winning season allowed the Phils to escape the indignity of posting more consecutive losing seasons than any other team in professional sports, as the Pittsburgh Pirates had posted 18 straight losing seasons as of 2010. From 1929 to 1933, Klein collected more than 200 hits in every season, led the NL in home runs four times and RBIs twice, and even set a major league record with 44 outfield assists in 1930.

Whiz Kids

In 1950, the Philadelphia Phillies ended 35 years of losing with a pennant-winning team whose starting lineup had an average age of 26—the youngest team in baseball history to win a pennant. Additionally, they won in exciting style, with bullpen ace Jim Konstanty revolutionizing relief pitching with a then-record 74 appearances and staving off the hard-charging Brooklyn Dodgers in the last game of the season with a dramatic 4–1 victory at Ebbets Field, won on a three-run homer by Dick Sisler in the 10th inning.

Unfortunately, the Whiz Kids' reign was short lived. Injuries to the pitching staff caused ace Robin Roberts to be overused, and by the World Series, the Phils were simply out of gas. They were swept by the Yankees in the Fall Classic and never contended for another pennant, likely because they were the last team in the National League to integrate.

The Pirates Ride a Roller Coaster in the '60 Series

In 1960, the Pittsburgh Pirates won the National League pennant for the first time in 33 years. Their opposition in the World Series would be the 1960 New York Yankees, who had won their 10th pennant of the past 12 seasons. The Bronx Bombers came into the series on a 15-game winning streak and were heavily favored to bring the World Series championship back to New York, but the Bucs won only two fewer games than the Yankees that season and boasted a lineup that included Hall of Famers Roberto Clemente and Bill Mazeroski, as well as National League MVP Dick Groat.

The Yankees learned early on that the Pittsburgh Pirates where not simply going to lie down before the might of the legendary New York lineup. In the first inning of game one, the Pirates shook the Yanks' pitching for three quick runs, scored two more in the fourth on a two-run homer from Mazeroski, and behind the pitching of Vern Law and Elroy Face, won the game by a final score of 6–4. Reeling from the unexpected loss, the Yankee sluggers regrouped in game two and absolutely destroyed the Pirates' pitching staff with a 16–3 victory, then won the third game at Yankee Stadium by an equally impressive 10–0 score behind ace starter Whitey Ford.

Determined not to suffer another embarrassing loss, the Pirates came into game four ready to shut down the mighty Yankee offense. Law returned to the mound and was able to stifle the Yankees batters for only eight hits and two runs. The Pirates mustered just seven hits, but they managed to get three runs to win the game, squeaking by the Yanks and tying the series.

Trying to regain the momentum from the team's two decisive wins, Yankees manager Casey Stengel made the controversial decision to start pitcher Art Ditmar, who had lost game one, in the hope that the Pirates would underestimate his abilities. But after giving up three runs in the top half of the second inning, Stengel pulled Ditmar from the game. Yankee relievers could do little to stop the Pirates, and Pittsburgh defeated the Yankees by a final score of 5–2.

Now the Yankees were backed into a corner, but they were not about to hand over the championship to the Pirates, especially after completely dominating them in two games. The 38,580 fans gathered in Forbes Field in Pittsburgh hoping to see their Pirates take home their first World Series since 1925 were sadly disappointed as the Yankees yet again toyed with the Pirates pitching staff, scoring 12 runs while Ford again shut out the Bucs. Over six games, the Yankees had managed to outscore the Pirates 46–17. Still, the series was tied, and one of the strangest World Series in history was going to come down to game seven.

The Pirates had the advantage of playing game seven at Forbes Field and seemed to put the seal on the game after Rocky Nelson's first inning home run and Bill "The Quail" Virdon's second inning single staked the Bucs to a 4–0 lead. Again, the Yankees' big hitters were up to the task and, buoyed by Moose Skowron and Yogi Berra home runs, were ahead 7–4 by the eighth inning. But the Pirates' fortunes were about to take a turn for the better.

After Gino Cimoli singled and Virdon's ground ball to shortstop Tony Kubek took a bad hop and hit him in the throat, thus allowing the Quail to reach base, Groat singled again to drive in one run. Two outs later, Clemente beat out an infield hit to drive in another run, putting the Pirates within one run of tying the game. All 36,683 Bucs fans were on their feet when Hal Smith stepped up to the plate. Smith responded with a three-run homer to give the Pirates a 9–7 lead going into the top of the ninth inning.

But the Yankees greeted Bob Friend, one of the greatest pitchers in Pirates history, with two singles, including one by Yankees pinch-hitter Dale Long, who, just four years earlier, had set a major league record with the Bucs by belting home runs in eight straight games. Pirates manager Danny Murtaugh then turned to Harvey Haddix, who had pitched 12 perfect innings in a game against the Milwaukee Braves the season before. Haddix retired three of the four batters he faced, but the Yanks were able to manufacture tying runs in large part because of the guile of Mickey Mantle, who managed to dive back onto first base rather than be caught in a rundown following the second out of the inning, thus allowing the tying run to score.

Pittsburgh second baseman Bill Mazeroski stepped up to the plate to lead off the bottom of the ninth. Facing off against the Yankees' Ralph Terry, Mazeroski let the first pitch go by for a ball, then smashed a now-historic home run to win the game, 10–9, and the World Series for the Pittsburgh Pirates. The Pirates had managed to beat the odds and defeat the Yankees in a series in which they were outscored, 55–27.

Bill Mazeroski

Bill Mazeroski was hardly a one-time wonder, and baseball historian Bill James has ranked Maz as the greatest defensive player in history. And, like Stargell and Clemente, he played his entire career, from 1956 to 1972, with the Pittsburgh Pirates.

Mazeroski's 161 double plays in 1966 are a record for a second baseman, and he led the NL in assists nine times. He was known for having a distinctive manner in catching the ball while turning a 6–4–3 or 5–4–3, where he would not so much catch the ball but rather trap it with his glove and then shuttle it to first.

What Mazeroski will forever be known for, of course, is hitting the World Series–ending home run in the bottom of the ninth inning of a 9–9 tie game against the New York Yankees, thus giving the Bucs their first world championship in 35 years. As of 2010, it is the only time in the history of the World Series that a seventh and deciding game has ended with a walk-off home run.

For years overlooked as a Hall of Famer, Mazeroski was finally enshrined in 2001. His humble nature made it impossible for him to complete his induction speech—he was overcome by emotion and broke down into tears—thus making it all the more memorable and cherished.

Harold Joseph "Pie" Traynor

A poll of sportswriters voted Traynor the all-time greatest third baseman during Major League Baseball's 100th anniversary celebration of professional baseball in 1969. A superb contact hitter during his 18-year career, spent entirely with the Pittsburgh Pirates from 1920 to 1937, Traynor had a career .320 batting average, drove in more than 100 runs for five straight seasons from 1927 to 1931, and led the NL in fielding categories 14 times in his career, including seven years leading the league in assists. He played for both the 1925 world champions and the 1927 pennant winners, then managed the team from 1934 to 1939, nearly leading the Bucs to the pennant in 1938 before falling on Gabby Hartnett's "Homer in the Gloamin'."

After his playing and managerial careers were over, Traynor became a popular sportscaster in Pittsburgh, doing everything from radio sports updates to professional wrestling commentary. *Pittsburgh Post-Gazette* sportswriter Bob Smizik has hailed him as the most popular Pirate in history. He was inducted into the Baseball Hall of Fame in 1948.

Ellis on LSD

On June 12, 1970, Pittsburgh Pirates hurler Dock Ellis pitched a no-hitter against the San Diego Padres. Fourteen years later, he claimed he pitched the game high on LSD. Ellis had been visiting friends in Los Angeles and ingested the drug at a party. He was under the impression that he was not scheduled to start that night but was given the start at the last minute.

Ellis took his place on the mound and proceeded somehow to fan six, walk eight and get a lot of help from his infield. As Ellis recounted in an interview with *High Times* magazine in 1984:

I can only remember bits and pieces of the game. I was psyched. I had a feeling of euphoria. I was zeroed in on the [catcher's] glove, but I didn't hit the glove too much. I remember hitting a couple of batters and the bases were loaded two or three times. The ball was small sometimes, the ball was large sometimes. Sometimes I saw the catcher, sometimes I didn't. Sometimes I tried to stare the hitter down and throw while I was looking at him. I chewed my gum until it turned to powder. I started having a crazy idea in the fourth inning that Richard Nixon was the home plate umpire, and once I thought I was pitching a baseball to Jimi Hendrix, who to me was holding a guitar and swinging it over the plate. They say I had about three to four fielding chances. I remember diving out of the way of a ball I thought was a line drive. I jumped, but the ball wasn't hit hard and never reached me.

High Fashion with Dock Ellis

Pittsburgh Pirates pitcher Dock Ellis made one of baseball's strangest fashion statements—correction, *the* strangest fashion statement—during a pre-game workout.

Always one to push the limits, Ellis was known particularly for his hairstyles. For the entire 1972 season, he proudly displayed a full afro. But he really caught everyone's attention when he appeared the following season during a pre-game workout at Wrigley Field in Chicago sporting several rows of large, white curlers in his hair. Fans looked on in amazement as Ellis tossed around the ball, wearing what they would most likely expect to see on their mothers rather than on a professional baseball player.

A quick-thinking photographer snapped a picture of the curlers, and the next morning, Ellis found himself on most sports pages across the country—not that it really bothered him. Unfortunately, it did bother the Pirates management. General manager Joe Brown sent down orders that the curlers should be removed for reasons of conduct unbecoming of a major league player.

Ellis was not amused by the decree from the fashion police. "I know the orders came from Commissioner Bowie Kuhn, and I don't like it. They didn't put any orders about Joe Pepitone when he wore a hairpiece down to his shoulders," said Ellis, who reluctantly removed the curlers before taking to the field.

Harold Arlin Makes History

On August 5, 1921, a quiet, 25-year-old foreman and part-time studio announcer carved a place for himself in the annals of baseball history. From a small, ground-level box seat at Forbes Field in Pittsburgh, using a converted telephone as a microphone and some rigged equipment, Harold Arlin called the first-ever broadcast of a baseball game on the nation's first commercial radio station, KDKA. The hometown Pittsburgh Pirates won the game that day 8–5 over the visiting Philadelphia Phillies. Just a few months later, radio stations in New York and New Jersey broadcast games of their own.

Pennsylvania Baseball Facts

- In the history of the major leagues, 1373 players have been born in Pennsylvania, 749 died in Pennsylvania, and 732 are buried in the state, according to www.baseball-reference.com. The 1373 players make Pennsylvania the second most prolific state for producing major league baseball players, trailing only California.

- Pennsylvania's baseball history stretches far beyond the major leagues. For example, outside Texas, no state has had more of its cities and towns (or boroughs, as they are often called in Pennsylvania) host professional baseball teams than the Keystone State. The following is a list of all the Pennsylvania locations that have had a minor league baseball team and the number of teams that have called each location home.

Allentown (54)	Homestead (2)	Piedmont (1)
Altoona (31)	Houtzdale (1)	Pottstown (2)
Ashland (2)	Jeannette (9)	Pottsville (8)
Bangor (3)	Johnsonburg (1)	Punxsutawney (2)
Beaver Falls (7)	Johnstown (50)	Quaker City (1)
Bellefonte (1)	Kane (3)	Reading (101)
Berwick (1)	Kensington (1)	Ridgway (1)
Bloomsburg (1)	Kittanning (1)	Scottdale (9)
Braddock (4)	Lancaster (49)	Scranton (78)

Bradford (29)

Butler (18)

Carbondale (7)

Carlisle (2)

Chambersburg (17)

Charleroi (13)

Chester (5)

Chester Thurlow (1)

Clearfield (1)

Coatesville (1)

Connellsville (5)

Coudersport (1)

Danville (5)

DuBois (1)

Dubois County (2)

Duquesne (1)

Easton (9)

Erie (76)

Frankford (1)

Franklin (4)

Germantown (1)

Gettysburg (3)

Greensburg (7)

Harrisburg (80)

Hazleton (21)

Lansdale (1)

Latrobe (1)

Lebanon (8)

Leechburg (1)

Lehigh Valley (2)

Lewiston (1)

Littlestown (2)

Lockhaven (2)

Mahanoy City (7)

McKeesport (15)

Middletown (1)

Milton (3)

Minersville (1)

Monessen (4)

Mt. Carmel (5)

Nazareth (6)

New Brighton (1)

New Castle (19)

Norristown (3)

Oil City (15)

Oxford (1)

Palmyra (1)

Patton (1)

Philadelphia Hilldale (13)

Phillipsburg (1)

Shamokin (9)

Sharon (7)

Shenandoah (3)

Slatington (1)

Slippery Rock (1)

Somerset (1)

St. Clair (1)

St. Marys (1)

State College (5)

Stroudsburg (7)

Sunbury (14)

Tamaqua (3)

Titusville (1)

Tyrone (1)

Uniontown (9)

Vandergrift (4)

Warren (8)

Washington (18)

Waynesboro (11)

Waynesburg (1)

West Chester (1)

Wilkes-Barre (63)

Williamsport (82)

Wilmerding (1)

York (57)

(Source: baseball-reference.com)

- Philadelphia Phillies manager Connie Mack holds the record for the most years as a manager. He held the position from 1901 to 1950. His 50 years as manager of one team will likely never be repeated as most managers in modern baseball are lucky to make it to five.

- Phillies super home run hitters include outfielder Chuck Klein, who hit four dingers on July 10, 1936, in a 10-inning game at Forbes Field against the Pittsburgh Pirates. The legendary Mike Schimdt joined the list when he hit four homers against the Cubs at Wrigley Field on April 17, 1976. The game lasted 10 innings, with the Phillies winning 18–16.

- The Philadelphia Phillies hold the dubious distinction of the most consecutive losses in the majors, with 23. In 1961, they ended the season with a record of 47 wins and 107 losses. It was a season to forget!

- In 1959, Pittsburgh Pirates pitcher Roy Face could do no wrong. At one point during the season, his record stood at a stellar 17 wins and 0 losses. He finished the season with just one loss for a final record of 18–1, which is a record-winning percentage of .947.

- Jack Nabors of the Philadelphia Athletics pitched so badly during the 1916 season that he won only one game in his 21 attempts and finished with the worst-ever winning percentage of .048.

- John Coleman of the 1883 Philadelphia Phillies was the team's ace pitcher but still had a dismal record of 12 wins and 48 losses.

- Johnny Burnett of the Cleveland Indians collected nine hits in 11 at bats in an 18-inning marathon game against the Philadelphia Athletics on July 10, 1932. For the most hits in nine innings, the record goes to Rennie Stennett of the Pittsburgh Pirates, who equaled the mark of Wilbert Robinson of the 1892 Baltimore Orioles on September 16, 1975, by collecting seven hits in seven at bats against the Chicago Cubs. The Pirates won the game by a score of 22–0, the worst shutout loss recorded after 1901.

Pennsylvania Baseball Quotes

"I never have been sick. I don't even know what it means to be sick. I hear other players say they have a cold. I just don't know what it would feel like to have a cold—I never had one."

—Honus Wagner

"In all my years of play, I never saw an ump deliberately make an unfair decision. They really called them as they saw 'em."

—Honus Wagner

"There ain't much to being a ballplayer, if you're a ballplayer."

—Honus Wagner

"Any time you have an opportunity to make a difference in this world and you don't, then you are wasting your time on earth."

—Roberto Clemente

"I am convinced that God wanted me to be a baseball player. I was born to play baseball."

—Roberto Clemente

"I am more valuable to my team hitting .330 than swinging for home runs."

—Roberto Clemente

"When I put on my uniform, I feel I am the proudest man on earth."

—Roberto Clemente

"Why does everyone talk about the past? All that counts is tomorrow's game."

—Roberto Clemente

"Roberto Clemente could field the ball in New York and throw out a guy in Pennsylvania."

—Broadcaster Vin Scully

"A World Series trophy is a wonderful thing to behold."

—Willie Stargell

"I eventually became proud of my strikeouts, because each one represented another learning experience."

—Willie Stargell, whose 1936 strikeouts are a National League record

"The umpire says, 'Play ball!' He doesn't say, 'Work ball!'"

—Willie Stargell

"The greatest feeling in the world is to win a major league game. The second greatest feeling in the world is to lose a major league game."

—Former Pirates manager Chuck Tanner, who was
famous for his positive attitude

"I had a spur which most baseball players do not have. The shadow of the coalmines was on me. I experienced all there was to experience and I never want to see a mine again."

—Plains native Ed Walsh, all-time major league
leader in lifetime ERA (1.82). Walsh lost his brother
in the coal mines, which afforded many Pennsylvanians
a living a century ago, but at a high cost, as there was
nearly one death per day recorded in the state's mines.

Chapter Six

The Greatest Baseball Teams of All Time

Among the Greats

The subjective question, "What's the greatest baseball team of all time?" will always remain a popular one. The most popular choice seems to be the 1927 New York Yankees, who swept the Pittsburgh Pirates in the World Series and posted a 110–44 regular season record. But Pennsylvania has at least three teams that can lay claim to this title.

The 1902 Pittsburgh Pirates

The case for the 1902 Pittsburgh Pirates is a simple one. They won the pennant by 27½ games. In the history of baseball, no major league team has ever had a bigger margin of superiority ahead of the second-place finisher. That year, the Bucs were 103–36 and second-place Brooklyn just 75–63. Furthermore, the Pirates' margin of victory in their games was 2.36 runs, a National League record that, as of 2010, was still valid, and was simply unheard of in the dead-ball era (1900 to 1919), when scoring was not as prevalent as it was after a cork center was placed in baseballs in 1920. If dominance over one's competition in a season is the deciding factor, then the 1902 Pirates are the greatest baseball team of all time.

The 1902 Bucs featured three Hall of Famers: shortstop Honus Wagner, outfielder Fred Clarke and pitcher Jack Chesbro. Ginger Beaumont led the NL in hits for the second straight season; pitchers Chesbro, Deacon Phillippe and Jesse Tannehill all won 20 or more games; and Tommy Leach became the first Pirate to lead the league in home runs when he walloped six, all of which were inside the park.

There was also one additional Hall of Famer in the Pirates' fold: owner Barney Dreyfuss, a cunning businessman who was responsible for building the Bucs dynasty of this era. What's more, he was the father of the modern World Series.

While the National League winner had often participated in a postseason series of some sort in the 19th century, often called the World Series, this practice diminished significantly after the American Association folded after the 1892 season. Enter the American League in 1901, which was raiding players from the National League in an attempt to become a "major" league. Chesbro, for instance, left for the New York Highlanders (now the Yankees) in 1903.

With the pennant wrapped up at midseason for the 1902 Pirates, there was little to hold the locals' attention. The team's attendance that year was 243,826, a good draw for the day but still lower than their previous three seasons. Even the lure of going for the National League's all-time single-season victory record was shallow; though the Bucs set the record on the last day of the season, only 1200 fans showed up, and the Cincinnati Reds were so upset at having to play the game under rainy conditions that they had their first baseman pitch and a pitcher catch. The Pirates did play a postseason series against the American League All-Stars, but that also failed to capture the public's attention.

The next season, Dreyfuss decided to challenge American League champion Boston to a postseason series. If nothing else, it would keep fans' interest throughout the year. Boston defeated Pittsburgh five games to three in the inaugural series in 1903. For connoisseurs of trivia, Pirates outfielder Jimmy Sebring hit the first World Series home run, and Boston's Cy Young further established his legacy by posting a 2–1 record with a 1.85 ERA. Though there was no series played the next year—John McGraw, manager of the pennant-winning New York Giants, refused to acknowledge the American League as equal—McGraw relented in 1905, and the World Series has been with us ever since.

And it likely was because the 1902 Pirates were so dominant!

The 1929–31 Philadelphia Athletics

The case for the 1929–31 A's as the best team ever states that with the Yankees at the height of their dynasty during the Babe Ruth years, it was the A's who beat them three years running. New York won their second straight World Series in 1928, but in the pennant race, the A's finished in second place by just 2½ games. They were beginning to get contributions for a 20-year-old prospect, Jimmie Foxx, who would take the place in the lineup of aging veterans such as Ty Cobb and Tris Speaker.

In 1929, Foxx exploded, hitting 33 home runs and leading the Athletics to the pennant 18 games ahead of the Yankees, with 104 victories and a World Series triumph against the Chicago Cubs.

The Athletics repeated in 1930, winning 102 games and finishing eight games ahead of second-place Washington and 16 ahead of New York. The A's beat the St. Louis Cardinals in the World Series, and though every starting position player for the Cardinals hit better than .300 that season, they fell to the superior pitching of Lefty Grove, George Earnshaw, Rube Walberg and Jack Quinn, and could only muster a .200 batting average in the Fall Classic. Grove was, perhaps, the most dominant pitcher for a three-year period in baseball history during this time. He posted an incredible 79–15 record from 1929 to 1931.

Even if the Yankees' one-two slugging duo of Babe Ruth and Lou Gehrig in 1927 and 1928 was slightly superior to Foxx and Al Simmons in subsequent seasons, they did not have a top end pitcher to match Grove. And though Foxx and Simmons failed to combine to hit 107 home runs the way Ruth and Gehrig did in 1927, Simmons bested them with batting averages of .365, .381 and .390 during the A's pennant streak, the latter two enough to take the American League title.

Add to the Athletics mix Hall of Fame catcher Mickey Cochrane, the inspiration for Mickey Mantle's first name and considered by many to be the best at his position, as well as a lineup featuring second baseman Max Bishop (.423 lifetime on base percentage); infielder Jimmy Dykes (.327 average in 1929); right fielder Bing Miller (.311 lifetime average), whose game-ending double won the 1929 series; and outfielder Mule Haas (.313, .299 and .323 from 1929 to 1931).

The team was so good that promising youngsters like Doc Cramer (.296 lifetime in a 20-year career) and proud veterans such as Eddie Collins, George Burns, Eddie Rommel and Howard Ehmke rarely got a chance to play. Ehmke, however, did start the first game of the 1929 World Series and set a since-broken record by striking out 13 Cubs.

The Athletics won 107 games in 1931, but St. Louis' Pepper Martin hit .500 to lead the Cardinals to victory in that series.

In 1932, the Yankees came back. Young players like shortstop Frankie Crossetti, outfielder Ben Chapman and pitcher Lefty Gomez were added to the roster, and key veteran pickups such as third baseman Joe Sewell and pitcher Red Ruffing were also obtained, allowing the Yankees to rebuild for one last run around Ruth.

The A's, meanwhile, made no real changes, but Earnshaw and Walberg were aging, and Roy Mahaffey was unable to pick up the additional load needed to support a staff. Foxx had his career year with 58 home runs, but the A's finished with a record of 94–60, 13 games back.

In another time, the A's might have found a couple of other pitchers and kept their club together to compete for future pennants. But this was the Depression, and the '32 Athletics drew only 405,500 fans that year. Although still above the league average, it was their worst gate showing since 1921, when Philadelphia finished in last place for their seventh straight year.

Manager Connie Mack began to sell off his players, just as he had nearly 20 years before, but this time, he could not rebuild. The A's would not win 90 games again until 1971, after the franchise had relocated to Oakland.

The 1934–36 Pittsburgh Crawfords

The argument for the Crawfords' greatness cannot really be recorded in numbers. They posted a .744 winning percentage in the Negro National League in 1934 with a 64–22 record, but their claim to the championship is disputed. The 1935 and 1936 Crawfords did, however, win the Negro National League championship outright. The main argument for the Crawfords as baseball's greatest team is simply that a listing of their roster reveals perhaps as much star talent as any baseball team in history.

At catcher there was Josh Gibson. On the mound, Satchel Paige. At first base and managing, Oscar Charleston. In the outfield, "Cool Papa" Bell. These players aren't just Hall of

Famers; they are probably the four most famous Negro League players of all time.

Add to this list lefty LeRoy Matlock, who went 18–0 for the Crawfords in 1935, and Roosevelt Davis, who was 12–4 that year, as well as Hall of Fame third baseman Judy Johnson and Ted "Double Duty" Radcliffe, and the Crawfords' roster reads like the greatest of All-Star teams.

Assembling this team was Gus Greenlee, who ran a numbers game in Pittsburgh (similar to today's Pennsylvania Daily Number drawing) and often gave money to charitable and business causes. In 1930, he was asked to buy a sandlot team named after the Crawford Street Bar & Grille. When he did, he decided to turn it into the best baseball team he could.

First Greenlee put his players on salary, then he went about signing the best players. When he found barnstorming to be inadequate, he resurrected the Negro National League for the Crawfords to play in. Greenlee even built his own ballpark, Greenlee Field, so his team wouldn't have to rent out stadiums owned by major league clubs, and purchased a bus for his players. This provided easy travel and scheduling privileges and gave the Crawfords "elite" status in Negro League Baseball.

Incredibly, the Crawfords were dismantled by Dominican Republic dictator General Rafael Truijillo. Greenlee and Paige never saw eye to eye on things, and when Truijillo offered Paige more money than he was making playing for the Crawfords, he not only jumped ship to play for Truijillo's San Pedro de Macoris team in Santo Domingo (then called Ciudad Trujillo), but he encouraged his Crawfords teammates to join him as well. After 1938, the Crawfords were no more, and Greenlee Field was demolished for an apartment complex soon afterward.

Chapter Seven

Basketball

Wilt Chamberlain and the 100-Point Game

It is, perhaps, basketball's most famous singular feat. It has been called a metaphor for black America, a record that will never be broken, and it is arguably the greatest moment in the history of both eastern and central Pennsylvania sports.

What was the feat? It was Wilt Chamberlain scoring an NBA-record 100 points for the Philadelphia Warriors against the New York Knicks on March 2, 1962, in Hershey.

At first glance, the particulars of the record speak for themselves. As the three-point line had yet to be instituted, Chamberlain accomplished the feat without the benefit of a three-point shot to pad his scoring total. It's the perfect total for a single-game NBA scoring record, a round figure that is easy to remember.

It's also a record held by a legendary player. Let us just say, for instance, baseball's equivalent to Chamberlain's achievement is Johnny Burnett of the Cleveland Indians collecting a record nine hits in a single game against the Philadelphia Athletics in 1932. But Burnett is a forgotten player from long ago. Chamberlain, of course, is a leading candidate to be called basketball's all-time greatest player, thus making his feat easier to remember for casual sports fans.

Yet this record is surrounded by as much folklore and fable as fact. There's no video of Chamberlain scoring his 100th point, and Bill Campbell's radio broadcast doesn't mention what kind of shot (dunk, layup, jumper) Chamberlain took to score it. The *Philadelphia Inquirer* didn't even send a reporter to the game. Only 4124 fans were in attendance at the Warriors' last regular-season contest in Pennsylvania before the team moved to San Francisco. For years, the common misconception was that the game ended immediately after Chamberlain scored his 100th point with 46 seconds left. Nobody knows for sure what happened to the game ball.

The record has its share of controversy, as well. The Knicks were without starting center Phil Jordon that day, and by the fourth quarter, the game hardly resembled traditional basketball, with both teams more focused on Chamberlain's individual feats than on winning or losing.

The story begins with Chamberlain, who lived in New York City and commuted to Philadelphia for games. Leaving New York at 8:00 AM that morning, he barely caught the Warriors' team bus for the two-hour ride to Hershey and later recalled in interviews that he had only had an hour of sleep prior to the game, which was not unusual for him. Chamberlain then spent much of the afternoon playing arcade games in the Hersheypark Arena.

While the arena is better known as the home of the Hershey Bears hockey franchise, it had been a common alternate venue for the Warriors since the early 1950s. Games played at alternate or neutral sites were commonplace in the then-15-year-old NBA, and this was the 13th game of the 1961–62 season that the Warriors would play under such conditions.

There was little on the line for the game, as the Warriors had already clinched the second postseason berth in the Eastern Division, and the Knicks were finishing out the season in last place.

The Warriors took an early 19–3 lead. Knicks backup center Darrall Imhoff got into foul trouble trying to guard Chamberlain and played for just 20 minutes, leaving third-stringers Dave Budd and Cleveland Butler to guard the scoring champion for much of the game. By halftime, Philadelphia had a 79–68 lead, and Chamberlain, buoyed by 13-of-14 shooting from the free-throw line, had 41 points.

Yet as impressive as this total was, for Chamberlain, such feats had been commonplace all season long. Less than three months earlier, he had broken Elgin Baylor's record of 71 points in a game by netting 78 against the Lakers. Chamberlain had already scored 60 or more points in 15 games, a record he would extend to 17 by the end of the season. While he was on pace to beat his young record, his first-half performance that night was par for the course during a season in which he averaged 50.4 points and 48.5 minutes per game.

It was at this point that Warriors' head coach Frank McGuire told his team to feed the ball to Chamberlain. Legendary Philadelphia basketball public address announcer Dave Zinkoff started informing the crowd of Chamberlain's scoring totals. He scored 28 more points in the third period, an NBA record, bringing his total to 69.

With the score 125–106 heading into the fourth period, there was little doubt who would win the game. The focus was on Chamberlain and how many points he could score. Just 4:09 into the period, Chamberlain scored his 79th point to break his own scoring record. But with 7:51 left, it was only the beginning.

"I heard the fans yelling for 100," Chamberlain recalled. "I thought, 'Man, these people are tough. Eighty isn't good enough. I'm tired. I've got 80 points and no one has ever scored 80.' At one point I said to [teammate] Al Attles, 'I got 80. What's the difference between 80 and 100?'"

Not wanting to suffer this ignominy, the Knicks began holding the ball on offense and fouling Chamberlain's teammates whenever they could. McGuire countered by putting in his second string around Chamberlain and ordering them to foul the Knicks. Imhoff fouled out, but Philadelphia continued to feed Chamberlain the ball, going to great lengths to do so. The seven-foot-one-inch "Wilt the Stilt" started taking the ball up the court, effectively playing guard. Teammates passed up easy shots to feed him the ball.

In all, Chamberlain took 21 shots from the field in the fourth period, five more than he took in the third and nine more than the first. He also shot 10 free throws, converting seven. With 1:19 left, Chamberlain scored his 98th point, allowing him to set the NBA record for most points scored in a period in successive quarters. He then stole the inbounds pass, but missed on his first attempt for 100 points, and the Knicks got the rebound. New York took the clock down to 1:01 before seldom-used Warriors' forward Ted Luckenbill fouled Richie Guerin, who then scored his team-high 39th point.

Campbell's call of the record on WCAU-AM 1210:

Let's see if they foul somebody quick. [Guy] Rodgers throws long to Chamberlain. He's got it. He's trying to get up. He shoots! No good, the rebound Luckenbill. Back to Chamberlain. He shoots! Up, no good, in and out. The rebound Luckenbill. Back to [Joe] Ruklick. In to Chamberlain, he made it! He made it! He made it! A dipper dunk! He made it! The fans are all over the floor! They stop the game! People are running out on the court! One hundred points for Wilt Chamberlain!

In addition to scoring 100 points, Chamberlain set NBA records for field goals attempted (63), field goals made (36), points in a half (59) and points in a period (31). A half-century later, all of these records but the latter still stand. He also converted 28 of 32 free throws in the game, a high percentage for a lifetime 51-percent free-throw shooter. Chamberlain was initially embarrassed by the record for taking so many shots, and Guerin said, "That game was not played as it should be played. The second half was a travesty....He took nearly every shot. In the normal flow, Wilt would have scored 80 to 85, which is mind-boggling when you think about it. I'm sorry, this may be basketball history, but I always felt bad about the game."

For his own part, Chamberlain always felt that a 1960 contest in which he grabbed an NBA-record 55 rebounds against Bill Russell's Boston Celtics was his greatest game.

As a side note, Darrell Imhoff was linked to Chamberlain in one other way. After playing two and a half seasons in San Francisco, Chamberlain was traded back to Philadelphia to the 76ers, the team that replaced the Warriors in Philadelphia. After leading the Sixers to the 1967 NBA championship, Chamberlain was traded to the Los Angeles Lakers during the summer of 1968. One of the three players Philadelphia obtained in the deal was Imhoff.

The Missing Ball

One of the lasting legacies of Chamberlain's 100-point achievement came over a debate about what happened to the basketball he scored his 100th point with that day. On October 6, 2000, Leland's Dynasties Auctions sold a ball they claimed to be the one Chamberlain used to set his famous record for $67,791. The ball had previously belonged to Kerry Ryman, who claimed that as a 14-year-old boy, he had picked up the ball during the on-court celebration that followed the record-setting point.

But Harvey Pollack, a public relations official for the Warriors, insists the ball was taken out of play, and Ryman had the ball that was used to play the final 46 seconds of the game. Ryman and Leland's counter that they had an affidavit signed by nine people who say they saw Ryman take the ball from Chamberlain during the melee that followed his historic basket, when an estimated 200 fans rushed the court.

What is known is that a basketball signed by Chamberlain was put on display in the lobby of a Philadelphia hotel as the "100-point ball" in the days and weeks that followed the game, but this ball was lost during the Warriors' move to San Francisco that off-season.

Ryman, for his part, claims that as an adult, he often tried to contact Chamberlain to give the ball back to him, but the great center showed no interest in obtaining the memento. Nobody doubts that Ryman took a ball used in the game; the only question is whether or not he had the one Chamberlain used to score his 100th point. But there was enough controversy surrounding the ball that Ryman's memento had to be auctioned twice. Before the controversy ensued, Leland's originally auctioned the ball for $551,844.

Chamberlain is not the only Pennsylvanian to score 100 points in a basketball game. Former major league pitcher Pete Cimino scored 114 points for Bristol High School in a 132–86 victory against Palisades High School on January 22, 1960, establishing the Pennsylvania high school record. Twenty-one years later, Linda Page of Philadelphia's Dobbins Tech scored 100 points in a 131–38 triumph against Mastbaum. Today, she gives private shooting lessons to basketball players.

Collegiately, Paul Arizin, Chamberlain's teammate in 1962, once scored more than 100 points in a game for Villanova against a junior college.

Championship Teams

National championships in college basketball didn't begin with the NCAA Tournament in 1939. Penn, who along with Yale became the first teams to settle on playing with five players per side, won the Helms Athletic Foundation National Championships in 1920 and 1921, finishing 43–3 during those years.

Pitt also won two national championships in the pre–NCAA Tournament era. In 1927–28, the Panthers, led by Charley Hyatt and coached by Henry "Doc" Carlson, patterned and weaved their way with a "Figure 8" offense to a Helms Title with a perfect 21–0 record, and then followed with another Helms Championship in their 23–2 campaign of 1929–30. Both Carlson, who often ran his team's practices without a ball to emphasize the proper execution of set plays, and Hyatt were part of the Basketball Hall of Fame's first class in 1959. Carlson was also the first coach to take his eastern team across the country to play western basketball teams (the Pitt football team would duplicate this feat by becoming the first team to travel across the country *by air* to play Washington in 1939) and, like many Pitt coaches of the era, earned a doctorate from the university's Department of Medicine.

Temple won not only a Helms Championship in 1938, but the National Invitational Tournament (NIT) as well. Coached by James Usilton, the Owls were 23–2 and beat Colorado, 60–36, in the championship final.

Although the NIT slowly but surely lost prestige through the years, many Pennsylvania teams have won it. The La Salle

Explorers, coached by Ken Loeffler and starring Tom Nola and Norm Grekin, took the NIT title in 1952.

Duquesne was a national power in the '50s as well, spending two weeks in 1954 ranked number one in national polls. Led by Sihugo Green and brothers Dick and Dave Ricketts, the Dukes won the 1955 NIT Tournament. Green would be the number one pick in the NBA draft in 1955 (ahead of Bill Russell), Dick the top selection in 1956, and Dave would become a catcher and go on to coach in Major League Baseball for the St. Louis Cardinals and the Pittsburgh Pirates.

Other NIT champs from Pennsylvania include Temple again in 1969, Kerry Kittle's 1994 Villanova squad and, most recently, the 2008–09 Penn State Nittany Lions under head coach Ed DeChellis.

Tom Gola and La Salle

In 1954, Philadelphia native Tom Gola led La Salle to a national title with a 92–76 victory against Bradley.

Gola seemed destined to play for La Salle. He attended La Salle High School, leading those Explorers to a Philadelphia Catholic League championship, and turned down offers to play at Kentucky and North Carolina State after La Salle offered two of his siblings athletic scholarships as well. He led the Explorers in scoring and rebounds in every season he played, including a 23-point average with 21.7 rebounds per game in the 1953–54 season.

No other player averaged as many as six points a game for the Explorers in 1953–54, but after Kentucky declined an NCAA bid to shamefully avoid playing against integrated teams and Indiana was upset in an early round, La Salle had a clear path to the title. Still, it was Frank O'Malley who scored the winning basket in the Explorers' 76–74 overtime victory against Fordham in the first round before Gola took over and led La Salle to triumphs against NC State, Navy and Penn State before besting the Braves in the finals.

Gola and the Explorers returned to the NCAA final in 1955, but this time, they were defeated by Bill Russell's San Francisco Dons. After graduating, Gola led the Philadelphia Warriors to the NBA championship in his rookie season.

The 1984–85 Villanova Wildcats

Pennsylvania's other NCAA men's basketball tournament champions were an even bigger surprise than the La Salle Explorers. In the 1985–85 season, the Villanova Wildcats hardly appeared to be the best men's basketball team in their own conference, let alone the nation. They finished the regular season with a 23-point loss to Pitt and only got as far as the semifinals of the Big East tournament before falling to St. John's, 89–74. Their 19–10 record failed to net them a national ranking and made them just an eighth seed in the Southeast region of the NCAA.

But the Big East was clearly the best conference in college basketball that season, sending three teams to the Final Four. Furthermore, the Wildcats had one of the league's best players in center Ed Pinckney and one of the best coaches in Rollie Massimino, a jovial sort in the Jim Valvano mold who was often seen at press conferences holding a fat cigar as Villanova advanced through the tourney.

Dayton fell first, 51–49, at the Dayton Arena. Then came an upset of top-seeded and second-ranked Michigan, 59–55, then Maryland, 46–43, and North Carolina in the regional finals, 56–44, giving Villanova sweet revenge on the Tar Heels for the 70–60 pasting that UNC had put on John Pinone's Wildcats in regional finals three years earlier.

Villanova then met Memphis State in the Final Four at Rupp Arena and struggled early in the game. Memphis State collected twice as many rebounds as the Wildcats in the first half, and the Wildcats only managed to tie the Tigers, 23–23. Villanova then went on an 8–0 run with Tigers center Keith Lee on the bench with foul trouble in the second half, but relinquished their eight-point lead and were tied, 41–41, with slightly more than three minutes remaining in the game.

Lee fouled out with 3:04 left on the clock, and Dwayne McClain, who hit 24 of the 25 free throws he attempted in the tournament, put Villanova up 43–41 from the charity stripe. Harold Pressley put the game away a minute later with a swooping slam from the right baseline, and when Massimino had the Wildcats play a spread offense, the game was effectively over.

Still, the Wildcats had to face top-ranked Georgetown in the finals. Georgetown was 35–2, the defending national champions and would be playing in their third final in four years. Pinckney would be facing the legendary Patrick Ewing under the boards, and the Hoyas had already topped the Wildcats twice.

But those previous two games against the Hoyas had been close affairs with low scores, reminiscent of Villanova's play in the NCAAs. The Wildcats had been the only team in the Big East to hold the Hoyas to fewer than 60 points in a game with their 2–3 zone. Furthermore, the Wildcats had done it twice.

Pinckney, fighting a stomach virus, held Ewing to only two field goals in the second half and outscored him in the game, 16–14. Villanova shot 78.6 percent from the field, including 9-of-10 shooting in the second half. Sophomore guard Harold Jensen hit a 16-foot jumper with 2:36 left to put Villanova on top 55–54 to start an 8–0 run, and the Wildcats won the national championship with perhaps the biggest upset in NCAA basketball tournament history, 66–64.

Pro Championships

The Philadelphia Warriors, named after a local basketball club and formed and coached by Ed Gottlieb in 1946, won the very first NBA championship in 1947 behind guard Joe Fulks, then followed up that title with the aforementioned 1956 title behind Gola and fellow native son Paul Arizin.

But after the Warriors moved to San Francisco following the 1962 season, the Syracuse Nationals moved to the City of Brotherly Love in 1963. Renamed the "76ers" (after 1776, the year the Declaration of Independence was signed in Philadelphia) after nine fans chose the moniker in a contest, the new team struggled initially, as many Philadelphia fans had trouble adjusting to cheering for the players they had previously rooted against when the Nats were one of the Warriors' chief rivals. Fans also did not warm to owner Ike Richman, an attorney who had assisted Gottlieb with the Warriors move to Frisco. Initially, the Sixers were a poor substitute for the Warriors and Wilt Chamberlain.

Meanwhile, even San Francisco's run at the NBA title in 1964 could not lure fans to the Cow Palace. When the Warriors slumped in 1965, nearly a third of their gate went to pay Chamberlain.

The answer for both teams was obvious—trade Chamberlain back to Philadelphia. During the 1965 NBA All-Star break in St. Louis, the team did just that. The reception for Chamberlain upon his return to Philadelphia was, as to be expected, overwhelming. The Sixers had been averaging less than 4000 patrons per game, but upon Chamberlain's return, fans literally lined the streets outside the Philadelphia Arena, where his first game back would be played.

In that game, the Sixers ironically beat the Warriors. In Chamberlain's second court appearance, the Sixers halted Boston's 16-game winning streak. Philadelphia won nine of their first 11 games after Chamberlain's return and had suddenly established themselves both with their fan base and within the league.

Two years later, since he'd set every other imaginable record in basketball at that time, Chamberlain was interested in becoming the first center to lead the NBA in assists. For the first time in his professional career, he averaged less than 30 points a game, 24.1, but he finished third in assists, allowing teammates Hal Greer, Chet Walker and future Sixers coach Billy Cunningham all to average 19 points a game. Philadelphia won 46 of their first 50 games and finished 68–13, a league record at the time.

Then, as if scripted, the Sixers beat the Celtics in the Eastern Conference semifinals, breaking Boston's eight-year championship reign. Finally, they took the NBA finals against, of all opponents, San Francisco in six games.

It wasn't just that this championship seemed to be poetic justice for Philadelphia basketball fans and Chamberlain—the win was his first championship since high school—it was also that the Sixers had made basketball history, and the 1966–67 team was voted the NBA's best ever during the league's 35th anniversary celebration in 1980.

A Title in Pittsburgh

But the Sixers weren't Pennsylvania's only pro basketball champions to play in 1967. The very next season saw the birth of the American Basketball Association (ABA), and with it, the Pittsburgh Pipers.

The Pipers were one of three professional sports franchises that debuted in Pittsburgh in 1967, a fact that likely contributed to their demise. The Pittsburgh Phantoms, a soccer franchise in the National Professional Soccer League, played at Forbes Field, and the Pipers joined the National Hockey League Penguins as tenants of the Civic Arena.

Led by Connie Hawkins, a former New York playground star who had turned professional with the Pittsburgh Rens of the failed American Basketball League a half-decade earlier, the Pipers played a freewheeling style of basketball the league would become famous for. Although they ended the season with only four of the players they started with, a roster retooling saw the Pipers win 15 games in a row, the longest winning streak that any professional sports team in Pittsburgh had enjoyed since the 1909 Pirates won 16 straight games.

Yet despite the talents of Hawkins, who averaged 26.8 points per game to lead the ABA, the Pipers were not a popular draw. Early in the season, game attendance was as low as 698, which was not uncommon for teams in the early days of the ABA, but was hardly conducive to making money. As the months went by, the team forged a 54–24 final regular season record, and the crowds improved but still averaged only 3000 in the 12,000-seat Civic Arena.

Crowds did not increase as the playoffs began. The Pipers swept the Indiana Pacers in the first round, 3–0, but the best-attended game in Pittsburgh had only 3141 patrons. The Minnesota Muskies were next, and the Pipers beat them in five games while averaging only 2800 fans per home game. By the time the championship finals against the New Orleans Buccaneers came around, Martin Luther King Jr. had been assassinated and armed troops had to be summoned to guard the Civic Arena from rioters.

Still, the Pipers took the seven-game series from the Bucs, led by future NBA coaches Doug Moe and Larry Brown.

In a back-and-forth final series between disciplined New Orleans and high-flying Pittsburgh, the Pipers won over not only their opponent, but also their fans, drawing 11,457 to the seventh game of the series, which ended 122–113 in the Pipers' favor.

Unfortunately, the team had lost $350,000 over the course of the season, so when owner Gabe Rubin received an offer from Minnesota businessman and lawyer William Erickson to buy the Pipers and move them to Minneapolis after the Muskies left for Miami, he saw a way to get out of debt. The Pipers would not have a chance to defend their title in Pittsburgh.

The Pipers did not fare any better financially in Minneapolis and did even worse on the court, finishing 36–42, so they moved back to Pittsburgh for the 1969–70 season and were renamed the Condors. They continued their free-wheeling style of play, and they led the league in points scored but finished last in defense in 1971–72. However, the move and absence of Hawkins, who joined the NBA in 1969, prevented the franchise from ever succeeding again in Pittsburgh. The Condors folded three years after their return.

The 1983 Philadelphia 76ers

When the ABA merged with the NBA in 1976, one of the teams that was absorbed was the New York Nets. But to finalize the merger, the Nets had to pay the New York Knicks a territorial fee, which proved to be too expensive to keep their star, Julius Erving.

Enter the Philadelphia 76ers, who bought Erving's contract from the Nets for $3 million and overnight changed their image from a struggling franchise that took a backseat to the Flyers to a perennial title contender.

Still, the Sixers always came up short of a championship, losing the NBA finals in 1977, 1980 and 1982. So prior to the 1982–83 season, they traded Caldwell Jones and a first-round draft choice for Houston center Moses Malone, who had single-handedly taken the Rockets to the NBA finals in 1981. Although he was the reigning Most Valuable Player in the league, he was available because the Rockets were rebuilding.

Malone made the Sixers unstoppable. They finished the regular season 65–17, then swept through the playoffs, losing only one game until they met the Los Angeles Lakers in the finals. The Lakers had beaten the Sixers twice before in the NBA finals, but this time, there was no stopping Philadelphia. Whereas the year before, the 76ers never so much as held a single lead at any point in their three games in Los Angeles in the NBA finals, in this encounter, Philadelphia swept the Lakers in four rather lopsided games.

The Sixers were so dominant that Philadelphia basketball fans have long argued whether the 1967 or the 1983 Sixers was the better team. Both teams overcame a long-time nemesis— in the former team's case, the Celtics, in the latter team's, the Lakers. Additionally, the '67 team gave Philadelphia fans the satisfaction of beating the franchise that had left the city a few years earlier, the San Francisco Warriors, and had a slightly better record, whereas the '83 squad, coached by Cunningham, was a bit deeper.

The question of which team is better likely depends on the era in which the person giving the answer grew up. But when the NBA selected their all-time greatest teams in 2004, both teams easily were included in the top 10.

Immaculata: The First Women's Basketball Dynasty

The early 1970s were a time of great change in women's basketball. First, in 1971, the game changed from the sport's six-player era, in which half a team's players stayed on one side of the court playing either offense or defense, to the five-on-five rules we know today. It was also in that same season that the Association for Intercollegiate Athletics for Women (AIAW) sanctioned the first championship tournament, thus marking the start of major women's college basketball.

The first team to dominate in this era, in the way that Connecticut or Tennessee would in later years, was Immaculata College. Located in the town of Immaculata, just outside Philadelphia, the Mighty Macs were pioneers in their sport, winning the first three AIAW national titles (1972–74) and playing for the first five championships. Along the way, Immaculata was the first women's basketball team to play on national television (in 1975, defeating Maryland) or play at Madison Square Garden.

The Mighty Macs wore tunics rather than the shorts and jerseys that players wear today. They had no home gym—it had just burned down—and no scholarships; head coach Cathy Rush was a part-time employee; the 16-team national tournament was held entirely at Illinois State; and Immaculata could only afford to take eight players to the tournament. They were accompanied by just five fans.

But in the championship final, the 15th-seeded Mighty Macs defeated West Chester, a team that had dominated the six-on-six player era, 52–48. From there, Immaculata not only became the premier women's program of the time, but the players who took the court for them also went on to become some of the premier coaches in the sport:

- Theresa Shank Gretz was named All-American in all of Immaculata's national championship seasons, scoring more than 1000 points, then went on to coaching greatness at St. Joseph's and Rutgers, Illinois, and the U.S. Olympic Team in 1992. She was inducted into the Basketball Hall of Fame in 2001.

- Rene Muth Portland also played on all three national title teams before becoming the head coach at Penn State for 27 years, leading the Lady Lions to two Final Four appearances.

- Marianne Crawford Stanley, who played from 1972 to 1976, was an All-American for the Mighty Macs' two national runner-up teams, then won three national championships at Old Dominion University.

- Guard Mary Scharff was not only an All-American during Immaculata's last national championship year, but after a stint playing professionally, she also returned to the Mighty Macs as their head coach from 1985 to 1997.

Immaculata's reign at the top of the college basketball world ended once Title IX began to take hold. Larger, more financially solvent colleges were forced to give women scholarships, and Immaculata was left behind. Cathy Rush left Immaculata after the Mighty Macs' last national championship finals appearance, finishing with a record of 149–15 at the school.

Today, Immaculata is just where it was in the 1970s, a non-scholarship program, only playing on a small-college level in Division III. Many record books don't even mention Immaculata, or for that matter West Chester, in their list of women's basketball national champions—their lists start in 1982, when the NCAA took over the women's basketball national championship tournament. Those record books are incomplete, because Immaculata and West Chester were truly the pioneers of women's college basketball.

Basketball Quotes

"Fo, Fo, Fo."

—Moses Malone, predicting the '83 Sixers would sweep through the playoffs with three four-game sweeps. He was only one off, as Philadelphia went 12–1 throughout the postseason, anticlimactically losing game four of the conference semifinals to Milwaukee. Philadelphia's championship rings would read "Fo, Fi, Fo."

"Your humor will do you no good if your superior frowns on it. Happily, Eddie Gottlieb put the stamp of approval [on me]."

—Legendary Philadelphia public address announcer Dave Zinkoff, explaining how he got his start and was able to entertain fans at the Spectrum with calls of baskets by Julius "Errrrrrrrving," among other famous phrases

"Nobody roots for Goliath."

—Wilt Chamberlain, nicknamed "Goliath," responding to critics

"Being a typical Pisces, I might have experienced mood shifts, but I don't remember any depression, or needing to do anything, or to have someone bring me out of being depressed."

—Julius Erving (this quote is notable because of his portrayal of Moses Guthrie of the Pittsburgh Pisces in the 1979 movie The Fish That Saved Pittsburgh*)*

"You want to hang me? Go ahead!"

—Villanova basketball coach Al Severance, also a local district magistrate. Supposedly, Severance kept a noose in his car and would present it whenever he faced critics of his coaching outside the arena.

"Learning the value of team play is to learn one of life's lessons."

—Pitt Hall of Fame basketball coach Doc Carlson

"I am not a role model."

—Former 76ers forward Charles Barkley in a popular advertising campaign

"I heard Tonya Harding is calling herself the Charles Barkley of figure skating. I was going to sue her for defamation of character, but then I realized I have no character."

—Charles Barkley

"We are not talking about the game I died for out there. I played every game as if it's my last. We are talking about... practice?"

—Sixers guard Allen Iverson, responding to a reporter who questioned his work ethic

"My dad used to say the grass is greener on the other side, but you still have to mow it."

—Penn State head basketball coach Ed DeChellis to a reporter while he was coaching at East Tennessee State and was rumored to be a candidate for the Nittany Lions' job

"He wins the Darryl Dawkins Award: five points, five fouls."

—Author Marky Billson, referring to an overly aggressive forward at Point Park College in the early 1990s

Chapter Eight

Boxing: The Men Who Made the State the Setting for *Rocky*

The State of Boxing

Philadelphia. Boxing. The two seem to go hand in hand. From Jack O'Brien to Joe Frazier, from Memorial Stadium to the Blue Horizon, Philadelphia has always been synonymous with boxing. Could anyone imagine another setting for Sylvester Stallone's *Rocky*?

Yet despite Philadelphia's reputation as the historic capital of boxing, the late Myron Cope often told his listeners on his talk show on WTAE-AM that Pittsburgh could match it. Granted, Cope, a respected sportswriter for many years before the Pittsburgh Steelers hired him as their color commentator in 1970, was a proponent of all things Pittsburgh, but in this case, he may have had a point.

For instance, no less of an authority than Bert Randolph Sugar called Pittsburgh a "fistic hotbed" in the 1930s, a decade in which the Steel City produced five champions. Sugar ranked Pittsburgh's Harry Greb as the third-greatest boxer in history in his 1984 book *The Greatest 100 Boxers of All Time*, behind only Sugar Ray Robinson and Henry Armstrong.

Armstrong's career began just outside Pittsburgh—he fought his first two pro bouts in Braddock and Millvale, respectively.

Furthermore, the first sporting event ever broadcast occurred in Pittsburgh—a Johnny Dundee–Johnny Ray fight at Motor Square Gardens on April 11, 1921, broadcast by KDKA.

Harry Greb

It is said that no other man fought in more professional bouts than Greb, who held the American light heavyweight championship from 1922 to 1923 and the world middleweight title from 1923 to 1926. In a 13-year career that began in 1913, Greb fought as many as 303 fights, including a record 44 in 1919.

Many of Greb's matches occurred in the "no-decision" era of boxing in the second decade of the 20th century, when, to prevent fights from being fixed, judges did not determine a decision after a bout, but instead let the sportswriters covering the fights determine the winner on the sports page. As a result, Greb's official record is 118–8–3 with 47 knockouts, but that doesn't begin to honor his legacy as a boxer.

Nicknamed "The Pittsburgh Windmill," Greb took on all comers, as his championships as both a middleweight and a light heavyweight show. His lasting legacy is that he was the only boxer to beat Gene Tunney, from whom he claimed the light heavyweight championship in 1922 with what boxing historians claim was one of the most savage beatings one fighter ever laid upon another. Incredibly, Greb won this bout with vision in only one eye, because he'd gone partially blind following a 1921 bout with Kid Norfolk.

Inside the ring, Greb was a brawler, and outside it, he is said to have lived just as hard, enjoying the company of beautiful women and drink well into Prohibition.

Greb died in 1926 at the age of 32 after falling into a coma while undergoing facial surgery following an automobile accident. At the time, he was viewed by many as the greatest fighter who had ever lived.

Newspaper reports have suggested that Pittsburgh mourned in a similar fashion to how a later generation reacted to Roberto Clemente's death in 1972, and it is even said that author Ernest Hemingway once referred to Greb as "one of our greatest Americans."

Tommy Loughran

"The Phantom of Philly" had a style that was so perfect, it was said he could fight for 15 rounds and not have a hair out of place. His techniques—stance, counterpunching, defense and footwork—are still taught to fighters today.

Loughran was arguably the greatest boxer to come from South Philadelphia, posting a record of 92–24–10. He held the light heavyweight championship from 1927 to 1929, only to give up the title after besting Jim Braddock at Yankee Stadium in the summer of 1929 to compete as a heavyweight.

He'd had success against heavyweights before, telling *Sports Illustrated* in 1979 of the time he sparred with Jack Dempsey in 1926. After Loughran got the best of Dempsey, the Manassa Mauler supposedly lost all his confidence and allowed Gene Tunney to best him in their championship fight at Sesquicentennial Stadium (later known as JFK Stadium) a few weeks later.

In 1934, after beating the likes of Max Baer, Pierre Charles and Jack Sharkey, Loughran took on Primo Carnera for the championship. Carnera was 6 feet, 5½ inches and weighed 270 pounds. Loughran was 5-foot-11 and 186 pounds. It was the biggest size difference ever between opponents for a heavyweight championship fight.

Loughran went the full 15 rounds against Carnera, even besting him in the minds of many onlookers. Loughran later said in interviews that he would have had to knock out Carnera to win the heavyweight crown, something Loughran only accomplished 17 times in his career.

After he retired from boxing, Loughran became a successful businessman and public speaker, a competitive bridge player, and even a contestant on the TV series *To Tell the Truth* in 1956. He lived his final years in a veteran's home in Holidaysburg and died in 1982.

A Pennsylvania historical marker honors Loughran in Philadelphia at the corner of 17th and Ritner streets, near Loughran's church, St. Monica's.

Billy Conn

What makes Billy Conn such a legend isn't necessarily the fact that he almost beat Joe Louis to win the heavyweight championship in 1941, but the story surrounding the bout. Prominent sportswriter Frank DeFord captured Conn's tale in 1985 in *Sports Illustrated*, and it is often regarded as DeFord's greatest piece.

The story starts with a young Irish teen who becomes a fighter to avoid a life working in the steel mills. He forms a bond with his Jewish trainer, Johnny Ray, who guides his 16-year-old protégé from an 8–7 career start to a 28–0–1 mark in his next 29 fights, often against top contenders. At the age of 21, Conn finds himself in Madison Square Garden in front of more than 15,000 fans, winning a unanimous decision against Melio Bettina for the light heavyweight crown.

Along the way, he falls in love with a young girl from the neighborhood, six years his junior, who happens to be the eldest daughter of an ex-baseball player, Jimmy Smith, something of a community leader—and the father does not want his daughter marrying a boxer. But if Smith doesn't love Conn, his daughter Mary Louise most certainly does, along with America's boxing fans. Conn's good looks, humor and fashion sense are enough for him to become a box-office star. The handsome prospect, after winning 16 straight bouts, is given the chance to fight Joe Louis for the heavyweight championship at the Polo Grounds in New York City in the summer of 1941.

Thousands of Pittsburghers take the train to New York City to see the fight. The Pittsburgh Pirates stop their night game against the Giants so the nearly 25,000 patrons at Forbes Field can hear the fight over the public address system, likely causing the 11-inning tilt to finish in a tie.

But Conn's mother hasn't tuned in. She's on her deathbed, stricken with cancer. The last time she saw her son, he promised her he'd return home champion of the world.

Louis outweighs Conn by 25 pounds, but after 12 rounds, Conn is ahead on two cards and even on the next. In what DeFord called boxing's most dramatic fight of all time, Conn merely has to stay away from Louis for the final three rounds and he'll have secured boxing's greatest prize.

However, a thought occurs to Conn—in a few days he'll marry Mary Louise, and folks will say her husband beat the great Brown Bomber for the heavyweight championship. But that's not good enough for her, he thinks. They have to say she's the wife of the fighter who *knocked out* Joe Louis.

So he continues the attack, and at 2:58 of the 13th round, Conn is counted out.

"What's the sense of being Irish if you can't be dumb?" Conn says after the fight.

Conn is cast as the lead in the boxing movie *The Pittsburgh Kid* soon after. A rematch against Louis awaits, or possibly a film career. But then comes Pearl Harbor, and then comes Smith, an angry father-in-law who wanted his daughter to marry into the wealth of the Philadelphia Main Line, not the working class of East Liberty, even if the pride of Shakespeare Street is, for all intents and purposes, on top of the world.

Smith provokes Conn in an argument, fisticuffs ensue, and "The Pittsburgh Kid" breaks his hand. The rematch against Louis will have to wait until after World War II.

By this time, Conn is no longer sharp, and Louis knocks him out in the eighth round of their 1946 rematch, effectively ending Conn's career.

But Conn would have one more fight. At the age of 73, after 50 years of marriage to Mary Louise, three sons and status in Pittsburgh as a man of the town, Conn broke up a robbery attempt at a Beechwood Boulevard convenience store down the street from his Squirrel Hill home.

Conn passed away in 1993. The corner of Fifth Avenue and Craig Street in Pittsburgh's Oakland section is alternatively named "Billy Conn Boulevard," both to honor Conn and the old Duquesne Gardens, the sports arena once located near this intersection where Conn fought one-seventh of the fights of his professional career.

Freddie Welsh

Many fighters from Philadelphia have become champions. But what about an *overseas* champ?

Such was the case with Freddie Welsh, a native of Wales born into wealth who decided to try his lot in life in North America as a teenager. A lifelong fitness buff, he took up boxing, which eventually became his source of income.

Born Fredrick Hall Thomas, he changed his name to "Welsh" in an attempt to hide from his mother the fact that he was a boxer. He moved to Philadelphia in 1905 to start a professional career, making a name for himself in 26 bouts over the course of the year, all but two in or around Philly.

Returning to Europe when his mother fell ill in 1907, Welsh did stunts such as fighting and knocking out three different opponents in one day to gain a reputation. But his mannerisms and voice had become Americanized during his stay in the U.S., and British audiences often rooted for his opponent. Welsh returned to America a year later and spent the rest of his career fighting on two continents.

A defensive fighter, Welsh registered only 34 knockouts in his 168-fight career. This explains why he didn't get a world lightweight title shot until 1914, when he bested Willie Ritchie in 20 rounds.

But Welsh had held European and British championships as far back as 1909 and was only knocked out once. Nineteen of his fights lasted 20 or more rounds, a sign of his endurance in the ring. His career record was 74–5–7, with the remainder of his fights claimed by newspaper decisions, of which Welsh took 48. Boxing historians Nat Fleischer, Charley Rose and Herb Goldman have ranked Welsh among the top 10 lightweights of all time, and Bert Randolph Sugar ranked him as the 48th greatest boxer of all time in 1984.

Joe Frazier

Joe Frazier is perhaps the most famous and successful of all the Philadelphia fighters. He was the heavyweight champion of the world from 1970 to 1973, and his rivalry with Muhammad Ali was clearly the greatest in modern boxing history.

Remember Rocky Balboa using slabs of meat as punching bags and running up the stairs of the Philadelphia Museum of Art? All taken from Frazier.

Frazier's story began when he won a gold medal in the 1964 Olympics. Upon turning pro, he was tutored by Eddie Futch, who refined him from being a brawler to more of a boxer with a defensive "bob and weave" style to combat taller opponents.

Frazier won his first 10 fights by knockout and took his 11th when Billy Daniels refused to answer the bell for the seventh round after being knocked down four times.

In 1968, in his 20th pro bout, he won his first title, the New York State Athletic Commission heavyweight championship. Held back by his trainers for the next two years to hone his skills, in 1970, Frazier became the undisputed heavyweight champ with a fifth-round knockout of Jimmy Ellis.

After a title defense to run his record to 26–0 with 23 knockouts, Frazier then faced Muhammad Ali in what was dubbed "The Fight of the Century" on March 8, 1971. It would be the first time two undefeated champions—Frazier current, Ali past but stripped of his title in 1967 for refusing induction into the army—would meet for a heavyweight title.

During the bout, "Smokin' Joe" used his famed left hook twice—once in the 11th round, and once in the 15th—to stagger Ali and hand him his first professional defeat.

Frazier retained his belt for two title defenses before being knocked out by George Foreman in 1973, the source of Howard Cosell's famous "Down goes Frazier!" call. One fight later, Frazier lost a rematch to Ali on decision in 1974, in large part because Ali was allowed by referee Tony Perez to hold the back of Frazier's neck throughout the fight.

It was obvious that a rubber match between the two fighters would be scheduled, and the next year, the two met again in the Philippines, in a fight titled "The Thrilla in Manila." Ali came on strong in the early rounds, but Frazier's tenacious training paid off, and he was able to wear down "The Louisville

Lip" in the middle rounds. But Ali was able to hang on, and in the 11th round, he started to land enough combinations to Frazier's face that the swelling made it difficult for "Smokin' Joe" to see. By the end of the 14th round, both fighters were seriously hurt, and Futch decided to stop the bout rather than risk further injury to Frazier, despite the boxer's protests. However, Ali was begging his own corner to stop the fight, saying he'd had enough, when Futch figuratively threw in the towel.

Ali, in his showman style, had insulted Frazier relentlessly during the three-fight series, causing a permanent rift between the two men. But after the Manila fight, Ali gave Frazier respect.

"Joe Frazier, I'll tell the world right now, brings out the best in me. I'm gonna tell ya, that's one helluva man, and God bless him," Ali said. "He is the greatest fighter of all times, next to me."

Frazier left boxing soon afterward with a career record of 32–4–1 and 27 knockouts. He had a cameo in *Rocky*, has been a frequent guest on Howard Stern's radio and David Letterman's television programs, and had his own gym in Philadelphia where he trained fighters through 2009. One of these boxers was his own son, Marvis, a heavyweight contender in the 1980s who amassed a 19–2 record with his only defeats coming from Larry Holmes and Mike Tyson.

Larry Holmes

One fight changed the way the public perceived Larry Holmes.

Granted, Holmes is regarded as one of the great heavyweight champions of all time. Equipped with a brutal left jab, many speculated during his championship reign whether or not Holmes deserved to be listed above Ali, Marciano and Dempsey. After all, Holmes had sparred with the best—Ali, Frazier and Earnie Shavers. He'd beaten Ali, admittedly when Ali was past his prime, but still dominated the fight that Ali's corner stopped after 10 rounds.

In all, Holmes defended the title he won from Ken Norton in 1978 20 times, took a stand when he fought Marvis Frazier on network television (which cost him his WBC heavyweight championship and ultimately forever divided the heavyweight division championship) for a larger payday than what he was offered to box top contender Greg Page, and amassed a 48–0 record that put him one shy of Rocky Marciano's record 49–0 mark.

But in 1985, Holmes, in his effort to tie Marciano's record, was defeated in 15 rounds by light heavyweight champ Michael Spinks, and then lost a rematch in similar fashion.

At age 36, it appeared Holmes' career was over. But after a brief retirement, he continued to fight and earned heavyweight title shots four times from 1988 to 1997. His most notable victory came in 1992, when he bested former Olympic gold medalist Ray Mercer in 12 rounds.

Holmes retired in 2002 with a 69–6 record and 44 knockouts. He currently runs a restaurant and lounge in Easton and sings in an eight-member group called Marmalade.

Charley Burley

Charley Burley is perhaps the least known of the fighters listed here because he never held a title, save for the California middleweight championship in 1944. This was not for lack of talent, but likely fear on the part of his potential opponents.

For instance, Art Rooney Sr. is said to have once tried to arrange for Burley to fight Billy Conn, but was rebuffed by

Johnny Ray, who told Rooney to "never mention [Burley's] name again!"

George Gainford, Sugar Ray Robinson's manager, considered Burley a versatile boxer who could adapt to any opponent's style, and Gainford would not allow the great champion to face Burley.

Burley was a welterweight fighting out of Pittsburgh from the 1930s to 1950, posting a record of 74–12–1 with 44 knockouts. On his way up, he defeated future welterweight champion Fritzie Zivic in two of three bouts in 1938 and 1939. Zivic responded by having his manager take over Burley's contract so he would not have to face him again.

Burley himself dodged one series of fights. He likely could have participated in the 1936 Olympics but declined the opportunity to protest the games being held in Nazi Germany.

Looking for any opponent he could fight to gather publicity, Burley often boxed out of his class, even taking on future heavyweight champion Ezzard Charles twice in 1942. Perhaps Burley's most notable victory came against Archie Moore in 1944, when Burley won a decision against the future light heavyweight champion, who called him "the toughest of all."

Even Joe Frazier's manager, Eddie Futch, called Burley the best fighter he ever saw. In his entire career, Burley was never knocked out. He was also August Wilson's favorite boxer, and the playwright patterned the character Troy in *Fences* after Burley.

Burley died in 1992 at the age of 75. On August 5, 2008, Pittsburgh's City Council recognized his career and life as a "loving family man" to his wife Julia and three children by declaring a "Charley Burley Day."

Philadelphia Jack O'Brien

Born Joseph Hagen, Jack O'Brien won only one title, the light heavyweight championship in 1905, and quickly abandoned it. But O'Brien belongs on the list of the all-time best fighters from Pennsylvania because he truly broke the mold in his era.

Sporting a 94–7–14 lifetime record with 56 knockouts, O'Brien took on all comers regardless of weight class or race. For example, in 1909 he took on Jack Johnson for the heavyweight championship, and despite a 205 to 162½ pound weight disadvantage, O'Brien battled Johnson to a draw.

Moreover, O'Brien was one of the great characters of his day. When he wasn't causing doubt in the minds of the sporting public by claiming that all of his early fights were fixed, he was playing the violin or socializing with Philadelphia's cultural elite at the opera or the symphony. In 1903, he toured Great Britain, claiming to be America's middleweight champion. He won three fights by knockouts in Newcastle Upon Tyne and earned the respect of the Geordies with his scientific, defensive style, patterned after Jim Corbett.

O'Brien fought professionally for 16 years and passed away in 1942 at the age of 64. Former *Ring* editor Nat Loubet ranked him as the greatest light heavyweight of all time.

Sonny Liston

Like Freddie Welsh, Sonny Liston was not a native of Philadelphia, but rather moved to the city to advance his career. Liston was one of boxing's most fearsome personalities, and not just because of his exploits in the ring. He was arrested 19 times, his contract was sponsored by the mob, and he died before he could retire.

Born into abject poverty, one of more than two dozen children born to an Arkansas sharecropper, Liston's upbringing was so Spartan that his birth date was never recorded. He ran away from an abusive father to be with his mother in St. Louis in 1944, but with no education, he turned to crime to support himself.

Liston learned to box in the Missouri State Penitentiary, which helped earn him a release after 28 months of incarceration in 1953. But after winning 14 of his first 15 fights, he was arrested again for assaulting a police officer in 1956, and after nine more months in prison, he moved to Philadelphia.

It was in Philly that Liston became a champion. He won his next 19 fights, 15 by knockout, though only one of these fights actually occurred in Pennsylvania. Finally, popular heavyweight champion Floyd Patterson gave Liston a long-awaited title shot.

Because of Liston's criminal past, many did not want him to have a chance at the championship. He made the most of his 1962 opportunity in Chicago, knocking out Patterson in the first round to become heavyweight champion and defending his title in a rematch with another first-round knockout a year later.

But Philadelphia did not embrace Liston. He often complained of being harassed by police, and after defeating Patterson to become champion, no fans came to greet him at the Philadelphia airport. This devastated Liston. He realized he would always be viewed as "the bad guy." Soon afterward, Liston moved to Denver, saying, "I'd rather be a lamppost in Denver than the mayor of Philadelphia."

Throughout the 1960s, Liston attempted to improve his image by speaking to children, visiting prisoners and appearing on *The Ed Sullivan Show, Love American Style* and in The Monkees' infamous film *Head*. He even appeared in a famous television advertisement with Andy Warhol for Braniff Airlines and on the album cover of The Beatles' *Sgt. Pepper's Lonely Hearts Club Band*.

Cassius Clay upset Liston in 1964 to take the heavyweight championship, then, after embracing the Muslim faith and changing his name to Muhammad Ali, knocked Liston out in a controversial 1965 rematch. After the second Ali fight, Liston continued to box as a ranked contender. One of his last fights was in 1968 at Pittsburgh's Civic Arena, when he knocked out Roger Rischer in the main event on the card of a benefit for Ben Anolik, Pennsylvania's first heart transplant patient. Liston and Sugar Ray Robinson are the only two boxers to headline cards at both Pittsburgh's Civic Arena and Duquesne Gardens.

Liston's final record was 50–4 with 39 knockouts. Chuck Wepner, the boxer on whom Sylvester Stallone based Rocky Balboa, has stated that Liston was the hardest puncher he'd ever faced. Liston was at least 38 when he knocked out Wepner, who also fought Ali and Foreman in his career.

Wepner was Liston's final bout. He was found dead in his home on Janurary 5, 1971, by his wife Geraldine. Liston's passing remains a mystery, and, like his birth, no one can say for sure what his exact date of death was.

Fritzie Zivic

Before Mike Tyson, Fritzie Zivic, a native of Pittsburgh's Lawrenceville neighborhood, was known as perhaps the dirtiest fighter of all time. He might stick his glove's finger into an opponent's eye, batter him with a low blow or a head-butt or even step on his feet. Usually, such a tactic was accompanied by "The Croat Comet" saying to his foe, "Pardon me!"

His record of 158–64–9 with 80 knockouts is not particularly outstanding; in fact, at one point in his career, Zivic lost eight straight fights. But he was such a prominent figure in Pittsburgh's boxing heyday, it seemed that nearly every contender of the 1930s and '40s had a fight with Zivic.

One such bout came in 1940, when Zivic fought Henry Armstrong for the welterweight title in front of a record Madison Square Garden crowd of 23,190. According to Zivic, Armstrong began fighting as dirty as Zivic typically did. Fearing a disqualification, Zivic did not retaliate in kind until the seventh round, after which referee Arthur Donovan Sr. told the fighters that such a style would be fine with him.

Zivic rallied in the late rounds. By the end of the 15th, Armstrong was on the canvas, and though he was saved by the bell, it was enough for Zivic to win the championship.

He would hold the title through 11 fights, including a rematch with Armstrong in which Zivic knocked out "Homicide Hank," and even lived up to his reputation in his first title defense when Al "Bummy" Davis, infuriated with Zivic's eye gouging, was disqualified for retaliating with low blows.

Later in his career, Zivic would beat Jake LaMotta at Forbes Field, and Freddie Cochran, the fighter who took Zivic's belt from him, at Madison Square Garden. He even went the distance with Sugar Ray Robinson.

Zivic retired in 1949 and became a bartender. He even owned a bar in Lawrenceville that displayed his picture on the building. Much like Sam Malone on *Cheers!*, he entertained patrons, including a young writer named Myron Cope, with stories of his athletic exploits.

Cope used these stories to write his first well-known sports piece, "The Art of Fighting Dirty," for *True* magazine, thus jump-starting his own legendary career in sports media.

Zivic died in 1984 of Alzheimer's disease. He was 71.

Michael Moorer

Michael Moorer, a Monessen native, became the first left-handed heavyweight champion when he won a 12-round decision against Evander Holyfield in 1994. Moorer was a dominant champion, winning his first 26 bouts by knockout en route to earning the World Boxing Organization (WBO) light heavyweight championship in 1988, just two years after turning pro.

Moorer was trained by some of the best handlers in the business: Emanuel Steward, Lou Duva and Teddy Atlas. It was with Atlas and his motivational style that Moorer beat Holyfield, which did as much for Atlas' reputation as it did for that of his protégé.

But Moorer lost the title in his first defense, getting knocked out by George Foreman, thus allowing Foreman to become the oldest heavyweight champion in history at 45. (The previous record was held by Joe Walcott, who was 37 when he knocked out Ezzard Charles at Forbes Field in 1951.) Undaunted, Moorer regained his title in 1996 when he beat Axel Schultz in a 12-round split decision. He had two title defenses before his relationship with Atlas became tenuous and the pair parted in 1997. Moorer lost his crown later that year when Holyfield knocked him down five times, finally earning a TKO in the eighth round. Moorer retired, made a brief but unsuccessful comeback in 2002, then retired again with a 52–4–1 record and 40 knockouts. He has since been a boxing commentator, a trainer and even a bodyguard for Tiger Woods.

Paul Spadafora

Perhaps Pennsylvania's best-known boxer in recent times has been McKees Rocks' Paul Spadafora, the International Boxing Federation (IBF) lightweight champion from 1999 to 2003 before he gave up the title to compete as a junior welterweight. He has been given Conn's old nickname, "The Pittsburgh Kid." Iron City Beer designed a can with Spadafora's picture on it, and he became a regular on HBO.

But in 2005, Spadafora was sentenced to prison and a bootcamp for attempted murder after he shot his pregnant girlfriend in 2003. He served 13 months. Between the shooting and his sentencing, he was also arrested for DUI and cocaine use.

"Spady" returned to boxing in 2006 after a 32-month layoff, but at 31, many felt he was past his prime. He has won seven decisions since his release, but is struggling to earn a ranking worthy of a title shot. As of January 2011, he has never been beaten in 46 career pro bouts.

Art Rooney Sr.

The founder of the Pittsburgh Steelers was an alternate on the 1920 United States Olympic boxing team. Professionally, he split two newspaper decisions in 1922 as a lightweight before pursuing other endeavors.

Boxing Quotes

Sonny Liston, in a 1963 interview with Howard Cosell, who questioned Liston's age:

Cosell: "How old are you now?"

Liston: "31."

Cosell: "Still 31?"

Liston: "Yeah."

Cosell: "Will you ever be 32?"

Liston: "No. I'm like Jack Benny."

"You're boxing. You're not playing the piano."

—Fritzie Zivic

"Rocky [Marciano] couldn't carry my jockstrap."

—Larry Holmes, after losing to Michael Spinks in 1985;
Holmes would later apologize for the remark

Chapter Nine

The Rivalries

Fighting Among Ourselves

How can a state with so much scenic beauty and so many things to do often be looked at somewhat negatively by its own citizens? Naturally, there are Pennsylvanians who are proud of their state, or commonwealth, as the case may be. But still, Pennsylvania often seems to be the butt of jokes that, frankly, may be undeserved.

For instance, Pittsburgh has consistently been named "America's Most Livable City" by the Rand McNally *Places Rated Almanac*. The hills, rivers and architecture give the city a distinctive, almost exotic beauty. Yet in 1979, Ron Fimrite wrote in *Sports Illustrated* that "Pittsburghers, anticipating familiar digs, were inclined either to defend themselves precipitously or to beat would-be detractors to the punch: 'How'd ya like the 'Burgh? Kinda dull, ain't it?'"

An argument can be made that to not like Philadelphia is to not like America. Isn't this where the nation started? Didn't the American Automobile Association use the Liberty Bell as the lone and defining symbol of the country for their road maps of the U.S.? But could Philadelphia native W.C. Fields ever resist taking a shot at his hometown? As *Daily News* writer Will Bunch summed it up in 2009: "Philadelphia...was a victim of a strange condition: low civic self-esteem. And what brought that on? A lot of things, some of them self-inflicted like our 'corrupt and content' political culture—but there was also a severe case of sibling jealousy, the sibling being our colonial cousin of New York City."

New York City? Perhaps. Philadelphia is, after all, closer to New York City than it is to Pittsburgh. Similarly, a Clevelander in Pittsburgh must almost always prepare him- or herself for some sort of comment, usually a boast about the Steelers, as Pittsburgh is closer to the Forest City than it is to Philly.

But in central Pennsylvania, the battle lines are drawn between Pittsburgh and Philadelphia in schoolyards, around water coolers, during call-in talk shows and the like. And whatever hatred is absent between the two cities, is alive and well in Harrisburg.

Could any of the self-confidence issues that Pennsylvania may or may not have be based on sports rivalry? The following is a list of well-known rivalries in Pennsylvania and what shapes them.

Non-football Rivalries

Pirates vs. Phillies

In 2011, the Pirates–Phillies rivalry doesn't seem like much. The two teams only play each other once a year in their own ballparks thanks to their placement in different National League divisions. Besides, the rivalry has become uncompetitive, with the Phillies entering 2011 holding the longest streak of consecutive postseason appearances, four, while the Pirates have endured a major league professional sports record of the most dubious distinction, having posted a losing record for 18 straight seasons. But at one time, and within the memories of many of their early 21st-century fans, the rivalry between the two cities was perhaps the fiercest in baseball, easily ranking alongside, if not above, the Red Sox–Yankees, Cardinals–Cubs or Dodgers–Giants.

For the first 25 seasons of divisional play in Major League Baseball, there were no wild cards, so to make the postseason, a team had to win its division. The one exception to this rule was in 1981, when because of a players' strike, the major leagues played a split season in which a divisional round of playoffs paired first- and second-half seasonal champions.

From 1970 to 1981, a Pennsylvania team finished in first place in every season except 1973, when the Pirates, grieving over the off-season death of Roberto Clemente, finished 2½ games behind the New York Mets. For four straight years, from 1975 to 1978, and then again in 1983, the Pirates and the Phillies finished one-two in the NL East standings. And in the last four years of pre-wild card divisional play, from 1990 to 1993, the Pirates won three division titles and the Phils took another.

During the 1970s and early '80s, there was a distinct dislike between the two franchises. It often seemed that when they played, the game wasn't complete unless there was a bench-clearing brawl. The 1977 pennant race, in which the Phils finished five games ahead of the Bucs in the standings, was heavily influenced by a brawl between the teams when Willie Stargell injured his elbow and missed the last 2½ months of the season as a result.

It eventually got to where even supposedly objective journalists got into the act. For instance, in 1985, after a decade of bitter rivalry, Bill Conlin used his "N.L. Beat" column in *The Sporting News* to take pot shots at Pittsburgh. "[Pittsburgh is] a city where Archie Bunker would have lived if Norman Lear had given him his choice of duplexes," he wrote in 1984. Conlin then openly questioned why the city was selected as America's Most Liveable the following year.

"I'd rather be dead than live in Philadelphia," countered KDKA sportscaster Bill Currie on his talk show, *Sports Huddle*, one-upping W.C. Fields. Currie had worked in Philadelphia prior to moving to Pittsburgh.

If that wasn't enough, the Phillies 1983 yearbook, which celebrated the franchise's 100th anniversary, ran a piece penned by Conlin imagining what the Phillies and life in general would be like in 2083. In his scenario, western Pennsylvania had been obliterated by a nuclear accident.

The next year, the Bucs countered, marketing their entire season on the phrase "I Don't Love the Phillies," complete with a "No" symbol over a heart between "I" and "the."

The rivalry really started to heat up in 1975, when the Pirates beat out the Phils by 6½ games to win the NL East, complete with an 11–3 division-clinching victory against Philadelphia at Three Rivers Stadium during the last week of the season. It was the first time in 75 years that the two teams finished in first and second place.

Then, after contending for the title the previous two years, Philadelphia took the first of three straight NL East championships in 1976 despite a furious run by the Bucs, who cut the Phillies' 15½ game lead on August 24 to just three by September 17 before falling off the pace. The 1978 race was very hotly contested, as the Pirates, 10 games under .500 and 11½ games behind the Phillies on August 12, caught fire by winning 37 of their final 49 games, including 24 in a row at home. The pennant race came down to the next-to-the-last game of the season between the two teams, when Philadelphia finally clinched it with a 10–8 victory, but not before Pittsburgh rallied for four runs in the bottom of the ninth inning and Stargell stepped up to the plate as the potential tying run.

The next year, the Pirates won the World Series, but first they had to get by the Phillies. The Bucs moved into first place in early August by sweeping a five-game series highlighted by a two-out, bottom-of-the-ninth, pinch-hit grand slam from John Milner to give Pittsburgh a 12–8 triumph. The next weekend, the Pirates won three of four games at Veterans Stadium, most notably a 14–11 victory in which the Bucs rebounded from an 8–0 deficit.

Then the Phillies, the only one of the original 16 franchises not to move or win a World Series, finally took the championship in 1980, but only after breaking a three-way tie for first place with the Bucs and the Expos on September 1, in large part by taking three of four games in September from the slumping Pirates.

In 1983, the Phils and the Bucs were tied for first place on September 17, but the Phils won 11 straight games down the stretch, highlighted by Steve Carlton's 300th victory on September 24 against St. Louis, thus making a three-game, season-ending series between Pittsburgh and Philly irrelevant.

After 1983, both teams fell on hard times. The Pirates finished in last place for three straight years, from 1984 to 1986; the Phils would find the bottom of the NL East in 1988, 1989 and 1992. When the Pirates became competitive again in 1988, they marketed the Mets, then their main competition for division supremacy, as their main rival.

But there were still moments to remember:

- Barry Bonds hit the first game-ending home run of his career to beat the Phils, 5–4, on September 23, 1986.

- The Bucs swept the Phillies on the final weekend of the 1984 season, complete with pitcher Don Robinson playing left field and captain Bill Madlock calling the shots for manager Chuck Tanner, to prevent Philadelphia from having a winning record, and in 1987, they did the same again, pulling themselves even with the Phils for fourth place in the division.

- Also in 1987, Mike Schmidt's 500th career home run was a two-out, ninth-inning, game-winning, three-run shot off Robinson to give the Phils a 7–6 victory at Pittsburgh on April 19.

- On June 8, 1989, the Phillies rallied from a 10-run, first-inning deficit behind Steve Jeltz's two home runs (he would only hit four in his entire career) from opposite sides of the plate to beat the Bucs, 15–11.

- On August 3, 1990, the Phils' Sil Campusano, batting .188 at the time, broke up a no-hit bid by Pittsburgh's Cy Young Award–winner Doug Drabek with two outs in the ninth and the Pirates up 11–0.

The rivalry has lost some luster with the Pirates' placement in the National League Central division and the Phillies in the East, not to mention the two teams' placements in the standings in the early 21st century. Eastern Pennsylvania natives attending the University of Pittsburgh have been known to wear Phillies caps and jerseys or even celebrate Phils victories by burning couches, while fellow Pitt students from western Pennsylvania have little to counter with. And whereas in a previous generation, fans argued whether Stargell or Schmidt was the better slugger, today, Phils first baseman Ryan Howard is often compared to the Bucs' great hitter. Furthermore, shortstop Jimmy Rollins went to the same high school as Stargell—Encinal, in Oakland, California.

But it's safe to say that Pirates' fans in central Pennsylvania still relish in rooting for the Phillies' opponents. And with the divisional set up, should the two teams ever meet in the National League championship series, it's likely the rivalry will become as bitter as it was in the '70s.

Penguins vs. Flyers

These two franchises began play in 1967, and almost immediately, the Flyers had the upper hand. When the Flyers were winning their second Stanley Cup in 1975, the Penguins faced bankrupcy. Even more notably, from February 7, 1974, to February 2, 1989, the Pittsburgh Penguins played the Flyers in the Spectrum 42 times and failed to win even a single game, posting a horrible 0–39–3 record. Since then, the Penguins have caught up in franchise prestige. As of 2011, the Flyers had not won the Stanley Cup in 36 years, but the Penguins had overtaken Philadelphia in total number of Cups with championships in 1991, 1992 and 2009.

What makes this rivalry so good is that not only are the two teams competitive with each other, but also that they have contrasting styles of play. The Penguins are owned by Mario Lemieux and preach a finesse type of game; the Flyers' general manager was Bobby Clarke, who still believes in the violent brand of hockey his Broad Street Bullies used in the mid-1970s to win back-to-back Cups. The Penguins are Sidney Crosby and Evgeni Malkin, both with scoring titles and only one season of 100 or more penalty minutes on their career record as of 2011. The Flyers are Daniel Carcillo, who led the NHL in penalty minutes in his first two full seasons. Furthermore, since Cleveland doesn't have a hockey team, the Flyers are unquestionably the Penguins' geographic rival.

Interesting moments between the two franchises include the Penguins' near miss of breaking the Flyers' 35-game unbeaten string, a major North American sports record, in 1979. The Pens had a 1–0 lead on the Flyers at the Spectrum on December 20, 1979, but Flyer Behn Wilson scored a tying goal at 15:52 that he actually kicked into the net. Had Wilson not scored, not only would the game likely have ended the Pens' winless streak in Philadelphia 10 years sooner, but the Flyers' unbeaten string would likely have stalled at 27, just short of the then-record.

It seemed that even when the Flyers weren't dominating the Pens, they were still beating them in the most dramatic and gut-wrenching ways. In 1989, the two teams met in the playoffs for the first time in the Patrick Division finals. Thanks to an incredible eight-point game from Mario Lemieux in a 10–7 game five victory, Pittsburgh had a 3–2 lead in the best-of-seven series. But after a 6–2 Philadelphia triumph in the Spectrum, backup goalie and future Penguin Ken Wregget stopped 39 shots in a 4–1 Flyers victory at the Civic Arena in the deciding game.

Eleven years later, Pittsburgh raced to a 2–0 series advantage against the Flyers; then, after a loss, they played Philadelphia to a 1–1 draw for four overtime periods at the Civic Arena. Finally, after 152 minutes and one second of hockey, Keith Primeau beat Ron Tugnutt to defeat the Pens and tie the series 2–2. Pittsburgh never recovered and lost the series in six games.

But if Lemieux and Jaromir Jagr couldn't beat the Flyers in the postseason, the Flyers, as of 2010, haven't been able to solve Crosby. The Penguins beat the Flyers in five games in the 2009 Eastern Conference finals as Marion Hossa scored in every Pittsburgh victory and native Pittsburgher Ryan Malone, son of former Penguin Greg Malone, scored two goals in the Pens' 6–0 series-clinching victory. The following season, Pittsburgh bested Philly again in six games thanks to four goals in the series by Crosby, a victory that began the Pens' journey to the Stanley Cup championship.

Forget the Pens' rivalry with the Washington Capitals based on Crosby and Alexander Ovechkin battling for individual supremacy in the NHL. Historically, Pittsburgh has had their way with the Capitals. The Flyers and the Penguins, as of 2011, will surely be fighting for control of their division for years to come, and the intrastate and geographic aspect of Flyers vs. Penguins makes this the premier contemporary rivalry in Pennsylvania.

Joe Frazier vs. Muhammad Ali

It was boxing's greatest rivalry, and whom one rooted for often spoke volumes about what kind of person he or she was. A Frazier fan stood for sportsmanship and honor, whereas an Ali fan was wild and intrepid. The exception was the Philadelphia metropolitan area, where cheering for Frazier meant rooting for the hometown hero.

The story began when Ali refused induction into the army in 1967 during the Vietnam War after applying for conscientious objector status with the Selective Service as a minister in the Nation of Islam. For this, Ali was stripped of his heavyweight belt and was absent from boxing for four of the prime years of his career. Enter Frazier, the dominating up-and-comer during this time. There were parallels between the two: Ali won a gold medal in the 1960 Olympics, and Frazier did the same in 1964; Ali was the unbeaten heavyweight champ in 1967, and in 1971, Frazier was the undefeated champion.

But Frazier hardly was trying to duck Ali. During Ali's four-year exile, Frazier worked to help Ali regain his boxing license, even meeting with President Richard Nixon to do so. But by the time Ali was reinstated and the two fought for the heavyweight championship in 1971, Ali was hardly gracious and instead began taunting Frazier in his showman style, thus beginning one of the bitterest feuds in sports history.

Ali slandered Frazier. Before their first fight at Madison Square Garden, Ali declared that any black person who would root for Frazier was a traitor, and as a result, unfortunate battle lines were drawn in what some were calling "the most extraordinary sporting event of all time." Frazier responded by knocking his opponent down in the 15th round and handing Ali his first professional defeat.

But Ali was not going away, and he continued to taunt Frazier when the two fought again in 1974. This time Ali won on decision, thanks in part to being allowed by referee Tony Perez to hold the back of Frazier's neck during the fight.

Now the heavyweight champion, Ali was even more merciless toward Frazier than he had been before. The Ali camp felt they were doing Frazier a favor by scheduling a third fight between the two boxers, the 1975 "Thriller in Manila," giving "Smokin' Joe" one last payday before retirement. In the lead-up to the bout, Ali repeatedly defamed Frazier, implying he was less than a man by calling him a "gorilla."

Fought on a muggy Philippines morning in reported 125°F temperatures, Ali won the early rounds by using his reach and punching power to stand toe to toe with Frazier in the center of the ring. Frazier came back by utilizing his right hand and, when Ali was not allowed to hold the back of Frazier's neck, "Smokin' Joe" began to dominate the middle rounds. After the 14th round, Ali told his corner to cut off his gloves and stop the fight. Even though Frazier had been blinded late in the fight when he took six phenomenal combinations in the 14th round from Ali, he continued to stand up.

"[Ali] was very close to killing [Frazier]," said Ali's doctor, Ferdie Pacheco. Frazier could barely see, and his trainer, Eddie Futch, had seen eight fighters die in the ring. He would not allow Frazier to be his ninth. In literally a race to see who could throw in the towel first, Futch won, and Ali took the match, only to collapse when he left his stool.

Afterward, Ali tried to apologize to Frazier for his taunting, but Frazier has been cool to such apologies, and has even taken some satisfaction in Ali's Parkinson's disease. But no matter what the official records are, both fighters believe they won all three bouts.

76ers vs. Celtics

In 1983, Jack Chevalier, the Philadelphia Flyers' beat writer in the old *Philadelphia Bulletin*, wrote in the April 25 issue of *The Sporting News* a list of what he felt were the top 10 rivalries in sports. Heading the list were the Philadelphia 76ers and the Boston Celtics. Sure, there's the sense that the Celtics are everyone's main rival, and today, it seems as if national media pushes the Celtics and Lakers as the top rivalry in the NBA.

But Sixers vs. Celtics isn't just about two teams or the two cities that Ben Franklin lived in. It's about Wilt Chamberlain and Bill Russell, and a generation later, Julius Erving and Larry Bird. Chamberlain, the one-man offensive machine who netted 100 points in a single game; Russell, the finest defensive center basketball has ever seen. Chamberlain, the conservative Republican; Russell, the liberal Democrat. Chamberlain, flaunting his lifestyle of sports cars and pretty women; Russell, who didn't sign autographs, thinking they were humiliating to the one who asked for them. Chamberlain, fascinated with individual statistics; Russell, the driving force behind eight consecutive NBA championships.

The Philadelphia fans' hatred of the Celtics began at this time. Chamberlain and Russell met on eight occasions in the postseason. Boston won seven times, a fact so hard to accept for Philadelphians that former 76ers owner Ike Richman died of a heart attack during a game against the Celts. And while the Chamberlain vs. Russell rivalry really dates back to the days when the Warriors were Philly's team, it brings up the question: What if the Warriors had beaten the Celtics in the '62 semis? Would the team have moved away? Could Frank McGuire have built a team that would have bested the Celtics with more consistency?

A generation later, the NBA's top individual rivalry was arguably between Julius Erving of the 76ers and Larry Bird of the Celtics. Both had built their teams up from ruin practically overnight. "Dr. J" was the proud veteran player who needed an NBA championship to make his legacy complete; Bird was the champion of rural America who won an NBA title in just his second year. Both players were poised to take the NBA to greater heights of popularity in the 1980s that Michael, Magic, Isiah and Charles would take even further. It even appeared that Erving and Bird had the same kind of gentlemanly relationship that Chamberlain and Russell did. Russell's family often enjoyed Thanksgiving dinner with Chamberlain; Erving and Bird appeared in Converse commercials together.

This time the rivalry was split. The Sixers bested the Celtics in the 1980 Eastern Conference finals, only to blow a 3–1 advantage against Boston in the best-of-seven conference finals the next year on the Celtics' road to the NBA championship. In 1982, the Sixers again jumped to a 3–1 advantage against Boston in the conference finals, only to lose the next two games and find themselves heavy underdogs in game seven at the Boston Garden. What made this contest so memorable was not only the Sixers' dominating 120–106 upset behind Andrew Toney's 34 points to put them in the NBA finals against Los Angeles, but also that, with 20 seconds left and the game decided, Boston fans chanted "Beat L-A!" in support of the Sixers as a show of sportsmanship.

Still, at the beginning of the 1984 season, Erving and Bird got into a fight during a 130–119 Boston victory. In some ways, this marked the turning point in the two stars' careers. The Celtics had overtaken the Sixers as NBA champions the season before and would top Philadelphia in five games in the Eastern Conference finals that season, as well. Furthermore, when the two players were ejected in the third quarter, Bird, who would go on to play until 1992, had 42 points while Erving, who retired in 1987, had just six.

The two franchises have only met once in the postseason in the quarter century since then, that being a 3–2 best-of-five Boston triumph in 2002 against the Allen Iverson–led Sixers.

Arnold Palmer vs. Jack Nicklaus

While most of the rivalries in Pennsylvania are extremely bitter, this rivalry seems to be punctuated by the gentlemanly nature of these two men. Arnold Palmer and Jack Nicklaus respect each other, and therefore we respect them.

It's well known that Latrobe native Palmer brought golf into the television era. He had a background that the masses could relate to—the son of a greenskeeper, he was a Coast Guard veteran whose brother was killed in an automobile accident. But he also had the charisma and looks for fans to be naturally attracted to him. Additionally, Palmer made golf exciting—he played with a freewheeling style, making spectacular shots others wouldn't even try.

Nicklaus, meanwhile, might not have had the physique of Palmer, but he certainly had the game. He nearly bested Palmer as an amateur in the 1960 U.S. Open at Cherry Ridge before Palmer came on at the end to win by two strokes, which probably served notice to Palmer's huge fan base, "Arnie's Army," that Nicklaus was on his way up.

Nicklaus hit his stride in 1962. At Oakmont in suburban Pittsburgh, the two were paired together at the U.S. Open, then went nip-and-tuck during the entire tournament. Nicklaus pulled even on the final hole, necessitating an 18-hole playoff. He beat Palmer by a stroke on the first hole and never looked back. Despite playing as essentially the "visiting team," Nicklaus won the playoff by three strokes, and a new chapter in golf history began as he won his first major.

Two years later, Palmer bested Nicklaus in the Masters by jumping out to a commanding lead on the first three rounds, shooting a 69, 68 and 69 before finishing with a 70, six strokes ahead of Nicklaus and Dave Marr, who tied "The Golden Bear" for second.

The pair defined golf in the '60s, with Nicklaus winning seven of his record 18 major championships in the decade and Palmer winning six of his seven. Nicklaus began to get the upper hand as he went along, but the two still remained highly competitive, with Nicklaus beating Palmer by four strokes in the 1967 U.S. Open at Baltusrol and Palmer taking the Thunderbird Classic at Upper Montclair that same year by a stroke over his rival. Six years later, Palmer bested Nicklaus by two strokes at the Bob Hope Desert Classic in Tamarisk. It was Palmer's last PGA Tour victory.

But the pair also played as a team many times. They won the Canada Cup in 1963, the World Cup in Mexico in 1967, and the Laurel Valley Country Club in Ligonier saw the duo take the National Team Championship (also known as the National Four-Ball Championship) in 1970 and '71, though it was only counted as an official PGA event in the latter year.

Even as their skills eroded with age, Palmer and Nicklaus never seemed to lose their popularity or their prominence within their sport. For instance, Palmer still strikes the first ball at the Masters and was named one of the 25 Coolest Athletes of All-Time by *Gentleman's Quarterly*. The Pittsburgh Steelers have created a special halftime ceremony just to honor him, and two days before his 80th birthday on September 8, 2009, Palmer threw out the first pitch prior to the Pittsburgh Pirates game at PNC Park against the Cubs. His brother Jerry runs the Latrobe Country Club, and his grandson, Will Wears, is a promising prospect for Latrobe High School.

Between Palmer's infectious personality and Nicklaus' success, golf's popularity boomed. It can reasonably be said, however, that golf would not be as prominent in American culture without Palmer and Nicklaus.

College Football Rivalries

Pitt vs. Penn State

In 1981, Tim Panaccio, who later made a name for himself covering the Philadelphia Flyers, wrote a book entitled *Beast of the East* about the Pitt–Penn State football rivalry. The cover of the book advertises the pairing of these two Pennsylvania schools as "America's greatest football rivalry." Thirty years later, Pitt–Penn State is America's greatest football rivalry that isn't played.

From 1893 to 2000, the Pittsburgh Panthers and the Penn State Nittany Lions engaged in a truly spectacular football rivalry that showcased to the rest of the country just how special football in Pennsylvania was. It was a competition defined by legendary coaches—Pop Warner, Jock Sutherland, Rip Engle and Joe Paterno—and a rivalry in which Dan Marino and Todd Blackledge could call signals against each other for four years, then wind up both being taken in the first round of the NFL draft.

Running backs? Try Tony Dorsett, John Cappelletti, Marshall Goldberg and Franco Harris. Linebackers? How about Jack Ham, Hugh Green, Shane Conlan and Joe Schmidt?

The Pitt–Penn State rivalry represented all the sappy story-book tales of young men from steel or coal towns playing college football at its highest level, earning stardom while acquiring an education. It meant bragging rights when the players returned home, and bragging rights for fans in the Keystone State throughout the year. And for much of the

1970s and '80s, the Pitt–Penn State matchup was the single most important regular season game in defining college football's national championship.

To understand the historical aspect of the rivalry, one has to remember that Pitt has won nine national championships. The first came in 1915, when Pop Warner arrived in Pittsburgh and, in addition to installing single and double wing formations and popularizing numbers on jerseys while coaching the Panthers, he also coached a young protégé, guard Jock Sutherland.

While Warner helped bring football out of its initial stages by creating plays that could capitalize on a player's speed rather than just brute force, Sutherland perfected them after becoming Pitt's head coach in 1924. From recruiting the "Dream Backfield" of the late '30s to creating a team that shut out 55 percent of the Panthers' opponents during his 14-year tenure to helping fund the construction of Pitt Stadium, Sutherland turned Pitt into *the* premier college football program in America in the 1930s. Together, Warner and Sutherland were 17–1–2 against Penn State and won eight national championships.

Following the 1938 season, Sutherland was forced to resign as the result of a power struggle with Pitt Chancellor John Bowman. The days of Pitt being a national power would be over for many years.

Soon afterward, Penn State slowly but surely started to build a championship football program. The Nittany Lions were nationally ranked in the final AP poll three times during the 1940s, and their undefeated squad of 1947 went to the Cotton Bowl, forging a 13–13 tie against Doak Walker and SMU.

Then in 1950, Penn State lured head coach Rip Engle from Brown. Engle brought with him a young assistant coach, Joe Paterno, who would later succeed him and dominate the rivalry, and college football, in the way that Warner and Sutherland had before him.

It's hard to imagine now in the age of Beaver Stadium, which holds 107,282 spectators, that at one time, Penn State played in a 30,000-seat facility about where the Nittany Parking Deck is today. Therefore, the vast majority of Pitt–Penn State games were played at Pitt Stadium, with exceptions being made for wartime travel restrictions or Penn State's 1955 centennial. But by 1960, Penn State football had reached the level where the stadium needed to be expanded to more than 46,000 and moved to its current location. The game started to be held at State College almost bi-annually, and the Nittany Lions began to dominate. Paterno, who became the Lions' head coach in 1966, immediately ripped off 10 straight victories in the series and didn't suffer a defeat at Pitt Stadium until 1987.

Much of this success stemmed from the demise of the Pitt Panthers, who suffered four single-victory seasons during this stretch. But when Johnny Majors came to Pitt as head coach in 1973 and brought Tony Dorsett with him, change was in the air. In Dorsett's first year, Pitt went to the Fiesta Bowl. By his second season, the game had to be moved to Three Rivers Stadium to accommodate national network television audiences. In his third, Penn State barely won, 7–6, thanks to four missed Panthers placekicks. In 1976, Pitt was ranked number one in the country, and Dorsett broke four major college football rushing records, including career yards, in a 24–7 Pitt victory that precluded the Panthers' national championship.

By now, the game between the two teams had become perhaps the most exciting annual event in college football. Penn State stopped a late two-point conversion to beat Pitt, 15–13, in 1977, and the top-ranked Nittany Lions overcame a late 10–7 deficit on a fourth down touchdown run by Mike Guman to win the following year, as well. Marino led Pitt to back-to-back victories in 1979 and 1980, only to see Penn State quell the top-ranked Panthers' national championship hopes in 1981 by overcoming an early 14–0 deficit and beating Pitt, 48–14.

Pitt was the preseason number one team in the country in 1982. After the 9–1 Nittany Lions beat the 9–1 Panthers, 19–10, it would be Penn State that would go on to win the national championship. This victory was followed by the controversy of time being put back on the clock for Penn State to kick a tying field goal with one second remaining in the 1983 game at Pitt Stadium, a 24–24 deadlock, the year Jack Chevalier called Pitt–Penn State "the rivalry of the future" in his *Sporting News* article.

Pitt gained revenge by knocking Penn State out of a bowl with a 31–11 victory in 1984. Penn State responded by beating Pitt 31–0 in 1985 and 16–13 in 1989, knocking Panthers head coaches Foge Fazio and Mike Gottfried out of their jobs.

During this era, it was not uncommon for Penn State fans to wear T-shirts reading "Shitt on Pitt." Pitt fans responded by chanting "Penn State sucks!" during the refrain of "Fight On," a Panthers fight song. Pitt fans supposedly sent death threats to Paterno during the mid-'70s, and Paterno countered by saying, when asked why he never left Penn State to go to the NFL, that he didn't want to leave college football to the likes of Barry Switzer and then–Pitt head coach Jackie Sherrill.

But in 1989, Penn State announced they would no longer compete as a football independent and instead would join the Big Ten Conference. This marked a seismic shift in the landscape of college athletics, effectively ending the days of major independents in football. It also marked the beginning of Super Conferences in college football, which ultimately resulted in the Big East Conference offering football.

It also triggered the end of the Pitt–Penn State football series. There are conflicting reasons as to why. Pitt fans say it was because Paterno was jealous that his vision of a conference involving Eastern schools was squashed when Pitt decided to leave the old Eastern Eight for the Big East instead. Penn State fans have said that Paterno didn't like it when Pitt made Penn State fans buy season tickets for the Panthers to get into the game.

So while many view Joe Paterno as the first major college football coach to win 400 games, many other fans see him historically as the man who ended one of college football's great rivalries.

The rivalry did start up again from 1997 to 2000. Penn State took three of the four contests, but the Panthers slowly crept up on their rivals, finally taking a 12–0 decision at Three Rivers Stadium in 2000, with Rod Rutherford catching, not throwing, a long touchdown pass in the second half to insure victory. Since then, Pitt and Penn State fans have had to settle for infrequent meetings in other sports such as men's basketball (as of 2010, the two teams had not met since 2005, when Pitt won their fifth straight game against Penn State), baseball (these games are often played at a minor league baseball park) and wrestling.

Without the opportunity to play each other, it could easily be said that both programs have suffered. For instance, without Pitt, Penn State does not have a true rival. Furthermore, the move to the Big Ten has opened up Pennsylvania as a recruiting area to other schools in the conference. Whereas native Pennsylvanians such as Terrell Pryor or Ty Law would likely have looked insular growing up in the Keystone State without Big Ten awareness, they instead signed with Ohio State and Michigan, respectively. Since joining the Big Ten, Penn State has often struggled to beat the Buckeyes and the Wolverines. Instead of "the Beast of the East," Penn State seems to be, more times than not, an also-ran in its conference. Pitt, meanwhile, appears to be undergoing something of a transition from a football to a basketball school because of their affiliation with the Big East. From 2000 to 2010, Pitt actually went to one more bowl game than Penn State, but by being in the Big East and razing venerable Pitt Stadium for the Pederson Events Center, they often fall behind Penn State in terms of public perception.

Still, even if the two teams don't play one another anymore, there is as much vitriol as ever between their fans. Pitt fans gleefully cheer any opponent of Penn State, and it has often been said that Panthers fans actually hate Penn State more than they like their own team. Penn State fans generally look down at Pitt for generally drawing half the number of fans at Heinz Field that the Nittany Lions do at Beaver Stadium. Penn State fans also often say that they don't care about the rivalry anymore, then break out into 30-minute conversations slamming the Panthers. And as a side note, the Pitt softball team beat Penn State, 2–1, in their first game on their new field at the Peterson Sports Complex on March 29, 2011, with Cory Berliner setting a Panthers' record with her 45th lifetime victory and Reba Tutt completing a rally started by Ellwood City's Ciera Damon with a game-ending, and winning, double. Pitt and Penn State are still playing against one another in other sports, so there is hope that when Paterno retires, the football series will come back from hiatus the way the Auburn–Alabama and Kentucky–Louisville rivalries did.

Lehigh vs. Lafayette

There is a school of thought that the rivalry between Lehigh University and Lafayette College is the greatest in all of college football. The games aren't aired nationally on television or attended by 80,000 people. It could even be said the two schools suffer from an identity crisis. Lafayette explored the possibility of dropping football around the turn of the century, while in the mid-1990s, Lehigh changed its century-old nickname of "Engineers" to the somewhat less unique "Mountain Hawks." But in all of college football, no two teams have played each other more often (146 times as of 2010) or have a greater hatred of each other.

Former Lehigh quarterback Kim McQuilken remembers the circumstances surrounding his freshman season of 1970. "If you were a freshman football player, you weren't eligible to play, so your job was to get into a fight on the field after the game," McQuilken told Michael Bradley in the book *Big Games*. Fights have been commonplace in this rivalry, which features two universities only 17 miles apart in the southeastern Pennsylvania communities of Easton and Bethlehem.

In other rivalries, when the home team wins, the fans pour out onto the field and tear down the goalposts. In the Lafayette–Lehigh rivalry, historically fans storm the field to tear down the goalposts when the *visiting* team wins, not only humiliating the vanquished loser, but sending a hefty bill to them for new goalposts as well. Goalposts, you say? They didn't last through the third quarter in the 1975 game, when fighting in the stands moved down to the field at halftime after Lafayette fans used a massive slingshot to pelt Lehigh rooters with debris.

In 1991, fans literally attacked security people trying to save the goalposts at Lehigh's Goodman Stadium. Remember John Belushi's food-fight scene in *Animal House*? In 1959, Lehigh students brought pears to the game and started one, hitting everyone from fans to players to security to officials. By the end of the game, nearly 700 people were involved in the violence. Even the bands have not been free from assault. There is at least one instance of Lehigh students attacking the Lafayette band and breaking their instruments.

What causes these two schools to historically enter into fits of rage? After all, these are not community colleges, but rather prestigious academic institutions. Perhaps it is the hard edge of the communities of Easton and Bethlehem. Both are known for the hardscrabble industries of coal and steel and derive much of their identities from the success of their teams. And being in such close proximity to each other, familiarity breeds contempt.

History also has produced animosity. There's the story of how Asa Packer, Lehigh's founder, was once approached by Lafayette to help start an engineering wing at the university. Packer refused on the grounds that the wing would be run by the Presbyterian Church, and instead founded Lehigh with the help of the Episcopalians.

Such animosities moved onto the gridiron when Lehigh played their very first game against Lafayette in 1884. Though they were routed in two contests against their Easton rivals that year, by 1885, Lehigh was competitive—perhaps too competitive. Late in the next game, Lehigh's center was ejected for rough play, and the Lehigh team walked off the field in protest, forfeiting the game, 6–0. In their second meeting that year, the two teams tied, 6–6.

The following season, a Lafayette team manager, H.L. Forceman, was called upon to officiate a game. Allegations of favorable calls to Lafayette were made, especially when one of their players picked up the ball and ran to the Lehigh three-yard line while Forceman was trying to figure out which down it was. When Lehigh walked off the field in protest, a Lafayette player merely picked the ball up again and crossed the goal line for the only score of the day.

The rivalry was on.

The two teams have met every year since 1897 and even met multiple times in the same season throughout the 19th century and for two years during World War II.

Both Lafayette and Lehigh have made significant football history. Lafayette halfback George Barclay was the first football player ever to wear a helmet in 1896, crudely strapping together pieces of leather to protect injury to, among other body parts, his ears. But Barclay did not play Lehigh that year, as the "Brown and White" protested his participation because Barclay had previously played semipro baseball in Chambersburg.

It was a pity because Lafayette claimed a national championship that season, as they did in 1921 and 1926. The latter two seasons, the Leopards were led by Hall of Fame coaches Jock Sutherland, better known for his prowess at Pitt, and then Herb McCracken, later of Allegheny College in Meadville.

Lehigh, meanwhile, won a Division II national championship in 1977 and played for the first-ever Division I-AA national championship in 1979.

Even today, without scholarships funding the football teams, there is often much on the line in the annual game between the two schools. From 1992 to 2010, either Lehigh or Lafayette won the Patriot League 10 times. The season-end contests of 2004 and 2005 decided the conference championship.

All this might help explain why Lehigh fans took to writing "Beat Lafayette" on Lafayette's field in 1936, only to be stopped in mid-phrase, or why Lafayette countered with "Lehigh Sucks" on the Engineers' field in 1973. Or how Lafayette students have been known to shave the heads of their counterparts from Lehigh. Or how the 1992 game kicked off at 10:45 AM to curb pre-game drinking.

"I do get nostalgic for the way it was," McQuilken said.

Geneva vs. Westminster

It is only natural that two Presbyterian colleges located 30 miles from one another in western Pennsylvania would become fierce rivals. But though these two Division III schools are small, their respective histories are significant.

The two teams first met in 1891 and have played each other almost annually since then. Geneva held the upper hand early, as they played at something of a major college level with games against current FBS opponents such as Pitt, Penn State, West Virginia, Boston College and Marshall, as well as then-powers like Washington & Jefferson and Ivy League schools.

In the 1920s, for instance, Geneva was led by head coach Bo McMillan and tackle Cal Hubbard. Hubbard is the only man in both the Pro Football and Baseball Halls of Fame. He led the Covies (later the Golden Tornadoes) to a New Years' Day Bowl game in Jacksonville following the 1926 season. McMillan, meanwhile, was 22–5–1 during his three-year stay in Beaver Falls, including posting an undefeated 8–0–1 record in 1927. Both men are in the College Football Hall of Fame.

Westminster would see its fair share of College Football Hall of Famers as well, beginning in the 1950s with head coach Harold Burry and quarterback Harold Davis, a three-time All-American. Later, Larry Pugh, a two-way lineman in the 1960s, would be enshrined in South Bend, as would coach Joe Fusco. In all, Westminster won six NAIA national championships before moving to NCAA Division III in 1998.

The rivalry was distinctly one-sided from 1957 to 1987, when Westminster took all 30 games played between the two schools. That changed in a most dramatic way in 1987, when Geneva posted a 16–15 victory at home with a late touchdown under harsh weather conditions in an NAIA playoff game. From then on, Geneva became more competitive, winning in

New Wilmington for the first time in 38 years in 1995, and then taking seven of the 10 games played between the two teams during the first decade of the 21st century.

Pro Football Rivalries

Steelers vs. Eagles

OK, we admit it. The Steelers and Eagles only meet once every four years in the regular season. *Sporting News Radio* talk show host David Stein once spent considerable time on his radio show dispelling any sense of a rivalry between the two franchises prior to their game in 2004. But that doesn't mean Steelers and Eagles fans in central Pennsylvania don't anticipate the game played every four years, or, for that matter, their annual preseason tilt. Furthermore, the Eagles and the Steelers once were the same franchise. And the official charter of the Pittsburgh Steelers that states they are in the NFL actually reads "Philadelphia Eagles," while the Birds' charter reads "Pittsburgh Pirates."

The story begins in 1940, when the NFL was in its infancy. After having lost $100,000 on the Pittsburgh Pirates, as the Steelers were known then, Art Rooney Sr. sold the team to a wealthy investor named Alexis Thompson, who wanted to move the team to Boston. Rooney used his share to buy into the struggling Eagles franchise, which would then play half its games in Pittsburgh.

But the move to Boston was not approved by the NFL, so instead, Thompson took the team to Philadelphia, and Rooney and Bell operated the old Philadelphia Eagles franchise in Pittsburgh.

Three years later, as mentioned earlier in the book, the Steelers and Eagles merged because of wartime player shortages and became, for a season, the "Steagles," finishing with a 5–4–1 record. Among the players on this team was quarterback Allie Sherman, who would coach the New York Giants to the NFL championship game 20 years later. Additionally, it was the first time the Eagles posted a winning record and would begin a streak of seven straight winning seasons—as of 2010, the longest in franchise history.

Then, in 1947, the Steelers and the Eagles again were linked when the franchises played their first playoff game against each other. After finishing in a tie with 8–4 records, the two teams met to decide who would play the Chicago Cardinals in the NFL Title Game. But the Steelers players staged a near-revolt prior to the game, with players going home and missing practice time because there was some question as to whether or not they would be paid. "All we got was a game salary," remembered running back Bob Cifers. The Steelers lost the playoff at Forbes Field, 21–0, and it was the last game Jock Sutherland coached the team.

The two teams met twice a year from 1934 to 1966, with the aforementioned exception of '47, when the two teams met thrice. In 1936, the teams played in Johnstown, which resulted in a 6–0 "Pirates" victory, and two years later, they met not in their Pennsylvania homes, but rather in Charleston, West Virginia, and Buffalo, with the Eagles taking both games. During the Eagles' NFL championship years of 1948 and 1949, they won all four games; in 1960, the two teams split, though it should be mentioned that the Eagles had already clinched their playoff berth and had home-field advantage by the time Pittsburgh took their 27–21 victory. In 1963, the two teams tied both their games. Despite Lou Michaels' then-Steelers record 50-yard field goal in the game, two conversion attempts failed, resulting in a 21–21 tie at Franklin Field. Then, on December 1, Michaels closed out the Steelers' Forbes Field era by kicking a late 24-yard field goal to forge a 20–20 tie and keep pro football's Gas House Gang's playoff hopes alive.

In 1967, when the NFL–AFL merger was announced, the Steelers moved into the NFL's Century Division and the Eagles went to the Capital Division, meaning that the two teams would only play once a year. When the Steelers went into the American Football Conference in 1970, regular season meetings became sporadic.

Still, there have been highlights. In 1970, the Eagles finished their Franklin Field era with a 30–20 victory against Pittsburgh (and punter Terry Bradshaw) despite a then-Steelers record 218 yards rushing from Frenchy Fuqua. The Steelers shut out the Eagles 27–0 en route to winning their first Super Bowl in 1974, and one of Philadelphia's biggest victories in the Dick Vermeil era was knocking off the Steelers, 17–14, at Veteran's Stadium in 1979. Merrill Hoge had his breakout game in a 27–26 loss to the Eagles in 1988; Donovan McNabb led the Eagles back from a 20–10 fourth quarter deficit at Pittsburgh in 2000 to hand the Steelers the only overtime defeat they ever suffered in Three Rivers Stadium, 23–20; and the Steelers dominated the Eagles, 27–3, during Philadelphia's Super Bowl season of 2004.

Finally, the Steelers and the Eagles both enjoyed a prosperous first decade of the 21st century. From 2000 to 2010, both teams endured only a single losing season each.

Steelers and Eagles Divisional Rivalries

The Steelers are generally regarded as the top rival of every team in the AFC North Division. Traditionally, the Steelers are the team to beat in the division and, as of 2010, they had all-time winning records against all of their divisional foes. Incredibly, since the AFL–NFL merger, the Steelers have never lost a playoff game to a division rival as of 2010 (the team is 3–0 lifetime against Baltimore, 2–0 against Cleveland, 1–0 against Cincinnati and 3–0 against the old Houston Oilers, when Pittsburgh was a member of the AFC Central). Rivalries against all of these teams have been bitter. For instance, Ravens defensive end Tony Siragusa, who played collegiately at Pitt, once suggested to reporters that Baltimore fans should "take care of business" against Steelers fans in the PSINet Stadium restrooms prior to a 2001 game against Pittsburgh. Two years later, Joey Porter and Ray Lewis once nearly came to blows outside Baltimore's team bus following Pittsburgh's season-opening victory against the Ravens.

Perhaps the cause of the Ravens' anger is that, as of 2011, not only have they never beaten the Steelers in the playoffs, but also, no Baltimore team has ever beaten a Pittsburgh team in the postseason. This includes the Steelers' two playoff victories against the Colts in 1975 and 1976, and the Pirates' two World Series triumphs against the Orioles in 1971 and 1979.

The Steelers–Browns conflict goes back much further. It is one of the NFL's great old traditional rivalries, dating back to 1950. Home teams traditionally have dominated, with the Steelers winning the first 16 games played between the two teams at Three Rivers Stadium and nine of the first 10 played at Heinz Field, whereas the Browns enjoyed winning streaks of six (1950–55) and nine (1965–73) in Municipal Stadium while taking 11 out of 12 contests played in Cleveland from 1982 to 1993.

Sure, there have been exceptions. The Browns trounced the Steelers, 51–0, in Pittsburgh to open the 1989 season, while the Steelers welcomed the Browns back into the NFL with a 43–0 whitewash in Cleveland in 1999. The last hurrah of the Steelers' Buddy Parker era was a 23–7 victory at Cleveland in the Browns' NFL championship year of 1964, a game in which John Henry Johnson scored three touchdowns and outrushed Jim Brown 200 yards to 59, the first time in Steelers' history that a back collected 200 yards rushing.

The rivalry was probably at its fiercest in the 1970s. In 1972, the Browns were considered the most prestigious franchise in the AFC Central Division, while the Steelers were trying to win their first-ever division championship in their 40th season. In week 10, the Browns beat the Steelers, 26–24, in Cleveland to tie Pittsburgh for first place in the division on a late Don Cockroft field goal. Two weeks later, with the division title on the line, the Steelers beat the Browns, 30–0, a game that forever changed the direction of the two franchises.

Because of the two teams' reversal of fortunes, the series became truly bitter. In the 1970s, the Steelers rolled up Super Bowls, and the Browns, who suffered through only one losing season in their first 28 seasons, posted three losing records in the 1970s alone. Wrote Jack Chevalier, when he ranked the Steelers–Browns the eighth-best rivalry in sports: "Pretend you live in Cleveland...you put up with...a long-struggling baseball team and a pro basketball loser...The entire sports year pretty much boils down to the Browns' attempt to beat out the Steelers for the AFC Central title."

Indeed, in 1994, Cleveland radio station WKNR promoted the Browns–Steelers week 15 affair for the AFC Central Division title as "the game you've waited for."

After that, Cleveland was especially hostile to Pittsburgh. So jealous are Browns fans of the Steelers' success that WWWE talk show host Pete Franklin referred to the franchise as the "Pittspuke Scumbags," and a popular T-shirt in Cleveland reads, simply, "S_itsburgh."

As might be expected as the rivalry has become more one-sided, Pittsburgh fans generally have not been as vitriolic, but a generation ago, Jack Lambert's fan club, "Lambert's Lunatics," are said to have left a car with an Ohio license plate in a Three Rivers Stadium lot in worse shape than when it came in, and Pittsburghers often will sneer at visitors from the Forest City. But when the Browns announced they were leaving Cleveland in 1995, Steelers fans wore orange armbands to the Browns–Steelers *Monday Night Football* game at Three Rivers Stadium in a show of support for their Ohio neighbors.

> <

Did someone say bitter? That's how Eagles fans react to the Dallas Cowboys.

Consider the history between the two teams. When the NFC East was formed in 1970, there were four franchises from the old, traditional NFL that played in baseball parks and for championships in bad weather. Then came the Cowboys, a team that was not only playing for division supremacy every season, but were a relatively young franchise that not only seemingly hadn't paid its dues, but also came from an entirely different geographical area and played in football-only stadiums. The Cowboys represented a kind of Texas swagger and lifestyle that clashed with Philadelphia fans, who generally were brought up to be humble.

The Eagles were Governor Ed Rendell, Democrat; the Cowboys were coach Tom Landry, who campaigned for Jesse Helms.

Besides, when the NFC was set up in 1970 with essentially a merging of the old Century and Capital divisions, it was designed with the idea that the Eagles would be the top rival of the Redskins. But if it was unusual for an upstart such as the Cowboys to come in and rule the old guard of the NFL, what was it like to see the Redskins, without a playoff berth since 1945, suddenly become the Cowboys top rival for division supremacy?

Not that there was a love affair between the Eagles and the rest of the division. Sadly, Philadelphia is the only team in the NFC East that, as of 2010, has not won the Super Bowl, and as of 2010, the Eagles had an all-time losing record against all of their divisional foes. But that hardly means the team hasn't been competitive against its NFC East opponents.

For instance, even though the New York Giants beat the Eagles the first two times they met in the postseason, Philadelphia countered by winning the next two postseason games against New York, a dramatic 23–20 victory in 2006 on a last-second David Akers 38-yard field goal and then a 23–11 triumph in 2009. The modern era of this rivalry seems to favor the Eagles, most notably a 12-game winning streak against the Giants from 1975 to 1981 highlighted by "The Miracle in the Meadowlands" on November 19, 1978, in which Herman Edwards' 26-yard touchdown run following a fumble recovery on a botched Giants handoff gave Philadelphia a 19–17 victory and propelled them to their first playoff berth in 18 years. The Eagles–Giants rivalry is also a large backdrop in the 2009 movie *Big Fan*, starring Patton Oswald.

The Eagles and Redskins, meanwhile, have only met in the playoffs once, a 20–6 Washington victory in 1990. This game was memorable for Eagles head coach Buddy Ryan's decision to replace quarterback Randall Cunningham in the third quarter with Jim McMahon. McMahon only managed to throw three incomplete passes, and Ryan was fired following the game.

The next season, behind Reggie White, Jerome Brown and defensive coordinator Bud Carson, the Eagles boasted the top defense in the National Football League but were besieged by injuries to their quarterbacks. They could only manage a 10–6 record and missed out on the playoffs on tiebreakers. There was a feeling of satisfaction, however, when Philadelphia beat eventual Super Bowl champ Washington, 26–24, behind quarterback Jeff Kemp in the season's final week.

Still, it's the rivalry with the Cowboys that generates the most fury and the greatest satisfaction for Eagles fans. The most notable game in all of the rivalry was the Eagles' 20–7 victory against Dallas in the 1980 NFC championship game. Buoyed by Wilbert Montgomery's 42-yard touchdown run in the first quarter, the game put Philadelphia into the Super Bowl for the first time.

That was only the beginning. From 1987 to 1991, the Eagles took eight straight games from the Cowboys. The animosity began during the 1987 players strike, when teams used strike breakers and replacement players to fill out their roster for three games. Reflecting the political culture of the two cities, Philadelphia fielded a weak replacement team, whereas Dallas had a strong one, resulting in a 41–22 Cowboys victory. Two weeks later, when the strike was settled, the Eagles ran the score up on the Cowboys in a 37–20 triumph, payback to veterans such as Tony Dorsett, Danny White, Too Tall Jones and Randy White who crossed the picket line.

The next year, the Eagles rallied from a 20–0 deficit to beat Dallas on two late Anthony Toney touchdowns, 24–23, and also beat Dallas in Tom Landry's last game as Cowboys coach. The following year, new coach Jimmy Johnson alleged that Philadelphia had placed a bounty on Dallas kicker Luis Zendejas in their Thanksgiving Day game, and when the two teams met in December at Veterans Stadium, the Cowboys were pelted with snowballs and other debris, with even future Governor Ed Rendell taking part in the melee. Dallas fans would counter in 1990 by throwing pork chops at Ryan only a few days after he'd choked on one during dinner, and eventually, Philadelphia's winning streak against the Cowboys ended in the next-to-last week of the 1991 season, when Dallas beat Philadelphia 23–15, thus putting the Cowboys in the playoffs and leaving the Eagles out.

Another notable game occurred in 1995, when the Eagles overcame a 17–6 deficit to win 20–17. Tied 17–17, Philadelphia stopped the gambling Cowboys on fourth and one with an

Emmit Smith carry on the Dallas 29-yard line with two minutes to play. The Eagles took over in field goal range, and Gary Anderson booted a 42-yard game winner, handing Dallas their last loss in a Super Bowl championship season.

In 2008, the Eagles played the Cowboys for a spot in the playoffs in the last week of the season and trounced Dallas, 44–6, at Lincoln Financial Field. The following season, Dallas returned the favor with a 24–0 triumph on the last day of the season in a game to decide the NFC East, then won their first playoff game in 13 years with a 34–14 victory against the Eagles.

Steelers vs. Cowboys

The Steelers and the Cowboys aren't divisional rivals, of course. In fact, they meet only as often as the Steelers and the Eagles do—once every four years.

But upon closer inspection, this rivalry is the football equivalent of the Yankees and the Dodgers or the Celtics and the Lakers. Not only have the Cowboys and the Steelers met in the Super Bowl a record three times as of 2011, but they also are the two most popular teams in the NFL.

It almost seems as if the two teams were destined for a rivalry. The Cowboys played the first game in their history against the Steelers in 1960, with Bobby Layne passing Sammy Baugh as the NFL's all-time leader in passing yards while throwing for four touchdowns in a 35–28 Pittsburgh triumph. The next season, the Cowboys won their first game in franchise history against the Steelers, 27–24, after Eddie LeBaron relieved Don Meredith and led Dallas to a victory in the last minute on a 27-yard field goal by Allen Green.

These teams represent the two most historically passionate football areas in the country. Furthermore, as mentioned in the section about the Eagles–Cowboys rivalry, there is a difference in the cultures of the two areas. Pennsylvania—Pittsburgh in this instance—is an area where humility is appreciated, sometimes to the detriment of even being able to praise the culture that the location has to offer. Texas—Dallas in this instance—constantly brags about how big and gaudy it is. This is often to the detriment of the public perception of the state—the rest of the country really doesn't care how big the horns of their cattle are and can't understand why Texans put the horns on the front of their cars.

Perhaps the image of the two teams can best be summed up this way: Who would you buy a used car from, Art Rooney Sr. or Jerry Jones?

The Cowboys are about marketing: the cheerleaders, the stadium and the old fight song they commissioned Charlie Pride to sing. The Steelers are about football: no cheerleaders, no decorated end zone and their old fight song is local DJ Jimmy Pol singing over a recording of the "Pennsylvania Polka." The Cowboys are Hollywood Henderson questioning Terry Bradshaw's intelligence before Super Bowl XIII; the Steelers are Bradshaw throwing four touchdown passes en route to victory and winning the game's Most Valuable Player award. The Cowboys are Cliff Harris trying to taunt Roy Gerela; the Steelers are Jack Lambert rising to the support of his teammate and slamming Harris to the ground. Ergo, the Steelers are about basics, and their support comes honestly and naturally. The Cowboys are about fads, and their support comes from advertising. And, oh yeah, a lot of the Steelers' support might stem from the fact that they've won the most and appeared in the most Super Bowls of any team as of 2011, including taking two out of three from the so-called "America's Team."

Go beyond the glory of the Super Bowls and you'll find some fascinating stories between the two teams:

- Tony Dorsett and Randy White were both from Pittsburgh, and Terry Bradshaw lived in Dallas after his playing career ended.

- Ernie Stautner, the only Steeler ever to have his number retired, was Tom Landry's defensive coordinator against the Steelers in the Super Bowl.

- In 1963, the Steelers beat the Cowboys to stay alive in the playoff chase on a fake punt by Ed Brown.

- Craig Morton sent the Steelers to a heartbreaking defeat with a last-second touchdown pass in 1967.

- The old Steelers vets from the '70s continued their dominance against a rebuilt Dallas team by stopping the Cowboys' streak of 17 straight opening-day victories with a 36–28 victory in 1982 on *Monday Night Football*.

- The Cowboys proved that Super Bowl XXX was no fluke with a 37–7 opening day victory in 1997.

- Jerome Bettis' touchdown in the final minute to beat Dallas 24–20 in 2004 became the springboard to a 15–1 record.

- Deshea Townsend's interception and touchdown return with two minutes left to beat the Cowboys 20–13 in 2008 was the springboard to a Super Bowl.

And remember, for all the bragging that Dallas does, they can never say that the Cowboys are from the City of Champions.

Quotes About the Rivalries

"Our victories were more than a pennant race for us, though. We were out to prove something to ourselves. We'd been held down by our cross-state rivals three years in a row. We wanted out from beneath their thumb. We wanted to win the pennant."

—Willie Stargell, on the Pirates beating the Phillies during the 1979 pennant race

"He wasn't just beating Ali. He was beating Ali up."

—Ali biographer Thomas Hauser, speaking of Frazier's dominance in the middle rounds of their third fight

"I said a lot of things in the heat of the moment I shouldn't have said. Called him names I shouldn't have called him. I apologize for that. I am sorry. It was meant to promote the fight."

—Ali, on Frazier, to the New York Times *in 2001*

"I thought it was the Klan."

—Julius Erving, upon seeing five Boston fans dressed up as ghosts to heckle the 76ers with "The Ghosts of Celtics Past" before game seven of the 1982 NBA Eastern Conference finals, which Philadelphia won, 120–106

"Aw, who the hell are the Cowboys? We beat them every time we play them!"

—Buddy Ryan, to a reporter following Philadelphia's 23–7 victory against Dallas in the 1988 season finale, Tom Landry's last game as Cowboys coach

"The kind of image [Arnold Palmer] projects [is] one of inclusion, not exclusion."

–Multiple PGA Tour winner Peter Jacobsen

"Neither. It's losing to Penn State."

–Pitt linebacker Sal Sunseri, when asked if his team's 48–14 defeat to the Nittany Lions was more painful because it came on head coach Jackie Sherrill's birthday or because it cost the Panthers their number-one poll ranking

Chapter Ten

Three Franchises That Aren't Here Anymore

Losing Teams

Pennsylvania has historically supported its teams so well that few have ever left the state for greener pastures. Pittsburgh, for instance, has never lost a major professional sports franchise that is still in existence. Philadelphia, meanwhile, has lost two—the basketball Warriors and the baseball Athletics. Ironically, both now reside in Oakland, California. This chapter is a look at the loss of the A's and the Warriors, and also tells the previously untold story surrounding the move of the pioneers of arena football, the Pittsburgh Gladiators.

The A's Move to Kansas City: An Inglorious End to a Proud Team

When the Philadelphia Athletics moved to Kansas City following the 1954 season, it could easily be argued that they had the second most successful history in the American League with nine pennants, five world championships and legendary figures such as Connie Mack, Jimmie Foxx, Eddie Collins and Lefty Grove.

The Phillies, meanwhile, had largely been known for losing. Their 1950 pennant was just their second in 67 years of play, the fewest any of the eight teams in the National League at that time had won. Why, then, did the A's move?

By 1954, the A's had fallen on hard times. After three straight winning seasons from 1947 to 1949, the club marketed "One More Pennant for Connie" in 1950, but instead, the A's finished dead last while the Phillies won their first pennant in 35 years. Following the season, Mack, aged 87, gave up the managerial reins that he'd held for 50 years, and ownership battles inside the Mack family resulted in Connie's sons Roy and Earle buying up controlling interest in the club. But to do so, they had to mortgage Shibe Park, putting the franchise deep in debt.

Behind batting champ Ferris Fain, sluggers Gus Zernial and Eddie Joost, and 20-game winner Bobby Shantz, the Athletics posted winning seasons in '51 and '52 to stay afloat, though they could not outdraw the Phillies, who had consistently outdrawn the White Elephants since 1948. But their luck did not last in 1953. Fain was traded, Shantz got hurt and Joost turned 37. The A's finished next-to-last, drew just 362,113 fans and lost more than $100,000.

The team was now $2 million in debt, and so broke that they were unable to pay for the uniforms the team would wear in 1954. Furthermore, a "Save the A's" ticket sales campaign promoted by the City of Philadelphia in 1954 failed miserably. The Athletics drew fewer than 1800 fans for four straight home games just three weeks after the campaign was announced. The team finished the season in last place, 60½ games out of first, and drew just 304,666 fans for the year. Just 1715 spectators attended their final home game, a Sunday afternoon tilt against the New York Yankees.

Numerous potential suitors came forth to make offers for the club, including future high-profile sports team owners Bill Veeck, Jack Kent Cooke, Clint Murchison and Charley O. Finley. Finley was the only one of the four who wanted to keep the team in Philadelphia, though there were other suitors prepared to do so.

The one that drew the most attention was Arnold Johnson, a shrewd businessman and former vice president of the Chicago Blackhawks. Johnson owned both Yankee Stadium and the stadium of their top minor league farm club, Blues Stadium in Kansas City. He convinced Kansas City that if they renovated Blues Stadium to the size needed to hold a big league club, he would buy the A's, move the team to Kansas City, and then sell the park back to the city.

Johnson's bid had a conflict of interest as he owned Yankee Stadium, but upon a final agreement for the sale of the club, he agreed to sell the stadium. He began to negotiating for the A's with the Macks early, and his bid seemed to be the strongest. American League president Will Harridge favored moving the A's, and the New York Yankees lobbied for the team's relocation as well, while bankruptcy loomed over the Mack family. At the end of the 1954 season, the AL approved the sale of the A's to Johnson as well as the team's relocation to Kansas City.

But the situation wasn't over yet. Jack Rensel, a former Phillies executive, headed up a syndicate of Philadelphia businessmen who wanted to keep the A's in town. He begged Roy Mack for one last chance, and Earle Mack reconsidered. The Macks decided to sell to the Rensel syndicate instead and called a press conference to do so, but Johnson telegrammed Roy after the deal was signed and gained a sympathetic ear by promising the Macks $250,000 more. Ten days later, at the American League meeting to gain approval for the sale, Connie Sr., 91, traveled to New York to try to win over his fellow owners on behalf of the Rensel syndicate, but was so ill he had to leave the meeting after an hour. Five hours later, there was strong evidence to suggest that Roy sabotaged his father's wishes and cast the deciding vote against selling the club to the Philadelphia group in order to keep Johnson's bid alive.

The Philadelphia syndicate quickly reorganized, but so did Johnson. Meanwhile, the trip to New York took its toll on the senior Mack, who became bedridden and did not eat regularly for days upon returning home. The new Philadelphia syndicate came to Connie's apartment on November 3 with an offer, but were turned away and told he was too ill to see them. Meanwhile, Roy and Johnson were pleading with Earle to sell, which he would only do if his father agreed.

There are two different stories about what occurred next. One is that the Philadelphia syndicate, at Earle's urging, arrived at Connie's apartment the next day with checks in hand, but his wife turned them away, demanding one check for the full amount. The Macks then met with Johnson, who finalized the deal. The other story is that Johnson arrived at Connie's apartment early the next morning, bribed Mack's chauffeur to gain entrance, and then completed the sale of the team before the Philadelphia group arrived, too late to stop it. What likely happened is that Connie's wife, Katherine, made the decision for her husband, though ultimately he had to sign off on the sale. Katherine made all the statements to the press after the meeting in New York, and her husband was simply too weak to attend any more owners' meetings to override Roy's vote. There was no guarantee that the new Philadelphia syndicate would have been approved by the American League as Johnson previously was, and creditors were scheduled to call on the team that very afternoon. Regardless, a crestfallen Earle left his father's apartment in tears.

Interestingly, neither Roy nor his son, Connie III, were ever given an executive position of real merit in Kansas City. Had he sold the team to the Philadelphia investors, he would have been a part owner of the club. The Kansas City A's never posted a winning season and were largely viewed as a glorified farm team for the Yankees. Thanks to Johnson's incestuous relationship with the Yanks, New York acquired stars such as Roger Maris, Ralph Terry and Ryne Duren from the A's in lopsided trades. After Johnson died, Finley bought the team, and after 13 losing seasons in Missouri, he moved the A's again.

Had the A's stayed in Philadelphia, without Johnson's relationship with the Yankees, it's likely that instead of watching the Phillies lose 23 games in a row in 1961, Philadelphia fans would have been able to see Maris chase Babe Ruth for the single-season home run record while their city's reputation as a sports town grew. After all, Philadelphia could have had two baseball teams instead of one, and the Eastern Seaboard would likely have become stronger American League territory, with the Orioles enhancing old rivalries with the A's, Yankees and Red Sox. Furthermore, it's likely that the Yankees, who won nine pennants in 10 years immediately after the A's left, would not have been as dominant in that era.

The Athletics had one last swan song in Philadelphia. It was customary for the A's and the Phillies to play exhibition games against each other before and/or after the regular season from 1903 through 1954 in what was called "The City Series." Prior to the 1955 season, the A's, now christened "Kansas City," played in the recently renamed Connie Mack Stadium one last time.

The Warriors Move to San Francisco

Following the 1961–62 season, the Philadelphia Warriors moved to San Francisco and the Cow Palace. In hindsight, however, an objective observer can ask if it was the best thing for the franchise.

The Los Angeles Lakers had moved from Minneapolis in 1960. By 1962, they had played for the NBA championship and nearly doubled their attendance from their final season in Minnesota. At this point, a group of Bay Area investors led by Franklin Mieuli offered Warriors' owner Eddie Gottlieb $850,000 for the team. The idea was that the Warriors could be, in effect, the Giants to the Lakers' Dodgers. Facilities would be improved, with the Warriors playing at the 14,000-seat Cow Palace instead of the 9600-seat Philadelphia Civic Center.

Gottlieb, the Warriors' former coach and general manager, had paid just $25,000 for the franchise 11 years earlier, and the San Francisco group was going to give him a $35,000-per-year job in the front office. With the Lakers needing a rival and a travel partner (their nearest opponent for their first two seasons in Los Angeles was St. Louis), the San Francisco offer was simply too good for Gottlieb and the NBA to refuse.

However, head coach Frank McGuire did not wish to come out west, as he had a son with cerebral palsy being treated by doctors in the East. Also, native Philadelphian Paul Arizin decided to retire after nine pro seasons rather than head to California. And Wilt Chamberlain was cool on the idea of playing for a coach other than McGuire. Chamberlain was eventually lured to the West Coast along with the rest of the team, but the Warriors had to pay him $85,000 a year to go, a contract that would eventually break the team.

Chamberlain was supposed to be the Warriors' drawing card, but he was also the archrival of Bill Russell, an Oakland native who had led the University of San Francisco to back-to-back NCAA tournament championships in 1955 and 1956. When the Boston Celtics came to the Cow Palace, San Francisco fans would often pull for Russell over the Warriors' meal ticket.

With the Giants in the 1962 World Series, any buzz surrounding the Warriors starting their first season in the Bay Area was gone. Their first game in San Francisco drew only 5000 fans, as it coincided with a middleweight championship fight at Candlestick Park. Furthermore, NBA teams of the time often had a strong local presence on their roster, and the Bay Area professionals that surrounded Chamberlain simply weren't on a par to the ones he'd played with in Philly.

The Warriors, who had played for the Eastern Conference title in their last year in Philadelphia, slumped to next-to-last place during their first year in San Francisco. They lost $1 million at the gate and finished dead last in attendance, drawing 50,000 fewer fans than they had during their last year in the east. During the first 50 years of the Warriors' stay in the Bay Area, they have only finished in the upper half of NBA attendance three times.

Whatever Happened to the Pittsburgh Gladiators?

As mentioned before, Pittsburgh is one of only five cities with three major sports franchises to not lose a major sports team that still is in operation. For the record, the others are Detroit, Miami, Phoenix and Tampa, though the Bay Area of Oakland–San Francisco may get a reprieve, since the Raiders actually moved back to Oakland from Los Angeles, and the California Golden Seals merged with the Minnesota North Stars after moving to Cleveland.

But there are two teams still in operation that used to be located in Pittsburgh. One is the American Hockey League's Rochester Red Wings, formerly the Pittsburgh Hornets. Their move was necessitated when Duquesne Gardens was torn down in 1956, and a new Hornets franchise was established in Pittsburgh when the Civic Arena opened in 1961. The second team is the Arena Football League's Tampa Bay Storm, which began as the Pittsburgh Gladiators, the winners of the very first game in AFL history.

The Gladiators operated in Pittsburgh for four seasons, making the playoffs every season and playing for the AFL championship twice. They led the AFL in attendance in 1987, averaging nearly 13,000 fans, and nearly drew the second-highest number of fans of the six teams the next year, averaging 8000 fans per game to the Chicago Bruisers' 8004.

But the early days of arena football were almost catastrophic. The inaugural league champion, the Denver Dynamite, did not return for a second season. The third season was just a four-game affair with teams playing mostly neutral site games. The Gladiators wound up playing more "home" games in Sacramento (two) than in Pittsburgh (one) in 1989, and nobody knew if the team was still in existence anymore. This writer, in fact, would walk around Pittsburgh wearing a Pittsburgh Gladiators pin, which often was met with the remark, "Oh, the *old* Gladiators," from fans who thought both the franchise and the league had folded. But they hadn't, and in 1990, they became the only franchise to play in each of the AFL's first four seasons.

"In 1990, we set up a new league and granted licenses for teams to play," said Bob Gries, a young businessman from Cleveland who bought the franchise prior to the season. "We got a late start, and we caught most of our games on the same night as the Pirates, who had a good season. That hurt us."

While the Gladiators and the Pirates only played once in Pittsburgh on the same day in 1990—July 14—the Pirates were having their best season since 1979. By comparison, when the Gladiators led the AFL in attendance in 1987, there were no scheduling conflicts with the Bucs, who had finished in last place for three straight seasons and were again mired at the bottom of the standings throughout the AFL season.

By the time the Gladiators kicked off their season on June 7, 1990, the Pirates had a five game lead in the National League Eastern Division. Couple this with the Gladiators' 0–2 start, and it's clear to see why it was difficult for Gries to get fans to come out to the Civic Arena to watch a struggling product on the field instead of watching an established winner in a popular sport on television, let alone attract the media attention needed to draw a fan base.

"I was going to fold the team at halftime of the third game," Greis said. "We lost the first two, and I'm going to lose so much money and this is no fun. So I decided if we lose this, I'll fold the team. We were losing at halftime, but came back in the second half and won, and the thrill of victory took over."

The Gladiators beat Washington, 55–32, in front of 5927 fans, the largest crowd of the season. Meanwhile, the Detroit Drive was averaging 13,191 fans during the regular season and even drew 19,902 for the championship game, though Greis was skeptical.

"If [Detroit Drive owner] Mike Ilitch had 20,000 fans, 18,000 were free tickets," said Greis.

By splitting their final six games of the regular season, Pittsburgh made the AFL playoffs but were beaten in the first round at Detroit.

"I lost $400,000 to 500,000," Greis said. "We didn't bring in any revenue. One hundred thousand dollars was all we brought in." And with no ties in Pittsburgh, Greis decided to relocate.

"The people were great, especially the DeBartolos," said Greis, referring to the Pittsburgh Penguins' owners at the time. "But I wanted to go to a market that had no baseball...Tampa was a good situation because they had no baseball [at the time]."

The announcement to move the team was actually mocked. One television sportscaster sarcastically used the line, "If you see people on the streets in mourning today, it's because the Pittsburgh Gladiators are no more," to report the news. None of the players or coaches went with the team to Tampa Bay, where the team still operates as of 2011.

But the lessons learned by the Gladiators may have helped the AFL survive. During the 1990s, the majority of AFL markets did not have Major League Baseball, and by 2000, the season began in March to get a heads-up in markets with baseball. Furthermore, when Ilitch bought the Detroit Tigers in 1992, he sold the Drive and allowed it to move to Worcester, Massachusetts.

Pennsylvania would not get another Arena Football League team until 2004, when a group led by Jon Bon Jovi was granted an expansion franchise in Philadelphia called the Soul. There was one link between the Gladiators and the Soul—Billy Osborn, a wide receiver/defensive back for the 1990 Gladiators, became the Soul's color commentator on radio broadcasts.

Quotes

"The [A's] fans cannot be blamed. The fans did not weary of Major League Baseball. They wearied of the dreary games played by the A's against rivals almost as dreary."

–Sports Illustrated, *November 8, 1954*

"Dad was in the league 54 years and only one time did he ask for a favor. He asked the other owners at the meeting in New York to keep the club in Philadelphia. He didn't care who owned the club as long as it stayed in Philadelphia. They turned him down. Fifty-four years in the league and they turned him down. That's what put Dad to bed."

–Earle Mack, after the American League rebuffed a group of Philadelphia businessmen who wanted to keep the Athletics in town. Had one more team approved the sale, the A's would not have moved.

Chapter Eleven

The Places

The Baker Bowl

The Baker Bowl housed the Phillies from 1887 to 1938, after which the Phils found it more economical to lease Shibe Park than continue upkeep on their own yard. On the plus side, the Baker Bowl, located on North Broad Street and West Huntingdon Street (hence the alternate names of Huntingdon Street Grounds, as well as National League Park), had unique dimensions, with 60 feet of space between all of the playing field and the stands, a feature that helped Grover Cleveland Alexander record his dominant statistics. Cut into a city block, the fence in right field was similar to today's Green Monster at Fenway Park, 60 feet high but only 280 feet away from home down the foul line and 300 feet in right center. This allowed Gavvy Cravath to hit 24 home runs in the Phils' pennant-winning season of 1915, a National League record for the dead-ball era.

The Baker Bowl also was the first ballpark in which a sitting president saw a World Series game (Woodrow Wilson in 1915), the site of Honus Wagner's 3000th hit, Babe Ruth's last game in 1935, and the home of the Philadelphia Eagles from 1933 to 1935. There was even a bicycle track built around the field in the 1890s.

In 1923, an incident at the ballpark led to fans being able to keep foul balls. Up until then, spectators were asked to return foul balls hit into the stands, though two years before, the Pirates had allowed their fans at Forbes Field to keep balls. Regardless, an 11-year-old named Reuben Berman refused to return a foul ball he caught while watching a game at the Baker Bowl, and the Phils management, incredibly, decided to have him arrested. Thankfully, the judge sided with Berman, and fans have been able to keep foul balls hit into the stands ever since.

As the stadium aged, it was derisively called "The Dump on the Hump" because centerfield had a literal hump to accommodate a railroad tunnel that went beneath the park. The Phillies were generally awful while they played there, winning just one pennant. The right field fence had a large billboard that advertised soap, reading "The Phillies use Lifebuoy" and leading local fans to remark, "and they still stink!" It is said that while the Phillies were on road trips, livestock grazed the field in lieu of lawnmowers.

Disasters were not uncommon at the park. Workers often went through the old wooden stands after games with buckets of water, looking for fires. A blaze in 1894 led to the park's reconstruction in 1895, with fewer posts to obstruct views. In 1903, a deck collapsed and killed 12 fans, and another part of a deck collapsed in 1927, injuring 50 people. And frankly, the ballpark and the views of old warehouses behind the outfield fences were not attractive.

The park held on for 12 years after the Phillies left; the owners tore down parts of the stands as time went by, and the venue hosted events such as midget auto races and ice skating.

Beaver Stadium

Home of Penn State football, Beaver Stadium was originally built in 1909. Situated on the lot of the modern-day Nittany Parking Deck, the 30,000-seat stadium was torn down, rebuilt and expanded to 46,284 seats at its present location in 1960. Various expansions have given it a seating capacity of 107, 282, thus making Beaver Stadium the fourth largest in the world behind Rungrado May Day Stadium in North Korea, Salt Lake Stadium in India and Michigan Stadium in Ann Arbor, Michigan. Named after former Pennsylvania governor James A. Beaver, who served on Penn State's Board of Trustees, the stadium was the home of the 1982 and 1986 National Football champions. There was a record crowd of 110,753 on September 14, 2002, for Penn State's 40–7 triumph against Nebraska.

Civic Arena

The first arena with a retractable roof when it was built in 1961, the Civic Arena (later named the Mellon Arena) was originally constructed for the Civic Light Opera, but ultimately provided professional hockey a chance to return to Pittsburgh after a five-year hiatus. Site of the first Arena Football Game in 1987, four Stanley Cup finals, one American Basketball Association final and three NCAA men's basketball tournament regionals, the stadium was home to the NHL Penguins, Duquesne basketball, the American Basketball League Rens, the ABA Pipers and Condors, the 1975 World TeamTennis champion Pittsburgh Triangles, the Major Indoor Soccer League Spirit, the Arena Football League Gladiators, the Major Indoor Lacrosse League Bulls, the Roller Hockey Phantoms, the Continental Indoor League Soccer Stingers, the MLL CrosseFire and the CBA Xplosion. The last event with the roof open was a 1994 Phantoms game. The Civic Arena was also the site of the first Arena Bowl and the "outdoor" arena football game in 1987. It hosted the last prizefight of legendary Sugar Ray Robinson in 1965, as well as numerous concerts, from Elvis Presley to Frank Sinatra to AC/DC (a 1990 concert blew out the sound system four times) to James Taylor and Carole King, who performed the last event at the arena in 2010. Bon Jovi's "Dead or Alive" video was filmed there. The stadium is located at 66 Mario Lemieux Place in Pittsburgh's Uptown neighborhood within walking distance of downtown. Its original capacity of 10,500 was ultimately increased to 17,132 in 1991.

Consol Energy Center

Built at a cost of $321 million, the Consol Energy Center opened in 2010 as the second home to the Pittsburgh Penguins and is located just below the old Civic Arena at 1001 Fifth Avenue. It seats 18,087 for hockey, in honor of Sidney Crosby's number 87, and has 66 luxury suites, in honor of Mario Lemieux's sweater number. Its completion allowed for the formation of the Pittsburgh Power Arena Football franchise. The stadium is the part-time home of the Pittsburgh Panthers and Duquesne basketball teams, and the Robert Morris hockey team, and it will be the site of the 2013 Frozen Four (NCAA men's hockey championships). The first event held in the facility was a Paul McCartney concert.

Before the first hockey game at the Consol Energy Center, Pittsburgh hockey legend Mario Lemieux christened the arena with a ceremonial pouring of melted ice water from Mellon Arena onto the new ice surface. For those looking to own a piece of that history, the Penguins offer bottles of the old ice surface to fans at the online store on NHL.com for $39.99. The website describes the bottle of water:

Nicknamed The Igloo, Mellon Arena has been home to the Pittsburgh Penguins since 1961. After almost 50 years, it was closed once and for all. On May 12, 2010, the ice from the stadium was melted and then bottled for a one-of-a-kind keepsake that you can now own. Proceeds from the sale will benefit the Pittsburgh Penguins Foundation.

Duquesne Gardens

Originally a trolley barn when it was built in 1891, Duquesne Gardens was the home of Pittsburgh hockey from 1895 until it was razed in 1956. Located at 110 North Craig Street near the intersection with Fifth Avenue, "The Arena" hosted America's first professional hockey league, the Western Pennsylvania Hockey League, and then the International Professional Hockey League in 1904. Billed as the "Largest and Most Beautiful Skating Palace in the World," the arena originally had a skating surface 50 feet longer than an NHL regulation rink, and the quality of the ice was such that the teams that played in the Gardens were able to lure players from Canada.

The arena made it possible for Pittsburgh to join the NHL for five years, from 1925 to 1930, but its 5000-seat capacity was not enough for the "Pirates" to continue operation. It was the home of the American Hockey League Hornets from 1936 to 1955, and the facility was also the first hockey rink to use glass above the dasher boards. Duquesne Gardens hosted six Calder Cup finals, 11 different professional, amateur and college hockey teams, as well as the Duquesne Dukes men's basketball team from 1904 to 1956 and the Pittsburgh Ironmen of the BBA (later the NBA) in 1946–47. It also hosted numerous boxing cards during Pittsburgh's boxing heyday in the 1930s, '40s and '50s. The intersection near where the arena stood is now called Billy Conn Boulevard. Bricks from the Gardens are now on display in the Consol Energy Center.

Exposition Park

Exposition Park was built in 1890 for the Players League's Pittsburgh Burgers, then served as the home of the Pittsburgh Pirates from 1891 from 1909. It was the first permanent home of the University of Pittsburgh football team and was also used by the Panthers' baseball team. Located approximately two blocks west of where PNC Park now sits, the yard was the first National League field to host a modern World Series game, and the Pirates became the first team to cover their infield with a tarpaulin. The field's expansive dimensions were 400 feet down the lines and 450 feet to centerfield, and the seating capacity was 16,000 at its peak.

Forbes Field

Built in 1909 across from the corner of Sennott and South Bouquet Streets in the Oakland neighborhood as one of the first two concrete-and-steel ballparks in the majors, Forbes Field was the home of the Pittsburgh Pirates from 1909 to 1970. The Pirates won the World Series in their very first season at the park, buoyed by rookie sensation Babe Adams' three victories against Detroit in the Fall Classic. The stadium seated 41,000 during the Pirates' 1925 World Championship season upon construction of a grandstand in right field, which was later reduced to 35,000.

The park's vast dimensions—365 feet to left field, 435 feet to center, 457 feet to a corner left center field, 408 feet to right center and originally 376 feet to right field (later shortened to 300 feet)—were such that a no-hitter was never thrown at the park, and J. Owen Wilson set a major league record that has stood for nearly a century by hitting 36 triples in 1912 for the Bucs. The stadium also featured a 110-foot distance from home plate to the backstop in 1909 (later shortened to 75 feet in 1959), so that any ball that got past the catcher often meant that runners on base could take two bases. Left field was shortened by 30 feet in 1947 upon the arrival of slugger Hank Greenburg to the Bucs, thus creating a bullpen by the fence and an area of the ballpark known as "Greenburg Gardens," which helped Ralph Kiner lead the National League in home runs for seven consecutive seasons.

Called the "House of Thrills," Forbes Field was also the location of the first baseball game called on radio (August 6, 1921, on KDKA; Pirates 8, Phillies 6), as well as Kiki Cuyler's two-out, three-run double in the bottom of the eighth inning off Washington's Walter Johnson to complete the Pirates' come-back from a three-games-to-one deficit in the 1925 World Series, thus giving the Bucs a 9–7 seventh game victory. It was also the site of Bill Mazeroski's legendary home run to win the 1960 World Series. Forbes Field was home to Pop Warner's national championship Pitt football squads, the Steelers' first-ever playoff game and Jersey Joe Wolcott's knockout of Ezzard Charles, which made him the then-oldest heavyweight champion in history at age 37.

Franklin Field

Arguably the most historic football stadium in existence today, Franklin Field has hosted the Penn Relays, the largest track and field meet in the U.S., since 1895. Home of the University of Pennsylvania Quakers football, soccer and track and field teams, Franklin Field also was the home of the Philadelphia Eagles from 1958 to 1970 and the Philadelphia Atoms NASL franchise in 1976. The stadium was the site of a USFL Philadelphia Stars' playoff victory against the New Jersey Generals, saw occasional use by the Temple Owls football team until 2002 and hosted the Army–Navy game from 1899 to 1935. Penn's baseball team even used the stadium in the first part of the 20th century.

Franklin Field was the site of the 1960 NFL championship game in which Philadelphia defeated Green Bay, 17–13, and the place where Jim Thorpe's Carlisle Indian School defeated Penn, 26–6, in 1907. It was also where Red Grange ran for 331 yards in Illinois' 24–2 victory against the Quakers in 1925 and hosted the famous 1968 game in which fans booed and threw snowballs at Santa Claus during a halftime show.

Located at South 33rd and Spruce Streets near Center City, the stadium's original capacity of 30,000 was rebuilt in 1925 to seat 78,000, but now holds 52,593.

Heinz Field

The home of the Steelers and the Pitt Panthers since 2001, Heinz Field seats 65,050, with a scheduled expansion in 2012 of 4000 more seats. It has been known to have a traditionally sloppy grass surface, making placekicks a chore, and an open view of the "Golden Triangle" from its location on Pittsburgh's North Side near the confluence of the Allegheny, Monongahela and Ohio Rivers. Other distinctive features include golden seats, the "Great Hall" celebrating both the Panthers' and the Steelers' histories, a statue of Steelers founder Art Rooney Sr. and Heinz Ketchup bottles "pouring" into the scoreboard whenever the home team crosses an opponent's 20-yard line. The stadium was also home to the 2011 Winter Classic hockey game between the Washington Capitals and the Penguins, and it hosted 10 Steelers playoff games in its first 10 years of operation, including four AFC championship games. Once expansion is complete, Heinz Field will likely be able to hold the largest crowd ever to see a sporting event in Pittsburgh.

Hersheypark Arena

Hersheypark Arena was built by Milton Hershey in 1936 to house the Hershey Bears. Skating and hockey had become a popular pastime at the Hershey Ice Palace, and the 7286-seat arena would prove to be the venue that would eventually get Hershey into the American Hockey League in 1938. Located 15 miles east of Harrisburg, the Hersheypark Arena has hosted 18 Calder Cup finals, Wilt Chamberlain's famous 100-point game, numerous concerts and even a birthday celebration for President Dwight Eisenhower in 1953. Replaced as the Bears' home venue in 2002 by the Giant Center, the arena still is used as the Bears' practice facility and is home to college hockey programs from Shippensburg University and Lebanon Valley College. It is also home to PIAA basketball and wrestling championships, and, from 1988 to 1991, the Hershey Impact indoor soccer team.

JFK Stadium

Built in 1925 for Philadelphia's Sesquicentennial Exposition the following year, this 102,000-seat stadium played host to the Army–Navy football game for 42 years as well as numerous concerts, including Live Aid, the Beatles, the Monsters of Rock (Van Halen, Scorpions, Dokken, Metallica and Kingdom Come), the Rolling Stones and Judy Garland. It was briefly the home of the Eagles in the late 1930s and 1941, as well as the World Football League Philadelphia Bell in 1974 and the 1926 American Football League champion Philadelphia Quakers. The stadium was also home to Navy football when the team hosted Notre Dame in the 1960s, and it was the original home of the Liberty Bowl from 1959 to 1963. The arena was the site of the Gene Tunney–Jack Dempsey heavyweight title bout in 1926 and the Rocky Marciano–Joe Wolcott fight in 1952. It also hosted high school football and soccer.

The stadium's unique architecture features arch-shaped entrances on the outside for every section in the stadium. It was condemned six days after the Greatful Dead played there in 1989, and the building was razed in 1992. Originally called Sesquicentennial Stadium, the name was changed to Philadelphia Municipal Stadium in 1926, and then the facility was renamed for John F. Kennedy after his assassination in 1963. Today, the site in the South Philadelphia Sports Complex is home to the First Union Center.

Lincoln Financial Park

Lincoln Financial Park is the home of the Philadelphia Eagles and the Temple Owls, as well as the Army–Navy game. Since 2003, it has seen a curbing of the violence that was once such a part of watching the Eagles at Veterans Stadium. The facility, which seats 65,532 and is located next to Citizens Bank Park at 1020 Pattison Avenue in South Philly, also has been the home of numerous soccer matches and concerts. The stadium hosted six Eagles playoff games in its first eight years of existence, including two NFC championship games.

The Palestra

"The Cathedral of College Basketball" opened in 1927 at 215 South 33rd Street and is home to several University of Pennsylvania sports teams as well as select Big Five games. Originally equipped with a seating capacity of 10,000, the Palestra has hosted a record 52 NCAA men's basketball tournament games and the Atlantic 10 tournament, as well as all Big Five (Penn, La Salle, Villanova, Temple and St. Joseph's) games until 1991. Current seating capacity is 8722.

Pitt Stadium

Hailed as the finest college football stadium in America when it was built, Pitt Stadium served as the home of the University of Pittsburgh Panthers football team from 1925 to 1999 and was one of the first true multisport complexes of its time. Funded in part by legendary head coach Jock Sutherland, the stadium was home to six national champions in football and two in basketball. Panther cagers played in Pitt Pavilion, located inside the stadium, until 1951. It stayed open until the building's demolition in 1999, allowing young fans to shoot baskets while their parents watched the football game. A crowd of 68,918 to see Pitt beat Fordham in 1938 was the largest gathering ever to watch a sporting event in Pittsburgh as of 2011.

The stadium also hosted baseball (with balls hit into the short right field stands counting as a double), soccer, track and field, and gymnastics, and was the home of the Steelers from 1958 to 1969, except for selected games (usually night) at Forbes Field through 1963. More than 100,000 people gathered in Pitt Stadium to hear Pope Pius XII speak in 1939. The facility received temporary lights in 1985, and permanent ones in 1987. Various improvements were made during the John Majors eras, from installing wooden lockers to putting in a weight room. Host to 46 Pitt–Penn State games, a distinctive cartoon "Panther" logo painted on the side of Pennsylvania Hall and overlooking the stadium was changed to "Hail to Pitt" in 1993. The original seating capacity of 69,400 was reduced to 56,500 in the 1940s. Located on the corner of Sutherland Drive and Terrace Street on top of "Cardiac Hill," the building was razed following the 1999 football season, and the site is now home to the Peterson Events Center.

Point Stadium

Located at the confluence of the Little Conemaugh, Conemaugh and Stonycreek Rivers, Point Stadium was built in 1926 on the land that Johnstown city founder Joseph Johns designated for a recreation ground in the early 19th century. The ballpark somehow can come off as being scenic and ugly, majestic and quirky, and it hosted minor league baseball, high school football and more.

The park is unique for three reasons: the unique outfield dimensions, which were designed to fit inside a city block bordered by Pennsylvania Route 56 and Washington, Johns and Main Streets; the fact that it is the only stadium directly served by an incline; and its incredible history. With its short outfield dimensions—originally 262 feet to left field, 385 feet to center and 251 feet to right field—Point Stadium could be a haven for home run hitters playing minor league baseball for the Johnstown Johnnies, but it may be better known as a football stadium. With an original seating capacity of 17,000, the stadium often sold out key high school football games of the area, including the annual Johnstown–Altoona game, and hosted an NFL game between Pittsburgh and Philadelphia in 1936, which was won by the Pirates, 6–0. The Steelers returned to the stadium in 1987, using it as a training ground for their replacement team. The 1983 football movie *All the Right Moves*, starring Tom Cruise, was filmed there, and it has been a concert venue for everyone from the Johnstown Symphony to Bon Jovi. Rebuilt in 2006, Point Stadium is now the home of Bishop McCort football games and the All-American Amateur Baseball Association World Series, featuring more spacious yet still quirky dimensions of 290 feet down the lines, 409 feet to center, 336 feet to left center and 395 feet to right center.

Shibe Park

Built just five blocks from the Baker Bowl at the corner of North 21st Street and West Lehigh Avenue, Shibe Park, named after Athletics owner Benjamin Shibe, was one of the first two concrete-and-steel ballparks in the majors, along with Forbes Field. The park hosted Major League Baseball for 62 seasons. The A's won the World Series in just their second season there and would go on to win five more at the ballpark, along with seven pennants. The Phillies, tenants from 1938 to 1970, won their 1950 pennant there. Shibe Park also hosted the snowy 1948 NFL championship game, which was won on a fourth quarter touchdown by Steve Van Buren.

The two most famous characteristics of the park were the French Renaissance dome above the home plate entrance that housed Connie Mack's office and the 36-foot "spite fence" that Mack put up in right field in 1935 to prohibit fans from watching games from the rooftops of 20th Street homes behind the stadium, arguably causing the demise of both the team and the neighborhood. The fence grew to 60 feet when the Ballantine Beer scoreboard was added in 1956.

The park also hosted the greatest comeback in baseball history—the Philadelphia A's scored 13 runs in the bottom of the eighth inning to beat Cleveland 17–15 on June 15, 1925 —and the greatest World Series comeback of all time as the A's scored 10 runs in bottom of the seventh of the fourth game of the 1929 series to overcome an 8–0 deficit and win, 10–8. Frank "Home Run" Baker earned his nickname there with his two-run homer to win game two of the 1911 World Series, and Lou Gehrig hit four home runs in a game in 1932. The park's original dimensions were 360 feet down the lines and 515 feet to center field, then 334 feet to left field, 329 feet to right, 390 feet to right center and 410 feet to center by the time the park closed.

Renamed Connie Mack Stadium in 1953, the building was razed in 1976 and the site was an empty lot for 15 years before the Deliverance Evangelistic Church was constructed there in 1991.

The Spectrum

Built in 1967, the Spectrum gave the Philadelphia 76ers a permanent home, so they didn't have to shuttle between various basketball venues, and convinced the NHL to give Philadelphia the Flyers franchise. Located in the South Philadelphia Sports Complex at 3601 South Broad Street, the Spectrum was home to 10 professional sports franchises and the only arena to ever host an NBA and NHL All-Star game in the same year when it did so in 1976. It hosted the Stanley Cup finals and the NBA finals in 1980, and featured one of the first matrix scoreboards in indoor sports, allowing fans to read messages and see animation.

The Spectrum also hosted the 1976 and 1981 Final Four, eight Atlantic 10 tournaments and three NCAA regionals. It was the site of Duke's Christian Laettner's buzzer-beating basket to beat Kentucky in the 1992 East regionals, the Flyers' 15-year, 42-game unbeaten streak against the Pittsburgh Penguins from 1974 to 1989, and Philadelphia's 4–1 exhibition victory against the Soviet Central Red Army Team in 1976.

The stadium is also the home of two Stanley Cup champions and one NBA champ. Six championships were won by the Philadelphia Wings indoor lacrosse franchise there, two by the Philadelphia Phantoms American Hockey League franchise, two by the Philadelphia Kixx indoor soccer team and one by the Philadelphia Soul arena football team.

AC/DC shot their "Moneytalks" video in the Spectrum in 1990, and Brian Johnson's father, Alan, saw him perform for the first time with AC/DC there in 1983, comparing the noise of the concert to the cannon fire he heard in North Africa during World War II. The stadium had a seating capacity of 18,369 for concerts, 18,136 for basketball and 17,380 for hockey. Statues of Kate Smith, Julius Erving, and Gary Dornhoefer scoring a game-winning goal to beat Minnesota in the 1973 playoffs surrounded the venue, along with, at one time, the famous statue of Rocky Balboa shown on the steps of the Philadelphia Museum of Art in *Rocky III*. The Spectrum was razed between November 2010 and April 2011.

Three Rivers Stadium

The Pittsburgh Pirates moved into Three Rivers Stadium halfway through their 1970 first-place season and stayed, along with the Steelers, through their 2000 campaign. Built on almost the same site as Exposition Park (the Bucs' home prior to moving to Forbes Field) the stadium allowed Pittsburgh to enter a glory-filled decade in which the Pirates won the World Series twice, the Steelers won the Super Bowl four times, and Pitt's 1976 national champions even beat Penn State there. Furthermore, the Pirates and the Steelers made the playoffs a combined 14 times in 20 seasons during the '70s, and the venue saw such historic occasions as the first World Series night game (game four of the 1971 Fall Classic), the Immaculate Reception (Franco Harris' 60-yard touchdown reception off a deflected pass with five seconds remaining to beat Oakland, 13–7, and give the Steelers their first-ever playoff victory), the first three no-hitters pitched in Pittsburgh since 1907 (by Bob Gibson in 1971, John Candelaria in 1976, and Francisco Cordova and Ricardo Rincon in 1997), eight AFC championship games, nine National League championship series and Roberto Clemente's 3000th career hit.

Although criticized, as many multipurpose stadiums of the era were, the artificial surface allowed the Pirates to incorporate a speed game into "The Lumber Company's" offense as a Pirate led the NL in stolen bases five times during the Bucs' 31 season tenure there from 1970 to 2000. The Steelers sold out their 1973 season there and have never failed to sell out a game since, except for the 1987 replacement players game. The field dimensions were 335 yards down the lines, 385 to the power alleys and 410 to center, with the power alleys and center field dimensions moved in 10 feet in later years. The football seating capacity of 59,000 was the NFL's smallest in 2000, the stadium's final season of use before it was imploded in 2001.

Veterans Stadium

Like many "cookie-cutter" stadiums that opened around the time "The Vet" did in 1971, this home of the Phillies and Eagles was criticized for being too sterile. But like other stadiums of the era, the teams that played there enjoyed unparalleled success. The Phillies won their first World Series in Veterans Stadium in 1980, and the Eagles clinched their first conference championship three months later. The facility also hosted 17 Army–Navy games, three World Series, two no-hitters and two NFC championship games. An infamous jail and magistrate office was set up for rowdy Eagles fans, especially those sitting in the notorious 700 level at the top of the stadium. The latest-finishing major league game, which was played on July 3, 1993, and ended at 4:40 AM, was played there. The stadium was also home to the North American Soccer League Philadelphia Atoms and Fury, Temple football and the United States Football League Stars in 1983–84. The Stars clinched a berth in the first USFL championship game with a 44–38 overtime victory against the Chicago Blitz, coming back from a 31–10 fourth-quarter deficit.

The baseball dimensions were 330 feet down the lines, 371 feet to the power alleys and 408 feet to center field, and seating capacity was originally 65,000 for baseball and 71,000 for football. The seats featured a distinctive Liberty Bell logo, and there was a Liberty Bell sign in centerfield. Elton John's song "Philadelphia Freedom" was played on the loudspeaker after Phillies games. Located at the corner of Broad Street and Patterson Avenue in South Philly, the Vet was razed in 2004.

War Memorial

The Cambria County War Memorial may be the most famous building in all of hockey. And while part of its renown is because its inception in 1950 predates any current NHL arena, the real reason is simple: *Slap Shot*, the 1976 Paul Newman movie that has been called not only the greatest hockey movie of all time, but also "The Greatest Guy Movie Ever Made" by *Maxim* magazine. Thankfully, the arena, located at 326 Napoleon Street in Johnstown, has not changed much since the film was made—the bricks, the entrances and even the press box remain practically the same.

Although Johnstown's minor league hockey teams, as of 2010, have gone the way of the fictitious Charlestown Chiefs of the film, in 2010–11, the War Memorial was used as an alternate venue for the ECHL Wheeling Nailers and is home to many amateur, high school, junior and college hockey programs. The arena was built with bonds to honor war veterans and to return hockey to Johnstown, where a team called the Blue Birds had played in 1941–42 at the Shaffer Ice Palace on McMillen Street. The hallway outside the seating areas features displays honoring Johnstown's past hockey teams, including the Jets, who played from 1950 to 1977, and the Chiefs, who were an original member of the ECHL for 23 years from 1988 to 2010. The building also houses the Cambria County Sports Hall of Fame.

The arena was the home of the 2000 Johnstown Jackals of the Indoor Football League, the 2001 National Indoor Football League J-Dogs, and the 2005–07 Riverhawks American Indoor Football Association franchise, all of whom featured many local players who played professionally, as well as the Johnstown Wings and the Red Wings of the Eastern Hockey League from 1978 to 1980. The building has also hosted numerous concerts featuring everyone from Alice Cooper to Willie Nelson. Its seating capacity is a modest 4001.

Chapter Twelve

Pennsylvania Hall of Famers

Baseball

Native Pennsylvanians in the Baseball Hall of Fame

Each name is accompanied by the city or town in which the athlete was born.

Roy Campanella (Philadelphia)

Nestor Chylak (Olyphant)

Stan Covelski (Shamokin)

Nellie Fox (St. Thomas)

Reggie Jackson (Wyncote)

Hughie Jennings (Pittston)

Tommy LaSorda (Norristown)

Effa Manley (Philadelphia)

Christy Mathewson (Factoryville)

Joe McCarthy (Philadelphia)

Bill McKechnie (Wilkinsburg)

Stan Musial (Donora)

Herb Pennock (Kennett Square)

Eddie Plank (Gettysburg)

Cum Posey (Homestead)

Bruce Sutter (Lancaster)

Rube Waddell (Punxsutawney)

Honus Wagner (Carnegie)

Bobby Wallace (Pittsburgh)

Ed Walsh (Plains Township)

John Montgomery Ward (Bellefonte)

Hack Wilson (Elwood City)

Baseball Hall of Famers Who Played or Worked in Pittsburgh (With the Year They Were Enshrined)

Jake Beckley	Pittsburgh Pirates	1st baseman	1971
Cool Papa Bell	Pittsburgh Crawfords	Center fielder	1974
Bert Blyleven	Pittsburgh Pirates	Pitcher	2011
Ray Brown	Pittsburgh Crawfords	Pitcher	2006
Leonard Buck	Homestead Grays	1st baseman	1972
Jim Bunning	Pittsburgh Pirates	Pitcher	1996
Max Carey	Pittsburgh Pirates	Center fielder	1961
Oscar Charleston	Pittsburgh Crawfords	1st baseman	1976
Jack Chesbro	Pittsburgh Pirates	Pitcher	1946
Fred Clarke	Pittsburgh Pirates	Left fielder	1945
Roberto Clemente	Pittsburgh Pirates	Right fielder	1973
Joe Cronin	Pittsburgh Pirates	2nd baseman	1956
Kiki Cuyler	Pittsburgh Pirates	Right fielder	1968
Frankie Frisch	Pittsburgh Pirates	2nd baseman	1947
Pud Galvin	Pittsburgh Alleghenies	Pitcher	1965
Josh Gibson	Homestead Grays	Catcher	1972
Rich Gossage	Pittsburgh Pirates	Pitcher	2008
Hank Greenburg	Pittsburgh Pirates	1st baseman	1956
Burleigh Grimes	Pittsburgh Pirates	Pitcher	1964
Ned Hanlon	Pittsburgh Burghers	Manager	1996
Billy Herman	Pittsburgh Pirates	Infielder	1975
Waite Hoyt	Pittsburgh Pirates	Pitcher	1969
Judy Johnson	Pittsburgh Crawfords	3rd baseman	1975
High Pockets Kelly	Pittsburgh Pirates	3rd baseman	1973
Ralph Kiner	Pittsburgh Pirates	Left fielder	1975

Freddie Lindstrom	Pittsburgh Pirates	Outfielder	1976
Al Lopez	Pittsburgh Pirates	Catcher	1977
Connie Mack	Pittsburgh Pirates	Manager	1937
Rabbit Maranville	Pittsburgh Pirates	Infielder	1954
Bill Mazeroski	Pittsburgh Pirates	2nd baseman	2001
Bill McKechnie	Pittsburgh Pirates	Manager	1962
Satchel Paige	Pittsburgh Crawfords	Pitcher	1971
Cum Posey	Homestead Grays	Executive	2006
Billy Southworth	Pittsburgh Pirates	Right fielder	2008
Willie Stargell	Pittsburgh Pirates	Left fielder	1988
Casey Stengel	Pittsburgh Pirates	Outfielder	1966
Pie Traynor	Pittsburgh Pirates	3rd baseman	1948
Dazzy Vance	Pittsburgh Pirates	Pitcher	1955
Arky Vaughan	Pittsburgh Pirates	Shortstop	1985
Rube Waddell	Pittsburgh Pirates	Pitcher	1946
Honus Wagner	Pittsburgh Pirates	Shortstop	1936
Lloyd Waner	Pittsburgh Pirates	Center fielder	1967
Paul Waner	Pittsburgh Pirates	Right fielder	1952
Vic Willis	Pittsburgh Pirates	Pitcher	1995

Baseball Hall of Famers Who Played or Worked in Philadelphia (With the Year They Were Enshrined)

Grover Alexander	Philadelphia Phillies	Pitcher	1938
Sparky Anderson	Philadelphia Phillies	2nd baseman	2000
Ritchie Ashburn	Philadelphia Phillies	Center fielder	1995
Frank Baker	Philadelphia Phillies	3rd baseman	1955
Dave Bancroft	Philadelphia Phillies	Shortstop	1971
Chief Bender	Philadelphia Athletics and Phillies	Pitcher	1953
Dan Brouthers	Philadelphia Phillies	1st baseman	1945
Jim Bunning	Philadelphia Phillies	Pitcher	1996
Steve Carlton	Philadelphia Phillies	Pitcher	1994
Ty Cobb	Philadelphia Athletics	Outfielder	1936
Mickey Cochrane	Philadelphia Athletics	Catcher	1947
Eddie Collins	Philadelphia Athletics	2nd baseman	1939
Jimmy Collins	Philadelphia Athletics	3rd baseman	1945
Stan Covelski	Philadelphia Athletics	Pitcher	1969
Ed Delahanty	Philadelphia Phillies	Left Fielder	1945
Hugh Duffy	Philadelphia Phillies	Outfielder	1945
Johnny Evers	Philadelphia Phillies	2nd baseman	1946
Elmer Flick	Philadelphia Athletics and Phillies	Outfielder	1963
Nellie Fox	Philadelphia Athletics	2nd baseman	1997
Jimmie Foxx	Philadelphia Athletics and Phillies	1st baseman	1951
Lefty Grove	Philadelphia Athletics	Pitcher	1947
Billy Hamilton	Philadelphia Phillies	Center fielder	1961

Bucky Harris	Philadelphia Phillies	Manager	1975
Waite Hoyt	Philadelphia Athletics	Pitcher	1969
Fergie Jenkins	Philadelphia Phillies	Pitcher	1991
Hughie Jennings	Philadelphia Phillies	Infielder	1945
Tim Keefe	Philadelphia Phillies	Pitcher	1964
George Kell	Philadelphia Athletics	3rd baseman	1983
Chuck Klein	Philadelphia Phillies	Right fielder	1980
Nap Lajoie	Philadelphia Athletics and Phillies	2nd baseman	1937
Connie Mack	Philadelphia Athletics	Manager	1937
Tommy McCarthy	Philadelphia Phillies	Outfielder	1946
Joe Morgan	Philadelphia Phillies	2nd baseman	1990
Kid Nichols	Philadelphia Phillies	Pitcher	1949
Herb Pennock	Philadelphia Athletics	Pitcher	1948
Tony Perez	Philadelphia Phillies	1st baseman	2000
Eddie Plank	Philadelphia Athletics	Pitcher	1946
Eppa Rixey	Philadelphia Phillies	Pitcher	1963
Robin Roberts	Philadelphia Phillies	Pitcher	1976
Ryne Sandberg	Philadelphia Phillies	2nd baseman	2005
Mike Schmidt	Philadelphia Phillies	3rd baseman	1995
Al Simmons	Philadelphia Athletics	Left fielder	1953
Tris Speaker	Philadelphia Athletics	Outfielder	1937
Sam Thompson	Philadelphia Phillies	Right fielder	1974
Rube Waddell	Philadelphia Athletics	Pitcher	1946
Lloyd Waner	Philadelphia Phillies	Outfielder	1967
Zack Wheat	Philadelphia Athletics	Outfielder	1959
Jud Wilson	Philadelphia Stars	3rd baseman	2006
Harry Wright	Philadelphia Quakers (Phillies)	Executive	1953

Football

Native Pennsylvanians in the Pro Football Hall of Fame

Each name is accompanied by the city or town in which the athlete was born.

Herb Adderley (Philadelphia)

Chuck Bednarik (Bethlehem)

Bert Bell (Philadelphia)

Fred Biletnikoff (Erie)

George Blanda (Youngwood)

Mike Ditka (Carnegie)

Tony Dorsett (Rochester)

Bill George (Waynesburg)

Harold "Red" Grange (Forksville)

Jack Ham (Johnstown)

Stan Jones (Altoona)

Jim Kelly (Pittsburgh)

Leroy Kelly (Philadelphia)

Dan Marino (Pittsburgh)

Joe Montana (New Eagle)

Lenny Moore (Reading)

Mike Munchak (Scranton)

Joe Namath (Beaver Falls)

Art Rooney (Coulterville)

Dan Rooney (Pittsburgh)

Joe Schmidt (Pittsburgh)

Joe Stydahar (Kaylor)

Charley Trippi (Pittston)

Emlen Tunnell (Bryn Mawr)

Johnny Unitas (Pittsburgh)

Randy White (Pittsburgh)

Pro Football Hall of Famers Who Played or Worked for the Pittsburgh Steelers

Bert Bell	1941–46
Mel Blount	1970–83
Terry Bradshaw	1970–83
Len Dawson	1957–59
Bill Dudley	1942, 1945–46
Joe Greene	1969–81
Jack Ham	1971–82
Franco Harris	1972–83
Robert "Cal" Hubbard	1936
John Henry Johnson	1960–65
Walt Kiesling	1941–44, 1954–56
Jack Lambert	1974–84
Bobby Layne	1958–62
John "Blood" McNally	1934, 1937–38
Marion Motley	1955
Chuck Noll	1969–91
Art Rooney	1933–88
Dan Rooney	1955–present
John Stallworth	1974–87
Ernie Stautner	1950–63
Lynn Swann	1974–82
Mike Webster	1974–88
Rod Woodson	1987–96

Pro Football Hall of Famers Who Played or Worked for the Philadelphia Eagles

Chuck Bednarik	1949–62
Bert Bell	1933–40
Bob "Boomer" Brown	1964–68
Mike Ditka	1967–68
Bill Hewitt	1937–39
Sonny Jurgensen	1957–63
James Lofton	1993
Ollie Matson	1964–66
Tommy McDonald	1957–63
Art Monk	1995
Alfred Earle "Greasy" Neale	1941–50
Pete Pihos	1947–55
Jim Ringo	1964–67
Norm Van Brocklin	1958–60
Steve Van Buren	1944–51
Reggie White	1985–92
Alex Wojciechowicz	1946–50

Pro Football Hall of Famers
Who Went to College in Pennsylvania

Chuck Bednarik (Penn State)

Bert Bell (Penn State)

Mike Ditka (University of Pittsburgh)

Tony Dorsett (University of Pittsburgh)

Russ Grimm (University of Pittsburgh)

Joe Guyon (Carlisle)

Jack Ham (Penn State)

Franco Harris (Penn State)

Wilbur "Pete" Henry (Washington & Jefferson)

Cal Hubbard (Geneva)

Rickey Jackson (University of Pittsburgh)

Howie Long (Villanova)

Dan Marino (University of Pittsburgh)

Mike Michalske (Penn State)

Lenny Moore (Penn State)

Mike Munchak (Penn State)

Art Rooney (Duquesne)

Dan Rooney (Duquesne)

Joe Schmidt (University of Pittsburgh)

Jim Thorpe (Carlisle)

College Football Hall of Famers from Pennsylvania Colleges

Reds Bagnell (Penn State)

Chuck Bednarik (Penn State)

Charlie Berry (Lafayette)

Hugo Bezdek (Penn State)

George Brooke (Swathmore, Penn State)

Harold Burry (Westminster)

John Cappelletti (Penn State)

Len Casanova (Pitt)

Jimbo Covert (Pitt)

Ave "Lil Abner" Daniell (Pitt)

Tom Davies (Pitt)

Harold Davis (Westminster)

Mike Ditka (Pitt)

Joe Donchess (Pitt)

Keith Dorney (Penn State)

Tony Dorsett (Pitt)

Rip Engle (Penn State Coach)

Albert Exendine (Carlisle)

Bill Fralic (Pitt)

Joe Fusco (Westminster)

Ed Garbisch (Washington & Jefferson)

Charlie Gelbert (Penn State)

Marshall Goldberg (Pitt)

Hugh Green (Pitt)

"Indian" Joe Guyon (Carlisle)

Jack Ham (Penn State)

Jack Harding (Scranton)

Truxton Hare (Penn State)

Dick Harlow (Penn State)

Harvey Harman (Haverford, Penn)

Howard Harpster (Carnegie Tech)

Jim Haslett (Indiana University)

John Heisman (Penn State, Washington & Jefferson)

Wilbur Henry (Washington & Jefferson)

Bob Higgins (Penn State)

Clarke Hinkle (Bucknell)

Bill Hollenback (Penn State)

Cal Hubbard (Geneva)

Jimmy Johnson (Carlisle)

Andy Kerr (Washington & Jefferson, Lebanon Valley)

Glenn Killinger (Penn State)

Chuck Klausing (Indiana University, Carnegie Mellon)

Ted Kwalick (Penn State)

Richie Lucas (Penn State)

Dan Marino (Pitt)

Pete Mauthe (Penn State)

Mark May (Pitt)

Herb McCracken (Pitt player; Allegheny and Lafayette coach)

Ed McGinley (Penn State)

George "Tank" McLaren (Pitt)

Tuss McLaughry (Westminster)

Leroy Mercer (Penn State)

Shorty Miller (Penn State)

John Minds (Penn State)

Skip Minisi (Penn State)

Lydell Mitchell (Penn State)

Ray Morrison (Temple)

George Munger (Penn State)

Edward "Hook" Mylin (Lafayette, Lebanon Valley, Bucknell)

Alfred Earle "Greasy" Neale (Washington & Jefferson)

Bob Odell (Penn State)

Dennis Onkotz (Penn State)

Win Osgood (Penn State)

John Outland (Penn State)

Joe Paterno (Penn State)

Bob Peck (Pitt)

Larry Pugh (Westminster)

Mike Reid (Penn State)

Glenn Ressler (Penn State)

Babe Rinehart (Lafayette)

Dave Robinson (Penn State)

Eddie Rogers (Carlisle)

George Savitsky (Penn State)

Hunter Scarlett (Penn State)

Joe Schmidt (Pitt)

Dutch Schwab (Lafayette)

Clark Shaughnessy (Pitt)

Frank Sheptock (Bloomsburg)

Joe Skladany (Pitt)

Andy Smith (Penn State)

Carl Snavely (Bucknell)

Herb Stein (Pitt)

Steve Stevenson (Penn State)

Steve Suhey (Penn State)

Jock Sutherland (Pitt, Lafayette)

Joe Thompson (Geneva, Pitt)

Jim Thorpe (Carlisle)

Bob Torrey (Penn State)

Dexter Very (Penn State)

Hube Wagner (Pitt)

Curt Warner (Penn State)

Pop Warner (Carlisle, Pitt, Temple)

Gus Welch (Carlisle)

Charles "Buck" Wharton (Penn State)

Harry Wilson (Penn State)

Mike Wilson (Lafayette)

George Woodruff (Penn State)

Andy Wyant (Bucknell)

Lloyd Yoder (Carnegie Tech)

Hockey

Hockey Hall of Famers Born in Pennsylvania

Hobey Baker (Wissahickon)

Hockey Hall of Famers Who Played or Worked in Pittsburgh

Sidney "Sid" Abel	Pittsburgh Hornets
George "Chief" Armstrong	Pittsburgh Hornets
John Ashley	Pittsburgh Hornets
Martin "Marty" Barry	Pittsburgh Hornets
Andrew "Andy" Bathgate	Pittsburgh Penguins (also Pittsburgh Hornets)
Leo Boivin	Pittsburgh Penguins (also Pittsburgh Hornets)
William Scott "Scotty" Bowman	Pittsburgh Penguins
Francis "Frank" Brimsek	Pittsburgh Yellow Jackets
Herb Brooks	Pittsburgh Penguins
Gerald "Gerry" Cheevers	Pittsburgh Hornets
Paul Coffey	Pittsburgh Penguins
Lionel Conacher	Pittsburgh Pirates (also Yellow Jackets)
Gordon Drillon	Pittsburgh Yellow Jackets
Ferdinand "Fernie" Flaman	Pittsburgh Hornets
Ron Francis	Pittsburgh Penguins
Frank Fredrickson	Pittsburgh Pirates
James "Jimmy" Gardner	Pittsburgh Pros
Douglas Harvey	Pittsburgh Hornets
William "Riley" Hern	Pittsburgh Keystones

Miles "Tim" Horton	Pittsburgh Penguins (also Pittsburgh Hornets)
R. Bob Johnson	Pittsburgh Penguins
Mike Lange	Pittsburgh Penguins
Mario Lemieux	Pittsburgh Penguins
Duncan "Mickey" MacKay	Pittsburgh Pirates
Dave Molinari	Pittsburgh Penguins
Joseph Mullen	Pittsburgh Penguins
Larry Murphy	Pittsburgh Penguins
Craig Patrick	Pittsburgh Penguins
Luc Robitaille	Pittsburgh Penguins
Glen Sather	Pittsburgh Penguins
Alfred "Alf" Smith	Pittsburgh Bankers (also Pittsburgh Duquesne, PAC)
Thomas J. Smith	Pittsburgh Bankers (also Pittsburgh Lyceum, Pros)
John "Black Jack" Stewart	Pittsburgh Hornets
Bruce Stuart	Pittsburgh Victorias
William H. "Hod" Stuart	Pittsburgh Bankers (also Pittsburgh Pros)
Frederick "Cyclone" Taylor	Pittsburgh Pros
Bill Torrey	Pittsburgh Hornets
Bryan Trottier	Pittsburgh Penguins
Roy "Shrimp" Worters	Pittsburgh Pirates (also Pittsburgh Yellow Jackets)

Hockey Hall of Famers Who Played or Worked in Philadelphia

William "Bill" Barber	Philadephia Flyers (also Philadelphia Phantoms)
Martin "Marty" Barry	Philadephia Arrows
Robert "Bobby" Clarke	Philadephia Flyers
Paul Coffey	Philadephia Flyers
Arthur "Art" Coulter	Philadephia Arrows
Emile Francis	Philadephia Falcons
Herbert "Herb" Gardiner	Philadephia Arrows
Gene Hart	Philadephia Flyers
Dale Hawerchuk	Philadephia Flyers
Sydney "Syd" Howe	Philadephia Quakers
Roger Neilson	Philadephia Flyers
Bernard "Bernie" Parent	Philadephia Flyers (also Philadelphia Blazers)
Darryl Sittler	Philadephia Flyers
Cooper Smeaton	Philadephia Quakers
Ed Snider	Philadephia Flyers
Allan Stanley	Philadephia Flyers

Hockey Hall of Famers Who Played or Worked for the Hershey Bears

William "Bill" Barber

Murray Costello

Ferdinand "Fernie" Flaman

Frank Mathers

Walter "Babe" Pratt

Basketball

Basketball Hall of Famers from Pennsylvania Who Played or Worked in the State

Paul Arizin (from Philadelphia; played for Villanova, Warriors)

Geno Auriemma (raised in Norristown; assistant coach at St. Joseph's)

Charles Barkley (played for 76ers)

Tom Barlow (played for Philadelphia SPHAS, Warriors)

John Beckman (Nanticoke Nans star)

Larry Brown (coached 76ers)

Henry Carlson (coach at Pitt)

Pete Carril (from Bethlehem)

Wilt Chamberlain (from Philadelphia; played for Warriors, 76ers)

John Chaney (coached at Temple)

Charles Cooper (played for Philadelphia Panthers, Saints)

Billy Cunningham (played, coached 76ers)

Chuck Daly (played for St. Mary's; coached at Penn; assistant with 76ers)

Bob Davies (from Harrisburg)

Julius Erving (played for 76ers)

Joe Fulks (played for Warriors)

Tom Gola (from Philadelphia; played for La Salle, Warriors)

Ed Gottlieb (coach of South Philadelphia Hebrew Association; established Philadelphia Warriors franchise)

Connie Hawkins (played for Pittsburgh Rens, Pipers)

Chuck Hyatt (played at Pitt)

Buddy Jeannette (played for St. Mary's; played at Washington & Jefferson)

Neil Johnston (played for Warriors)

Alvin Julian (from Reading)

John Kundla (from Star Junction)

Harry Litwack (Temple coach)

Kenneth Loeffler (from Beaver Falls; coached at Geneva, La Salle)

Moses Malone (played for 76ers)

Pete Maravich (from Aliquippa)

Red Mihalik (from Ford City)

Earl Monroe (from Philadelphia)

Ralph Morgan (from Philadelphia)

Jack Ramsay (from Philadelphia; coached for St. Joseph's, 76ers; executive for 76ers)

Mendy Rudolph (from Philadelphia)

Cathy Rush (coached at Immaculata)

Lynn St. John (from Union City)

Maurice Stokes (from Rankin; played for St. Francis College)

Vivian Stringer (from Edenborn)

Earl Strom (from Pottstown)

Jack Twyman (from Pittsburgh)

Golf

Pennsylvania Golfers in the Golfing Hall of Fame

Dwight Eisenhower (retired to Gettysburg)

Betsy King (Reading)

Arnold Palmer (Latrobe)

Carol Semple Thompson (Sewickley)

Chapter Thirteen

Did You Know?

General

- Because of blue laws, Pennsylvania professional sports teams could not play legally on Sunday until 1934.

- Christina Aguilera of Wexford has often sung the national anthem prior to Pittsburgh sporting events. She started as a 10-year-old girl, singing the "Star Spangled Banner" prior to the Steelers' 24–3 triumph against the New England Patriots at Three Rivers Stadium on December 3, 1990— Chuck Noll's 200th head coaching victory. Then at age 11, she sang the anthem before the second game of the 1992 Stanley Cup playoffs, a 3–1 Penguins triumph against the Chicago Blackhawks. She sang the anthem prior to the Pirates last home opener at Three Rivers Stadium in 2000, at the Penguins home opener in 2005 and at Super Bowl XLV, a matchup between the Steelers and the Packers.

- Legendary sportscaster Bob Prince was a swimmer at the University of Pittsburgh.

- The St. Joseph's Hawk mascot flaps its wings/arms throughout the games it attends.

Baseball

- Former Pirates slugger Ralph Kiner once dated Elizabeth Taylor.

- In 1952, the Pittsburgh Pirates were the first team to mandate that their players wear batting helmets while hitting.

- Former Pirates relief pitcher Terry Forester has the highest lifetime batting average of any major leaguer, with 75 or more career at bats at .397 (31 for 97).

- One of the most effective protests against Prohibition occurred during the 1929 World Series when Philadelphia fans chanted, "We want beer!"

- On the same day the Pirates played their first game as a member of the National League, April 30, 1887, the Phillies opened up the Baker Bowl.

- The Pirates' Willie Stargell hit the longest home run in the history of Veterans Stadium in Philadelphia, and the Phillies' Greg Luzinski hit the longest home run in the history of Three Rivers Stadium in Pittsburgh.

- The seventh game of the 1960 World Series, famous for Bill Mazeroski hitting a game-ending home run to give the Pirates the world championship against the New York Yankees, is the only game in World Series history in which not a single batter struck out.

- As of 2010, Pirate Benny Distefano was the last left-handed-throwing catcher in the major leagues when he caught three games for the Bucs in 1989. Distefano is also the only minor league player ever snogged by Morganna the Kissing Bandit, when he played in the first-ever AAA Minor League All-Star Game in 1988.

- More Major League Baseball players have been born in Pennsylvania than any other state except California.

- Former Philadelphia Athletics and Phillies outfielder Elmer Valo missed being a four-decade Major League Baseball player because he was actually an ineligible player when he took his first major league at bat in 1939.

- In 1979, Willie Stargell became the only player to ever be named Most Valuable Player in the League Championship Series, World Series and regular season in the same year.

- Emerson "Pink" Hawley, 1890s Pirates pitcher, got his nickname because of the pink outfits his mother made him wear as a baby. Knowing she was expecting twins, she made both pink and blue outfits for her babies, assuming one twin would be a girl, but she was instead blessed with two boys. Hawley holds the Pirates record for home runs in a season hit by a pitcher, with six in 1895, and his 31 games won that season has not been eclipsed by a Pittsburgh hurler since.

- The Pittsburgh Pirates were the first team to field an all-black starting nine on September 1, 1971: Al Oliver (1B), Rennie Stennett (2B), Dave Cash (3B), Jackie Hernandez (SS), Gene Roberto Clemente (RF), Clines (CF), Willie Stargell (LF), Manny Sanguillen (C) and Dock Ellis (P).

- In 1990, Pittsburgh's Point Park College won 41 straight baseball games.

- Pennsylvania is not only the home of the Little League World Series in Williamsport, but the Pony League World Series in Washington, as well.

- The Pirates' Babe Adams was the only player to play for both the 1909 and 1925 World Champions. As a rookie in '09, he was 12–3 with a 1.11 ERA and won three games against the Detroit Tigers in the World Series. As a wily veteran in 1925, he won six games for the Bucs and pitched a scoreless inning in the fourth game of the World Series.

- The Phillies became the first team to lose 10,000 Major League Baseball games on July 15, 2007.

- Steve Carlton won a then-record four Cy Young awards for the Philadelphia Phillies in 1972, 1977, 1980 and 1982.

- Jerry Reuss is the only player to be on the roster of both the 1979 world champion Pirates and the 1990 Pirates, who were the next Pittsburgh baseball team to finish in first place. Reuss was on the Bucs roster for the first three days of the '79 season before being dealt to Los Angeles, then came back in 1990 to close out his career as a spot lefty out of the bullpen during the pennant race.

- Reuss and John Candelaria are the only two Pirates to play for managers Danny Murtaugh, Chuck Tanner and Jim Leyland.

- The Pirates never had a home run champion during the lively ball era because of the vast dimensions of Forbes Field until Ralph Kiner arrived in 1946. Kiner then led the NL in home runs for a record seven straight seasons.

- Gus Suhr of the Pirates held the National League record of 822 consecutive games played until he was passed by Stan Musial in 1957.

- Donora's Stan Musial was the National League's all-time career hit leader with 3630 until Pete Rose, playing for the Phillies, surpassed him in 1981.

- Musial was Willie Stargell's favorite player growing up, and they both finished with 475 career home runs.

- Because of flooding at old Exposition Park, located on the banks of the Allegheny River, the Pirates opened their season on the road every year, beginning in 1894. This tradition continued until 1954, 45 years after the Bucs moved to Forbes Field.

- The Pittsburgh Pirates' Paul and Lloyd Waner, "Big Poison" and "Little Poison," are the only brothers to be enshrined in the Baseball Hall of Fame. Part of the Bucs' vaunted lineup of the 1930s of "L. Waner, P. Waner, [Arky] Vaughn and [Pie] Traynor," the duo collected more hits, 5611, than any other brother act in baseball history, including the trios of Matty, Felipe and Jesus Alou, and Joe, Dom and Vince DiMaggio.

Basketball

- In 1950, Duquesne's Chuck Cooper was the first black basketball player to be drafted by the NBA.

- College basketball began at Geneva College in Beaver Falls. Geneva fielded intramural teams in February 1893, and a varsity team played the New Brighton YMCA two months later.

- Longtime Villanova men's basketball head coach Alexander Severance died on the same day that the Wildcats won the NCAA men's basketball tournament—April 1, 1985.

- While Cathy Rush was coaching Immaculata to the women's basketball national championship in 1972, she was taking graduate courses at West Chester, whom the Mighty Macs beat in the championship final, 52–48.

- Pitt was ranked number one for the first time in men's basketball when the 14–0 Panthers took the top spot on January 5, 2009.

- Duquesne was the top-ranked men's basketball team in the country in the AP Poll on February 16, 1954, and again on February 23, 1954.

Bowling

- Pennsylvania has 43 different Bowling Halls of Fame.

Boxing

- Journeyman Pittsburgh boxer Billy Wagner, who compiled a 19–9–1 record in a 12-year professional career from 1951 to 1963, has something in common with boxing legends Sugar Ray Robinson and Sonny Liston. They are the only three men ever to box professionally at both the Duquesne Gardens and the arena that replaced it in Pittsburgh, the Civic Arena.

Football (Pro and College)

- The "Miracle in the Meadowlands" was the only fumble recovery of Herman Edwards' 10-year NFL playing career.

- Dan Marino's boyhood home on Parkview Avenue in Pittsburgh had a backyard that touched the backyard of Andy Warhol's boyhood home on Dawson Street.

- Marino often played catch with Willie Stargell as a teenager in Oakland.

- The Pitt–Penn State football game was played at Three Rivers Stadium annually from 1974 to 1976, and in every one of those years, a quarterback from Sto-Rox High School saw action (Robert Medwid for Pitt in 1974, Chuck Fusina for Penn State in 1975 and 1976).

- A Studebaker showroom was once located in Forbes Field, and Pontiac displayed their new models during Steelers games at Three Rivers Stadium in the corner of the end zone where right field was for baseball games.

- Prior to the 2011 season, Mt. Carmel High School's football teams had amassed 789 victories, the most in Pennsylvania and the fifth highest total in the nation. In fact, four of the top 25 winningest high school football programs come from Pennsylvania; Easton, Berwick and Steelton-Highspire (Steel High) are the other three.

- The coldest football game at Three Rivers Stadium (5°F on December 17, 1989; Steelers 28, Patriots 10) produced that stadium's smallest crowd ever—26,594—for a Steelers game, but the coldest game at Heinz Field (8°F on January 23, 2011; Steelers 24, Jets 19) produced that stadium's largest—66,662.

- In 1908, the Pittsburgh Panthers became the first football team to wear numbers on their uniforms to identify their players.

- Duquesne has played in the Orange Bowl Classic football game (in 1937), but the University of Pittsburgh never has.

- Connie Mack created the first professional football team in Philadelphia. In 1902, he organized a Philadelphia Athletics football club that included Rube Waddell and led the team to the Eastern Professional Championship. The team lasted only a year, but their photo is prominently displayed in the Pro Football Hall of Fame in Canton, Ohio.

- NFL commissioner and Philadelphia native Bert Bell died of a heart attack at an Eagles–Steelers game in 1959.

- Pitt Stadium did not have light standards until August 31, 1985, when the Panthers defeated Rod Woodson and Purdue, 31–30, under temporary fixtures. Permanent lights were not installed until 1987.

- The Steelers have won more Super Bowls than any other team in NFL history.

- The longest touchdown reception in Steelers' history, 90 yards against Seattle in 1981, was pulled in by future quarterback Mark Malone. It was the only pass reception of Malone's career.

- Although he did not score a touchdown on the play, Dwight Stone also caught a 90-yard pass, in 1990 against Denver, tying him with Malone for the longest reception in Steelers history. The next year, Stone caught an 89-yard touchdown pass from quarterback Neil O'Donnell. It was the first pass completion of O'Donnell's career.

- Pittsburgh Steeler Terry Bradshaw set a national record in high school by throwing a javelin 245 feet.

- The Eagles' Wilbert Montgomery set an NAIA record by scoring 76 touchdowns at Abilene Christian.

- Steve Van Buren is the first NFL player to record back-to-back seasons of more than 1000 total yards from scrimmage. Van Buren actually accomplished the feat three years in a row en route to leading the Eagles to NFL championship game appearances from 1947 to 1949.

- Van Buren was the NFL's leading career rusher before Jim Brown.

- Brothers Ty and Koy Detmer have both started games at quarterback for the Philadelphia Eagles. Koy actually replaced Ty on the Eagles roster in 1998.

- Former Eagles quarterback A.J. Feely kept a picture of Jennifer Lopez in his locker while he courted his wife, professional soccer player Heather Mitts.

- In 2010, the Steelers were the most popular team in the NFL in terms of merchandise sold, and the Eagles were the fourth most popular.

- "The Polish Rifle," Ron Jaworski, and backup quarterback Joe Pisarcik both received medals from Pope John Paul II when he visited Philadelphia in 1979.

- Doug Shields, president of Pittsburgh's city council from 2008 to 2010, played the Steelers' mascot, "Stevie Steeler," from 1983 until 1990.

- Huntingdon's Juniata College, today a Division III program, went to the Tangerine Bowl (now the Capital One Bowl in Orlando) following an 8–0–1 season in 1955. The Indians tied Missouri Valley State, 6–6. This was two years after future NFL head coach Chuck Knox graduated, though the Indians also went undefeated in his senior season of 1953.

- Andy Gustafson, who helped establish the football program at the University of Miami, scored the first touchdown in the history of Pitt Stadium in 1925.

- Johnstown's Carlton Haselrig won six NCAA wrestling championships in the 1980s for Pitt-Johnstown as he was allowed to compete both at the Division III and Division I levels. His exploits were such that he was drafted by the Pittsburgh Steelers in 1989, where he became an All-Pro lineman in 1993.

- Western Pennsylvania has produced six quarterbacks that are in the Pro Football Hall of Fame: Joe Montana (Monongahela), Joe Namath (Beaver Falls), Dan Marino (Pittsburgh), John Unitas (Pittsburgh), Jim Kelly (East Brady) and George Blanda (Yorkville).

- The last pro football game at Tulane Stadium was Super Bowl IX, where the Steelers won their first Super Bowl by defeating Minnesota, 16–6.

Hockey

- The Hershey Bears' nickname is a derivative of Hershey "B'ars."

- The Hershey Bears have won 11 Calder Cups as of 2010, the most of any team in American Hockey League history.

Horse Racing

- Smarty Jones (2004) and Lil E. Tee (1992) are the only Pennsylvania-bred horses to win the Kentucky Derby, but three horses bearing the name of Pennsylvania cities or boroughs—Johnstown (1939), Apollo (1882) and Baden Baden (1877)—have won the Derby.

- Meadows harness jockey Dave Palone led his track in victories and earnings for the 20th straight year in 2009, and led all harness racing jockeys in victories in 1999 and 2000.

Notes on Sources

Websites

ABC News/ESPN Sports: abcnews.go.com/Sports/

Arena Football: www.arenafan.com

Arnold Palmer: www.arnoldpalmer.com

Baseball Almanac: www.baseball-almanac.com

Baseball-Reference.com: www.baseball-reference.com

Baseball-Statistics.com: www.baseball-statistics.com

BoxRec Boxing Records: boxrec.com/index.php

Charley Burley: charleyburley.com

The Cyber Boxing Zone: cyberboxingzone.com

ESPN: espn.go.com/

Fayette County Sports Hall of Fame:
fayettecountysportshalloffame.com/index.html

Fun Facts About Pittsburgh's Ball Parks: home.mindspring.
com/~gearhard/stadiums.html

Golf.com: www.golf.com/golf/

Harry Greb: harrygreb.com

Hockey-Reference.com: www.hockey-reference.com

The Internet Hockey Database: hockeydb.com

Jim Thorpe: www.cmgww.com/sports/thorpe/index.php

Linda Page Shooting Clinic: www.lindapage100points.com

NBA: www.nba.com/playoffs/2011/index.html

NHL.com Network (Penguins): penguins.nhl.com

Pennsylvania Basketball Hall of Fame: www.pahoops.org/events.htm

Philly.com (Sports): www.philly.com/philly/sports/

Pittsburgh Panthers.com: www.pittsburghpanthers.com/sports/
m-footbl/spec-rel/06-media-guide.html

Pittsburgh Post-Gazette online (Sports): www.post-gazette.com/
sports/

PopWarner.com: www.popwarner.com/

Pro Football Hall of Fame: www.profootballhof.com/default.aspx

ShrpSports: www.shrpsports.com/index.html

Three Rivers Rowing Association: www.threeriversrowing.org

TribLIVE.com (Sports): pittsburghlive.com/x/pittsburghtrib/
sports/?_s_icmp=nav_sports

A Tribute to Wilt Chamberlain: wiltfan.tripod.com/index1.html

United States Trotting Organization: www.ustrotting.com

WNBA: www.wnba.com

Magazines

Sports Illustrated

The Sporting News

USA Today

The Baseball Research Journal

Books and Periodicals

Bradley, Michael. *Big Games*. Dulles, VA: Potomac Books, 2006.

Finoli, David, and Bill Ranier. *Pittsburgh Pirates Encyclopedia*.
Champaign, IL: Sports Publishing LLC, 2003.

Murphy, Cait. *Crazy '08: How a Cast of Cranks, Rogues, Boneheads, and Magnates Created the Greatest Year in Baseball History.* Washington, DC: Smithsonian Books, 2007.

O'Brien, Jim (ed.). *Hail to Pitt: A Sports History of the University of Pittsburgh.* Pittsburgh: Wolfson Publishing, 1982.

Peterson, John E. *The Kansas City Athletics: A Baseball History.* Jefferson, NC: McFarland, 2003.

Roberts, Randy (ed.). *Pittsburgh Sports: Stories from the Steel City.* Pittsburgh: University of Pittsburgh Press, 2000.

Ruck, Rob. *Sandlot Seasons: Sport in Black Pittsburgh.* Champaign, IL: University of Illinois Press, 1993.

Stargell, Willie, and Tom Bird. *Willie Stargell: An Autobiography.* New York: Harper & Row, 1984.

Sugar, Bert Randolph. *The 100 Greatest Boxers of All Time.* New York: Bonanza Books, 1984.

Taylor, John. *The Rivalry: Bill Russell, Wilt Chamberlain, and the Golden Age of Basketball.* New York: Random House, 2005.

Taylor, Ted. *The Ultimate Philadelphia Athletics Reference Book: 1901–1954.* Bloomington, IN: Xlibris, 2010.

Warrington, Robert D. "Departure Without Dignity." *The Baseball Research Journal*, Fall 2010.

Wright, Jerry Jay. "The 1884 Altoona Unions." *The National Pastime* 13: 53–56.

Film and Video

Sonny Liston: The Mysterious Life and Death of a Champion. Jeff Liebermann (director). With Sonny Liston, William Nack, Jerry Izenberg, Geraldine Liston. New York: HBO, 1995.

ESPN SportsCentury (TV series, 222 episodes, 1999–2006).

The Thriller in Manila. John Dower (director). New York: HBO Documentary Films, 2008.

Marky Billson

Marky Billson has lived all over the Commonwealth, from the Main Line of Philadelphia to the City of Pittsburgh to the small, central Pennsylvania boroughs (never "towns") of Shippensburg and Huntingdon. His work has appeared in a variety of publications, including the *Pittsburgh Post-Gazette*, the *Johnstown Tribune-Democrat*, the *York Daily Record*, the *Uniontown Herald*, the *Beaver County Times* and the *Philadelphia Metro*, covering everything from the Pittsburgh Steelers to high school hockey. Additionally, he has been a sportscaster, both hosting talk shows and calling play-by-play in western Pennsylvania and beyond. He believes that anyone who doesn't have the word "yinz" in their vocabulary talks funny.

J. Alexander Poulton

J. Alexander Poulton is a writer, photographer and genuine sports enthusiast. He's even willing to admit he has "called in sick" during the broadcasts of major sports events so that he can get in as much viewing as possible. He has a BA in English literature and a graduate diploma in journalism, and has over 15 sports books to his credit, including books on hockey, soccer, golf and the Olympics.